Theories of International Political Economy

An Introduction

Stéphane
Paquin

OXFORD
UNIVERSITY PRESS

OXFORD
UNIVERSITY PRESS

Oxford University Press is a department of the University of Oxford.
It furthers the University's objective of excellence in research, scholarship,
and education by publishing worldwide. Oxford is a registered trade mark of
Oxford University Press in the UK and in certain other countries.

Published in Canada by
Oxford University Press
8 Sampson Mews, Suite 204,
Don Mills, Ontario M3C 0H5 Canada

www.oupcanada.com

Library and Archives Canada Cataloguing in Publication
Paquin, Stéphane, 1973-, author
Theories of international political economy : an
introduction / Stéphane Paquin.

Includes bibliographical references and index.
ISBN 978-0-19-901896-3 (paperback)

1. International economic relations--Textbooks.
2. Economics--Textbooks. I. Title.

HF1359.P36 2016   337   C2015-908522-5

Cover image: sumkinn/Shutterstock.com

Oxford University Press is committed to our environment.
Wherever possible, our books are printed on paper which comes from
responsible sources.

Printed and bound in Canada

1 2 3 4 — 19 18 17 16

Contents

Acknowledgements   vi
Introduction   vii

1   The Invention of IPE   1

Historical Foundation of the Field   2
What Is IPE?   5
Economists and IPE   8
Theoretical Perspectives in IPE   12
The Dividing Lines between the Orthodox and Heterodox Schools   17
Conclusion   22

2   Theorizing International Political Economy   26

Epistemology in IPE   27
What Is Positivism in Orthodox IPE?   29
Types of Theory   32
Theorizing According to the Orthodox Approach   36
Theorizing According to the Heterodox Approach   39
Theorizing among the Neo-Gramscians   40
Theorizing According to Susan Strange   43
Conclusion   47

3   The Realist Perspective in IPE   50

Basic Assumptions of the Realist Perspective in IPE   51
The Myth of Globalization   57
Globalization, War, and Peace   61
Power and Hegemonic Stability Theory   64
Power and Interstate Relations   70
Conclusion   73

4   The Liberal Perspective   77

Basic Assumptions of the Liberal Perspective in IPE   78
Globalization, War, and Peace   84
Peace through Democracy   85
Peace through International Institutions   86
Economic Interdependence as a Factor of Peace   87
Globalization and Transnationalism   90
Liberal Institutionalism   93
The Rational Design of Institutions   101
The Debate on Compliance   103
Conclusion   105

5   Domestic and Open Economy Politics   108

Interests   111
Institutions   114
The Second Image Reversed   121
Ideas   127
Conclusion   131

6   From Marxism to Neo-Gramscianism   134

Marxist Approaches in IPE   135
Dependency Theory   138
The World-System Approach   140
The Neo-Gramscian School   141
Robert Cox   143
The Rediscovery of Gramsci   145
The Structural Power of Capital   151
The Politics of Mass Production   155
Conclusion   156

7   The British School   159

The Heterodox British School in IPE   160
Globalization   165
Structural Power   168
Markets   173
Finance   176
Conclusion   179

8   Green and Feminist IPE   182

Green IPE   183
The Orthodox Approach in Green IPE   183
Critical Green IPE   187
Feminist IPE   191
Feminist Ontology in IPE   191
Feminist Epistemology in IPE   196
Conclusion   197

Conclusion   200
Bibliography   206
Index   223

Boxes and Figure

Boxes

1.1   International Political Economy or Global Political Economy   7
3.1   Mercantilism and the Realist Perspective   54
3.2   Do Multinationals Have a Nationality?   58
4.1   The Prisoner's Dilemma and International Cooperation According
      to Robert Keohane   98
6.1   The Expansive Logic of Capitalism According to Marx and Engels
      in the Manifesto of the Communist Party of 1848   138
7.1   American Structural Power According to Susan Strange's Model   172
8.1   International Environmental Agreements, Regimes, or Institutions   186

Figure

2.1   Orthodox IPE Researchers' Steps in Theorizing   39

Acknowledgements

This book would not have been possible without the help of many colleagues, students, and friends. I am deeply grateful to those who, despite their busy schedule, agreed to read and comment on the chapters of this book. I also thank those who sent me references, articles, and additional information.

My gratitude goes especially to François Bafoil from CERI-Sciences-Po Paris, Bertrand Badie from Sciences Po Paris, Dario Battistella from Institut d'Études Politiques de Bordeaux, Érick Duchesne from Université Laval, Christian Deblock from Université du Québec à Montréal, Mathieu Arès from the Université de Sherbrooke, Jérémie Cornut from McGill University, and John Groom from the University of Kent (from whom I took this idea of dividing the theories of IPE on the world academic scene by adopting Immanuel Wallerstein's concepts of core, semi-periphery and periphery).

I also thank Benjamin Cohen, Robert Keohane, Helen Milner, Peter Katzenstein, Robert Jervis, Ron Rogowski, Anne-Marie Slaughter, Michael Doyle, Beth Simmons, Jeff Frieden, Kenneth Oye, Jana Von Stein, Jonathan Kirshner, and Thomas Oatley for answering my emails and sending me their syllabi, when possible, and the required reading lists for general examinations in their institution.

I would also like to thank Nancy Dunham for her much needed help in the translation and revision of this manuscript.

A thank you also to the team of Presses de Sciences Po in Paris, and notably Marie Genevieve Vandesande, for allowing me to reproduce large parts of my previous book that was first published in French in 2013 as: *Théories de l'économie politique internationale. Cultures scientifiques et hégémonie américaine* by Presses de Sciences Po, Paris, France, 377 pages.

Introduction

Economists desire to be able to explain 99% of all economic phenomena with three laws. That's what physicists can do. In fact, we have 99 laws that explain maybe 3% of all phenomena.
— Andrew W. Lo, Finance professor, MIT

The transformations in international political economy (IPE), from the collapse of the USSR to the financial crisis of 2008, have taught those who aspire to build comprehensive and rigorous theoretical explanations of political and economic global phenomena a serious lesson in humility. If few theorists were actually able to predict these major events, then why should we care about studying IPE theories? To borrow from Andrew W. Lo, do the 99 theories in IPE explain only 3 per cent of the phenomena?

Many practitioners, journalists, and even university professors have agreed to minimize the importance of the theoretical approach in the social sciences, an approach that has often been characterized as an exercise exclusively for academics disconnected from reality, isolated in their ivory tower, and protected by job security. Moreover, in a context increasingly dominated by Big Data, can we not simply bypass theories and get directly to the facts?

IPE is so vast a research field that one might think a good dose of naïveté is required to attempt to theorize it. There are so many actors (states, international organizations, multinationals, non-governmental organizations, social movements, markets, international finance, not to mention billions of individuals), with their own history, identity, capabilities, and logics, that it seems illusory to believe that we could one day formulate a satisfactory theory. In IPE, the explanations are multiple, and the details never-ending, making it impossible to understand all these logics in their entirety.

Paradoxically, it is this lack of easily understandable meaning that makes efforts at theorizing necessary. Attempting to think about IPE without any theoretical tools seems even more naïve than the alternative. Researchers need a guide in order to know where and what to research, because, without theories, the world is a jungle. Asking a student or a professor to expound all the aspects of a question in IPE is like asking a geographer to reproduce a life-size map of part of the Earth. The undertaking would certainly be impossible regardless of the quantity of empirical data available. Geographers, just like IPE specialists, must select and hierarchize the important facts in addition to giving them a meaning. In a word, they must inevitably theorize the world. The choices made by researchers imply a theory, even if only an implicit one (Rosenau and Durfee, 2000).

According to international relations theorists John Baylis, Steve Smith, and Patricia Owen, "a theory is a kind of simplifying device that allows you to decide which facts matter and which do not" (2011: 3). They believe that theories are a little like glasses with different-coloured lenses that we use to see the world: with pink glasses, the world seems pink, with yellow glasses, it seems yellow, etc. The glasses may be different, but the world remains the same. A theory is a tool that is used to identify important variables and to hierarchize them for analysis and comprehension.

Theory is not an option. Theories are everywhere—in politicians' speeches, in editorials, in experts' opinions, and in professors' and students' reflections. These opinions, visions, and speeches about the world contain theories—simplified and abstract visions of the world and how it works.

Some more skeptical researchers claim not to be interested in theories but rather in "facts." For example, many historians, sociologists, and political scientists maintain that their work relies on empirical material and facts, not on theories. This statement is naïve, for in a context where millions, or even billions, of facts exist, selecting the most important "facts" and hierarchizing them requires a theory, however implicit. Researchers are not always aware of their theories, which may be inherited from their family, their peers, their education, and the media. A fact does not exist without a frame of reference, without a preliminary theory. As Karl Popper remarked, observations are influenced by previously acquired knowledge and theories (Popper, 1963, 1972; see also Kuhn, 1962).

The "facts" do not speak for themselves; what we find depends on how we come to select the events and trends we deem important and to discard others that seem more trivial. Once we have selected some important facts versus others, thereby creating a hierarchy among them, we are theorizing. The more our theory is simplified, the more it explains vast and important events with just a few variables and the more we climb up the ladder of theoretical abstraction. According to some theorists, the ultimate goal is to explain something big with something small.

Given that all research in the social sciences involves theorizing work, however weak, it is preferable to make the theoretical approach explicit when discussing as vast a subject as IPE. Being explicit represents a fundamental element in the theoretical enterprise. The more a theory is expounded simply and clearly, the easier it is to contest it during academic debates and to revise it if necessary. Even though IPE researchers agree that no "grand universal theory" actually works in IPE, we can still eliminate the worst theories.

There is a more practical reason for studying theories. Before writing poetry, one must learn basic grammar rules. Learning theory in order to become a specialist in a field of study is the equivalent of learning compulsory figures in figure skating for the Olympics. It is impossible to be identified as a specialist and get hired at a university without minimal knowledge of the main theoretical debates, especially in IPE. Theory is simply the discipline's centre of gravity. In fact, as IPE theorists Peter Katzenstein, Robert Keohane, and Stephen Krasner maintain, since its beginnings in the 1970s, IPE in the United States has been built less on research themes than on theoretical perspectives (1998: 645). The importance of IPE theories ensures that it is difficult today to wield influence in debates on international questions while completely ignoring IPE theories. A tourist approach to IPE is not an option.

The Aim of the Book

The aim of this book is to identify the differences between the scientific cultures of the orthodox and the heterodox schools and between the principal theoretical debates in IPE since its beginnings. *Scientific culture* refers to a system of meaning that the members of an IPE community use in their interactions. The book borrows the terms *orthodox school* and *heterodox school* from economics. Several theoretical perspectives (liberal, realist, neo-Gramscian, feminist, etc.) cut across each of these schools. Nowadays the field of IPE is largely divided between the American orthodox school and the heterodox school, which is dominant in Great Britain and has a strong presence in Canada and around the world.

In the United States, the orthodox school derives from political science departments. Its level of analysis lies mainly at that of medium-range theories. Its research agenda focuses on subjects such as cooperation, efficiency, governance, power relations, globalization, and especially American hegemony. Its objective is to understand how the world works without passing normative judgments. The American school is not very open to disciplines other than economics and political science. This school rests on the two pillars of traditional hard science: rationalism and positivism. It also bears an allegiance to quantitative methods. The American school prioritizes the scientific method based on the natural science model. It favours causal theories. Over time, it has adopted a scientific culture close to that of neoclassical economists. The style is reductionist and demonstration is generally based on controlled empirical tests. The majority of its authors favour methodological individualism and rational choice theory. The school's orthodoxies have a predominantly materialist and neo-utilitarian vision of the world. Constructivism and reflective ideas-based analyses are largely absent from the analysis. This orthodox school is very focused on quantitative methods and increasingly on formal modelling (Cohen, 2007, 2008, 2014).

Characterized by a critical orientation to IPE and the works of the American school, the heterodox school does not accept the world as it is (Cox, 1981; Strange, 1984). Compared to the American school, the heterodox school is more explicitly normative and focuses on questions of justice, ethics, morality, and equity in IPE. The heterodox school does not believe in the idea of adopting the scientific method of the hard sciences model. The hard sciences approach is deemed inadequate for understanding the real world in which we live, the world of the social sciences. The heterodox school is predominantly non-positivist or even postpositivist. It rejects quantitative methods and formal modelling. It is also very critical of rational choice theory and willingly develops holistic approaches. It is much more open to the roles of ideas, identity, and values. Its works are closer to the tradition of research in interpretive historical sociology—quite the opposite of reductionism. The heterodox school, which neglects themes linked to the governance of international negotiation or of monetary policy, concentrates on very big questions such as, who has power in the global economy? What are the key steps in the evolution of the world? How can we change the world? To answer these much bigger questions, researchers must take into account a much wider range of factors. Positivist epistemology is thus largely useless, as the parameters are changing and all relevant factors must be analyzed (Cohen, 2007, 2008, 2014).

A warning is necessary: it is true that these debates and this opposition between the scientific culture of the orthodox school and the heterodox school give a good overview of what the IPE discipline is today, but they do not do justice to the great diversity of the works since its founding. As an example, Robert Gilpin or Peter Katzenstein of the American orthodox school never abandoned their historical analyses. As well, the differences appeared only gradually and they are now at their peak. They are especially visible among the new generation of orthodox authors.

The orthodox and heterodox schools are ideal types. That is, they exaggerate certain traits in the thinking of several authors and link ideas that make it possible to give meaning to the reality. This typology forms and structures ideas in a more logical and homogeneous way than the reality. In other words, orthodox authors are orthodox to varying degrees, just as heterodox authors propound varying degrees of heterodoxy. Therefore, instead of seeing this divergence between orthodox and heterodox in terms of two totally opposed schools, it is preferable to imagine it as a continuum on which the orthodox approach is on one end and the heterodox on the other. In the end, however, as this book will show, the division with regard to IPE theories is very real and is based on different scientific cultures that are largely incompatible and irreconcilable.

How the Book Is Divided

To build a big picture of theories of IPE on the world academic scene, we can adopt Immanuel Wallerstein's concepts of core, semi-periphery, and periphery. Based on the research of a team of professors working on the

Teaching, Research, and International Policy (TRIP) project who conducted several studies on international relations and IPE around the world, and based on the introductory textbooks, syllabi, and reading lists for the general examinations at major universities, we can conclude that the core of the theoretical production in IPE is indisputably constituted of the American orthodox school. Even critics of orthodox IPE concede the American orthodox school has produced the principal debates and theories and has dominated the discipline since the 1970s. It is difficult to call oneself an IPE specialist without having a strong knowledge of the American orthodox school authors. The semi-periphery is formed by the works of the heterodox school: the neo-Gramscian school and the British school. The other works in IPE—namely, green and feminist IPE—make up the periphery.

The first chapter of this book sets out the history of the field, the definition of IPE, its relationship with the economics discipline, and the various debates about the theoretical perspectives in IPE. Chapter 2 explains how the orthodox and heterodox schools theorize IPE. What is a legitimate theory in IPE for each of the two schools? The differences in scientific culture are very evident here. The chapters that follow look at the principal theoretical perspectives of the discipline. Chapters 3, 4, and 5 focus on the various theoretical perspectives within the orthodox school. Chapter 3 deals with the realist perspective in IPE, notably with its conception of globalization, power distribution, and hegemonic stability theory. Chapter 4 examines the liberal perspective, the predominant perspective in IPE. The debates hinge on the theorization of globalization, complex interdependence, cooperation, and democratic peace theory, which bridges the theories of security and of IPE. Chapter 5 discusses the domestic politics perspective and Open Economy Politics.

Chapters 6 and 7 consider the semi-peripheries of the works in IPE: those of the neo-Gramscian school and the British school. Chapter 6 examines in greater depth the works of the neo-Gramscian school whose leader, Robert W. Cox, is the most influential IPE researcher outside the dominant trend. Chapter 7 sets out the broad framework of the British heterodox perspective and focuses in particular on the works of the woman who is often considered the founding mother of IPE, Susan Strange. Chapter 8 explores the works on the periphery—that is, the green and feminist perspectives in IPE. While green IPE is divided between the orthodox and heterodox school, feminist IPE is clearly predominantly heterodox.

1 The Invention of IPE

Chapter Contents

- Historical Foundation of the Field
- What Is IPE?
- Economists and IPE
- Theoretical Perspectives in IPE
- The Dividing Lines between the Orthodox and Heterodox Schools
- Conclusion

Reader's Guide

Most specialists date IPE's birth to the year 1970, when British scholar Susan Strange published an article titled "International Economics and International Relations: A Case of Mutual Neglect." The American version of the discipline was born in the United States at almost the same time, in June 1971, when Joseph Nye, a young professor at Harvard University, and Robert Keohane published a special issue of the journal *International Organization*. Although the definition of IPE is still the subject of debate, researchers agree that IPE is concerned with international politics and international economics, that is to say, politics and economics beyond state borders. IPE focuses especially on the power relations between the world of states and that of economic actors on the international scene. The goal of this chapter is to explain the logic behind the invention of IPE as a discipline, the debates over the definition of what IPE is, the relationship between IPE and the economics discipline, the various debates about the theoretical perspectives in IPE, and the development of divergent ontology, epistemology, and methodology between the orthodox and the heterodox schools.

If IPE has to have a founding moment, it would be precisely 15 August 1971. On that date, US President Richard Nixon suspended the monetary system established by the Bretton Woods Agreement in July 1944 during the Second World War. With this action, the American head of state planted a seed of doubt: Had the world's most powerful country begun its decline, just like the British Empire before the First World War? If so, would history repeat itself? Would the decline of the United States plunge the world into a maelstrom of instability marked by a new economic crisis like that of 1929 and a global conflict like the Second World War? To remain stable, does the international system require a "stabilizer," a hegemony that has enough power to ensure the system operates smoothly? These debates gave rise to hegemonic stability theory, the founding theory of IPE. The answers to these questions, and to many others, would structure the evolution of the debates in IPE from the time of its foundation in the early 1970s.

The goal of this chapter is to explain the logic behind the invention of IPE as a discipline, the debates over the definition of IPE, the relationship between IPE and the discipline of economics, the various debates about the theoretical perspectives in IPE, and the development of divergent ontology, epistemology, and methodology between the orthodox and the heterodox school.

Historical Foundation of the Field

The field of IPE emerged in the 1970s in Great Britain and the United States and subsequently in other parts of the world. Why then? Prior to the 1970s, international relations specialists, at the time few in number, focused mainly on security issues. The Cold War dominated the questionings of researchers and practitioners. Post–World War II, the nascent Bretton Woods institutions attracted little attention in political science departments. At the time, monetary and commercial transactions were very strictly controlled and, for many, the creation of operating rules for international economic institutions was a technical issue reserved for legal scholars and economists. Only a small group of political science researchers took an interest in these questions.

In the 1960s and 1970s, several international factors contributed to the growth of IPE. The decline of the United States, at least in relative terms, combined with the emergence of new economic giants such as Germany and Japan, sparked a series of debates on the decline of American power or hegemony. In 1945, the US economy was approximately three times that of its closest rival, the USSR, five times that of Great Britain, and twenty times that of Japan, but these gaps would rapidly narrow.

In 1945, Western Europe and Japan still depended on the United States for investments and foreign aid. However, as of 1971, the United States found itself in a trade deficit situation. For some, President Nixon's suspension of the monetary system established under the Bretton Woods Agreement was another sign of the decline of the American Empire. According to several authors, the only explanation for this decision was the decline of American power on the international scene (Keohane and Nye, 1977; Krasner, 1976; Gilpin, 2001; Strange, 1988a).

The postwar period was further marked by a wave of independencies among former European colonies. Developing countries emerged as vital international actors. Starting in the 1970s, newly independent countries called for a different international economic order. These actors gradually became members of various international organizations, which made it more difficult not only for the United States but also for the other Western countries to exercise leadership on the international scene and to adopt standards that would achieve consensus in international organizations.

Other factors helped launch IPE. The détente between the United States and the USSR, and the easing of tensions created by this bipolar relationship, meant that the international relations discipline was able to direct part of its attention away from questions of military security. The creation of the Organization of the Petroleum Exporting Countries (OPEC) in 1960, the first oil shock in 1973, the problems of economic growth and stagflation in the 1970s, and the debt crisis of third world countries in the 1980s caused great anxiety regarding international economic stability. The economic interdependence and internationalization of major corporations were also part of the picture. Consequently, researchers slowly became aware of the phenomenon that today we call globalization.

With the return of the Cold War and the hardening of East–West relations in the late 1970s and early 1980s, specialists once again focused on security issues. Neorealism in international relations theory then emerged with force. However, with the collapse of the Soviet Union and the accelerated development of new information technologies, IPE reached a tipping point in the 1990s. The multiplication of studies on globalization permitted IPE to become enduringly institutionalized in political science departments. Hence, the debates about economic interdependence, globalization, and the decline of American power marked the birth of IPE as a field of inquiry.

Most specialists date IPE's birth to the year 1970, when British scholar Susan Strange published an article titled "International Economics and International Relations: A Case of Mutual Neglect." In this article, Strange argued that most university courses in international relations and in economics did not provide an adequate understanding of the changes occurring in international economics. Teaching and research in international relations promoted the broadening and deepening of the divide between international economics and international relations; any bridge building was therefore impossible. In spirit, IPE is a form of necessary synthesis, a *via media* or middle road, between the discipline of international relations and that of international economics. The two disciplines could no longer ignore one another.

The American version of the discipline was born in the United States at almost the same time, in June 1971, when Joseph Nye, a young professor at Harvard University, and Robert Keohane, then a professor at Swarthmore College, both members of the editorial committee of *International Organization*, published a special issue of this journal. The issue included contributions by Robert Gilpin, Robert Cox, Peter Evans, and Raymond Vernon, among others. It was not about IPE as such—the term was adopted only gradually in the United States—but about transnational relations and world politics. In that issue, Nye and Keohane called into question the dominant perspective in international relations—realism—according to which the state is at the centre of international action and its chief agents are diplomats and soldiers. The authors noted that economists are less inclined to accept the state-centric perspective than are political scientists and diplomats (Nye and Keohane, 1971).

According to Nye and Keohane's conception, which was systematized in a work published in 1977, IPE is an extension of transnational relations (Keohane and Nye, 1977). The extension of transnational relations probably explains why, in their rereading of works that appeared in *International Organization* since 1971, Peter Katzenstein, Robert Keohane, and Stephen Krasner consider works focused on globalization, trade, but also constructivism as part of the IPE field. Their visioning of the field almost excluded works about international security issues (Katzenstein, Keohane, and Krasner, 1998).

In the early 1970s, Strange, Nye, and Keohane took a position against the realist theorists' conception of international relations that had dominated the international relations research field since the 1950s and 1960s. According to the three authors, the realist, and later on neorealist, conception of international relations was very clearly in crisis as of the end of the 1960s and the early 1970s on three fronts. The first crisis was one of issues, as it became obvious that the realists' narrow conception of international relations was no longer adequate given the diversification of international problems. This crisis of issues led to the second crisis: that of actors. To assume the centrality of the state was very clearly excessive, as evidence grew that other actors such as multinationals, international organizations, and non-governmental organizations were becoming more and more central in international relations. These two crises naturally lead to the final crisis: that of explanation. It was disconcerting to realize just how incapable realist theorists were of predicting or even explaining numerous international issues.

According to Stephen Krasner, no IPE course was offered in the United States prior to the first half of the 1970s. The first textbook on the subject, by Joan Spero, was not published until 1977 (Spero, 1977). After 1970, however, interest in IPE grew rapidly. These changes can be explained by the fact that, in American universities, the typical research program in international relations began to lose steam. Hans Morgenthau's major work, *Politics among Nations*, was published in 1948. The most cited works by Thomas Schelling on conflict and arms control strategies were published in the 1960s (1960, 1966; Schelling and Halperin, 1961). (Schelling went on to win the 2005

Nobel Prize in Economic Sciences for his application of game theory to the understanding of conflict and cooperation between states.) Legal scholars practically held the monopoly on the study of international organizations as US economists favoured the formal modelling of econometrics and dismissed macroeconomics. Seeing that international economic and political issues were clearly becoming more important and that the field was open, young political scientists stepped into the breach.

IPE has since grown dramatically. It is now an academic discipline with a coherent set of concepts, theories, research programs, and reference works. It has its founding authors, and many professors describe themselves as specialists in this discipline. In the United States alone, more than 30 per cent of university professors in the broad field of international relations list IPE as their first or second field of research, making it the second most popular field in international relations after security issues. The situation is similar in Canada with 26 per cent and in Great Britain with 24 per cent of professors identifying IPE as one of their primary fields of research (Maliniak, Peterson, and Tierney, 2012: 28–9).

What Is IPE?

Although the definition of IPE is still the subject of debate, researchers agree that IPE is concerned with international politics and international economics, that is to say, politics and economics beyond state borders. IPE focuses especially on the power relations between the world of states and that of economic actors on the international scene. Nowadays, the most cited definition of IPE comes from one of its founding fathers, Robert Gilpin, who has spent his career at Princeton University. For him, IPE is "the reciprocal and dynamic interaction in international relations of the pursuit of wealth and the pursuit of power" (Gilpin, 1975b: 43).

In 2000, Jeffry Frieden and David Lake defined IPE more simply as "the study of the interplay of economics and politics in the world arena" (1). In the *Routledge Encyclopedia of International Political Economy*, British author R. J. Barry Jones offers a similar definition of IPE. According to Jones, IPE "addresses the complex interrelationship between political and economic activity at the level of international relations (IR)" (2001: 813–14).

In the same vein, John Ravenhill writes in 2014, "Global political economy is a field of enquiry, a subject matter whose central focus is the interrelationship between public and private power in the allocation of scarce resources" (18). In this definition, the global or international dimension of the research is not made clear, which is rather surprising as Ravenhill's textbook is entitled *Global Political Economy*.

While these definitions are the most agreed upon, other definitions exist as well. In his major work, *The Political Economy of International Relations*,

Gilpin himself presented IPE as the study of interactions between states and markets (1987, 8). In a more recent work, Joseph Grieco and John Ikenberry also chose this formulation (2003). Likewise, Susan Strange called her 1988 textbook *States and Markets: An Introduction to International Political Economy*. However, in her book *The Retreat of the State*, Strange declares her regret over the choice of this title (1996: 3). She would have preferred "*Authority and Markets*" because, according to her, the state is no longer the main source of authority in the international system.

Jeffry Frieden and Lisa Martin believe that the emphasis placed on economic dimensions most distinguishes this field of research from other fields that look at international issues. According to these authors, the field of IPE includes "all work for which international economic factors are an important cause or consequence" (Frieden and Martin, 2002: 118). For Helen Milner, the emphasis on the economic dimension refocuses IPE on its fundamental purposes, as opposed to a very broad definition of IPE that tended to include all international relations theories, other than those to do with security issues, in the category of IPE (2002).

In contrast, Stephen Krasner, one of the most important realist theorists of IPE in the United States, maintains that IPE "is concerned with the political determinants of international economic relations" (2008: 108). Krasner says that IPE can be contrasted with studies in traditional economy. Economists and IPE specialists ask the same types of questions, but the answers to the former emphasize economic factors such as interest rates, labour market rigidity, or education level. IPE specialists instead emphasize political factors such as the distribution of power between the actors or the relations between states and markets. While it is necessary to have good basic education in political economy to understand the key works in IPE, it is even more important to know the consistently referenced theoretical debates in international relations.

For Stephen Krasner, IPE is part of the broad discipline of international relations. According to him, internationalists who study security issues ask different questions than do IPE researchers, questions such as, what are the causes of war? Or in what context are alliances likely to be stable? But they propose answers whose logic is comparable to the answers of IPE researchers (Krasner, 2008).

Roger Tooze also maintains that IPE emerged from international relations rather than from economics or political science. At the analytic level, IPE emphasizes international or global phenomena, while economists and political scientists concentrate instead on the nation-state as the unit of analysis (Tooze, 1984). IPE proposes a fusion of research fields that were separated in the past, fields such as international economics, international politics, political science, and national economics. IPE specialists believe that these disciplines are inseparable and that one cannot be understood without taking the others into account. IPE thus emerged from a growing dissatisfaction with economists' and political scientists' explanations of matters such as economic interdependence, trade liberalization, American power, and so on.

Even though the phenomenon is more marginal, some IPE authors, especially in the realist tradition, also cross over into security issues. This theme is of particular significance in the works of Robert Gilpin (1981, 1987, 2001). For him, no country can become a power through weapons alone; wealth is also required. The accumulation of power goes hand-in-hand with the accumulation of wealth. Susan Strange as well insisted that the two objectives are inseparable. In her textbook *States and Markets*, she developed a conception of structural power in which the security structure is one of the pillars (1988c). Security issues are also vital in Richard Rosecrance's works that focus on the transformations of the nation-state into the virtual state and the effects of these transformations on international conflicts (1999; Rosecrance et al., 2002). The works of Michael J. Hiscox (2002) factor in issues related to international trade and political conflicts, and those of Jonathan Kirshner (2007, 1995) discuss monetary manipulations as a tool of coercion and the aversion to war of bankers and the financial world.

For most researchers, IPE is a subdiscipline of international relations, alongside security issues. For her part, the ever-provocative Susan Strange maintained that international relations are a subdiscipline of IPE (1994). Strange's position can be explained largely by the fact that she was very critical of the way in which IPE developed in the United States and wanted

---

> ### Box 1.1   International Political Economy or Global Political Economy
>
> According to Ronen Palan, those who consider IPE a subdiscipline of international relations (the orthodox) would prefer to call their discipline "international political economy," while those with a more multidisciplinary conception of IPE (the heterodox) would prefer the term "Global Political Economy" to show that global political economy does not focus solely on the politics of international economic relations (Palan, 2000). But this distinction is not rigorously respected. For example, Robert Gilpin called his 2001 book *Global Political Economy*, despite the fact that in it he uses the term *international political economy*. The same is true for the textbook edited by John Ravenhill. As well, the flagship journal of the heterodox school is titled *Review of International Political Economy*. Certain authors with heterodox leanings also use the term *new international political economy* to distinguish it from the orthodox approach.

to express her dissent regarding the dominant approaches that focus mainly on the politics of international economics issues. In her works, she drew an unflattering portrait of IPE as practised in the United States. According to her, it is not true IPE, but rather a mediocre and unsound political approach to international economic relations based on a narrow conception of economic relations between states. She thought IPE should be related to many more subjects than just interstate relations.

Nowadays, according to Geoffrey Underhill, the majority of IPE specialists adhere to three core ideas: (1) economics and politics cannot be separated, and to understand one, you must also study the other; (2) the state is essential to the functioning of the market, and political interactions are the main factor by which the market's economic structure is established and transformed; (3) there is an intimate relationship between domestic politics and international politics and therefore we cannot artificially separate the two (2000). Beyond this observation, fundamental divergences do exist, as we will see in this book.

Economists and IPE

Are IPE specialists not simply "economists" who work in political science departments? No, because not many economists think about international economics as it is understood by IPE specialists. With its aim to describe and explain power relations in relation to economic and financial issues on the international scene, IPE differs from the traditional international economics. Economists rarely pay attention to international matters in terms of power relations. Economists have little interest in questions such as, does America have enough authority to make their standards be accepted in an international economic forum? Thus, to the questions, who governs? or who gets what, when, and how? economists offer no convincing answers. Instead, they tend to study international economics based on the general market logic and rational choice theory.

Economists prefer to concentrate on the private sphere and on the behaviour of individuals. As Paul Krugman explains, "Economics is about what *individuals* do: not classes, not 'correlations of forces,' but individual actors. This is not to deny the relevance of higher levels of analysis, but they must be grounded in individual behavior. Methodological individualism is of the essence." Furthermore, he states that individuals are self-interested and intelligent. As he points out, "Hundred-dollar bills do not lie unattended in the street for very long." Thus, fundamentally, the primary concern of economics is the interaction between these individuals (Krugman, 1996). If we accept Krugman's definition, we realize that economists have neither the interest nor the theoretical tools needed to properly think about the public sphere and the state. Certain concepts, such as power, authority, hegemony, social movements, ethics, and values, are foreign to their analyses. Consequently, the state, international organizations, and transnational actors, as economic actors, are more or less absent from their studies (except in creating market imbalance or failure).

To overcome this problem, many economists endogenize the state; that is, they postulate its actions based on precepts of individual economic rationality. Economists are also more generally interested in the results of a policy than in its processes. They assess policies but do not seek to explain their development, which includes the negotiations, compromises, and inevitable political arbitrations in any political process. The power relations in policy development are not really taken into account, except in an approximate and unsystematic way.

This does not mean that economists have had no impact on IPE studies. The influence of certain economists, besides Marx and Keynes, in the rise of IPE as a research field is unquestionable. Several founding texts were even written by economists. Hungarian economist Karl Polanyi can rightly be considered one of the founding fathers of the discipline. In his major work *The Great Transformation*, published in 1944, Polanyi developed the thesis that the market economy does not exist without the nation-state, that in fact the market is created and structured by the state. They are not two separate phenomena but a single phenomenon that he called the market society. Polanyi's reasoning was that states brought about changes in social structures in order to promote capitalism, while capitalism requires a strong state to mitigate its worst effects. For Polanyi, the system collapses due to the impacts of the self-regulating market on society, which, naturally wanting to protect itself from that market's effects, develops a protectionist reflex.

We owe to economist Albert Hirschman a classical thesis on national power and the structure of trade. In this 1945 study, Hirschman sought to explain how governments use trade to increase their power. His starting point was that two countries that trade with one another do not reap the same benefits. In this asymmetrical relationship, the less dependent country may try to instrumentalize the situation to strengthen its power. In his analysis, Hirschman demonstrated how Nazi Germany used its trade policy to expand its zone of influence in Eastern Europe in the period between the two world wars (Hirschman, 1945).

In a book published in 1948, Canadian economist Jacob Viner was one of the first researchers to explore the relationship between power and plenty as foreign policy objectives. Richard Cooper's influence is also undeniable. In his book *The Economics of Interdependence* (1968), Cooper was among the first to examine the effects of economic interdependence on state sovereignty. He had a definite influence on the work of Nye and Keohane. Charles Kindleberger also had a huge influence in the IPE field with his 1970 work *Power and Money*, which examined the effects of political interdependence.

His 1973 book *The World in Depression, 1929–1939,* in which he developed what Robert Keohane would later call the hegemonic stability theory, was even more influential. Raymond Vernon's book *Sovereignty at Bay,* published in 1971, proposed one of the most influential analyses of multinationals as key political actors on the international scene.

Despite these fundamental contributions, economists as a whole threw in the towel in the early 1970s. Several reasons explain this situation. According to Benjamin Cohen, in the 1970s, in the context of the Cold War and the rivalry between capitalist and communist systems, few American economists wanted to be identified as being critical of the market economy and liberalism. To manifest communist sympathies was the best way to sink into obscurity within an economics department. To include criticisms of the market economy in economic analyses was often perceived at the time as an ideological bias. Political scientists had no such constraints (Cohen, 2008, 2014).

The emergence of IPE as a discipline occurred at a time when economics departments in the United States were resolutely turning towards econometrics and accepting more broadly the postulates of utilitarian economists and the rational choice approach. The study of qualitative and descriptive political economy was discouraged, while the use of quantitative and formal modelling methods was promoted to the point of becoming hegemonic. In a survey conducted among economics students at the end of the 1980s in the United States, "only 3% thought that 'having a thorough knowledge of the economy' was 'very important' for achieving success in the profession, and 68% thought it 'unimportant'" (Wade, 2009: 99). The priority was the acquisition of mathematical and statistical bases from which to develop better models.

Neoclassical economics, which today forms the orthodoxy in the economics discipline, arose from the synthesis of Keynesianism with classical theories. The very great majority of theoretical models by neoclassical economists were envisaged in a closed economy as opposed to a globalized one. The fundamental research area was therefore the national or domestic economy of countries and not the economic relations between countries. International trade, monetary relations, international finance, and the relations between countries came second. For example, in the 19th edition of the neoclassical reference text *Economics* by Paul Samuelson and William Nordhaus, of a total of 31 chapters, the four chapters dealing with international trade and finance appeared in the sixth section of the book, even though these themes are fundamental in IPE. A number of IPE specialists think neoclassicists traditionally underestimate the importance of IPE (Samuelson and Nordhaus, 2010).

From the epistemological viewpoint, economists' reservations about studying international questions are the most important issue. Economists are naturally reticent to analyze problems that cannot be dealt with using the tools developed by neoclassical economists. Economics has become, admittedly more in the United States than elsewhere, an abstract and disincarnated discipline. As Benjamin Cohen asserts,

> For a century, especially in the United States, the [economic] discipline had been growing increasingly abstract, relying ever more on deductive logic and parsimonious theoretical models to pare messy reality down to its bare essentials. The style was reductionist. The aim was to uncover core relationships—"to predict something large from something small," as economist Harry Johnson put it. (2007: 206)

The very complex reality that IPE envelops makes it uninteresting for economists. From the 1960s and 1970s on, American economists bothered less and less with research problems that could not be measured or quantified. In their analyses, they emphasized deductive logic and the creation of parsimonious theoretical models in order to explain with very few variables an important economic phenomenon. The nascent IPE contrasted too greatly with the criteria of professionalism in American economics departments. IPE's research areas—American hegemony, international regimes, and cooperation—are not natural research areas for economists. Concepts such as power, authority, national interest, social movements are foreign to their analyses. Only a small number of economists are interested in political institutions and in the decision-making processes within states.

According to Susan Strange, economists' works are inadequate for analyzing the problems that should constitute IPE. She asserted that a critical look at their work reveals several flaws. Economists are partial, she claimed. Most American economists implicitly seek in their work to preserve order and stability in order to defend America's national interest. They are also naïve, as they tend to think that political factors can be set aside (Strange, 1970).

Nonetheless, we cannot conclude that economists have completely ignored international political economy questions. Several very well-known economists, such as Paul Krugman, Joseph Stiglitz, Dani Rodrik, and Jeffrey Sachs, have produced works in the fields of development, climate change, trade, and international finance. Other authors have proposed analyses on free trade, the International Monetary Fund, financial crises, and the World Trade Organization, but these works reside on the periphery of mainstream economic theory.

It is because of this situation that several political scientists decided in the 1970s to create the new discipline that became IPE. The IPE objective was to compensate for the failure of economists to explain key international political economy issues. Most IPE specialists believe that economists attempt to understand the world with economic models that, while sophisticated, are much too separated from reality. IPE notably revives the classical political economy approaches, but applies these approaches to international questions that embrace economic issues. Political economy was then envisaged as a social science discipline rather than a field of application of mathematical models.

Theoretical Perspectives in IPE

How do we distinguish between the various theoretical perspectives in IPE? In the early 1970s, IPE was fundamentally a very eclectic and profoundly innovative multidisciplinary undertaking. In the words of Susan Strange, the person who invented the concept "international political economy," the IPE research field was an open range, accessible to educated individuals of all professions and all political persuasions (1984: ix). IPE was a new undertaking developed by a small number of very dynamic researchers who opened new areas of thought and research.

IPE's founding mother and fathers, Susan Strange, Robert Keohane, Joseph Nye, Robert Gilpin, Stephen Krasner, Benjamin J. Cohen, and Robert Cox, carried out research that clearly differed from the classical analyses of macroeconomists and international relations specialists who focused on military security issues. The new works were critical of the dominant approaches and called for researchers to reconsider existing theories and analytic models. Following the publication of the first works in IPE, it became impossible to conceive of the world and international politics as before. And since the 1970s, theoretical perspectives have also been refined and developed.

Robert Gilpin was the first to propose a typology of theoretical perspectives in IPE in an article that appeared in the *International Organization* journal in 1975. In this article, he developed typologies based on various political economy schools. In his original typology, Gilpin proposed three theoretical perspectives. The first was the "sovereignty at bay" model, the name taken from the now classic work by Raymond Vernon (1971). This paradigm stressed economic interdependence and the decline of the nation-state. The second perspective, "dependency" or "dependencia," focused on relations of dependence between northern and southern countries. The last perspective, called the "mercantilist," emphasized economic nationalism and protectionism.

In Gilpin's 1987 textbook, the "sovereignty at bay" perspective became the "liberal" perspective, "dependency" became "Marxist," and "mercantilist" became the "economic nationalism" perspective.[1] In his 2001 textbook, Gilpin reused the latter triptych, but observed that it was less relevant than before. He claimed that Marxism was in decline, that liberalism had grown dramatically and was now dominant, but that he nevertheless adhered to the state-centric realism perspective that is a synthesis of the realist approach to international relations and the approach focusing on economic nationalism (Gilpin, 2001).

Following Gilpin's typology, IPE specialists still identify three very general perspectives or schools of thought in IPE (Hülsemeyer, 2010). Of these three, only the liberal approach is used in almost all IPE textbooks. Other authors have replaced the "nationalist" perspective with the "mercantilist" or "realist" or even the "state-centric realist" perspective. The Marxist perspective has also been called alternately the "structuralist," "dependency," "world-system," and even at times "critical theory" approach. The constructivist approach, apart from a few exceptions, remains marginal in IPE. It seldom appears in introductory texts and scientific publications (Abdelal, Blyth, and Parsons, 2010).

While these perspectives are the most important for understanding the debates in IPE, an increasing number of authors are stressing the irreconcilable epistemological differences (What is legitimate knowledge? That is, how do researchers know what they know?) between the approaches in order to distinguish between the different schools. In the 2014 edition of his textbook, John Ravenhill presents Gilpin's three approaches mainly to criticize them and to show their obsolescence; Matthew Watson (2014) follows suit in the same publication. Watson identifies, based on a two-by-two matrix, no fewer than 19 distinct traditions that are related by complex ties. Although Watson demonstrates great learnedness, his matrix is just the opposite of a parsimonious approach and is too sophisticated to be the basis of a textbook.

According to Craig N. Murphy and Douglas R. Nelson, and subsequently Benjamin Cohen and Mark Blyth, the distinction between the approaches is no longer between the three perspectives developed by Gilpin, but rather between the American conception of IPE, that favoured by the *International Organization* journal, and the British conception of IPE (in which are also included the works of Robert Cox and the neo-Gramscian school) (Murphy and Nelson, 2001; Cohen, 2008, 2014; Blyth, 2009).

For Cohen, five critical points divide the American and British schools: (1) ontology, (2) agenda, (3) purpose, (4) openness, and (5) epistemology (2014: 5). In Cohen's view, the American school is not very open to social science disciplines other than economics and political science. Its research agenda focuses on subjects such as international regime, cooperation, power relations, and especially American hegemony. Its level of analysis lies mainly at that of medium-range theories. Its objective is to understand how the world works without passing normative judgments. This school is positivist and prioritizes the scientific method based on the natural science model. It is very focused on quantitative methods and increasingly on formal modelling (Cohen, 2007, 2008, 2014).

Compared to the American school, the British is more critical and explicitly normative. According to British school authors, the American school proposes *problem-solving* theories because it focuses on political problems with the desire to solve them, but without questioning more deeply the system within which these problems emerge. Instead of being problem-solving, the British school is *problem-posing*. Its overall goal is not to make the world work better but to change it! As heterodox authors are more multidisciplinary, they are also more open to studies from disciplines other than political science and economics, disciplines such as sociology, history, philosophy, and so on. For the British school, positivist epistemology is largely useless, as the parameters are changing and all relevant factors must be analyzed (Cohen, 2007, 2008, 2014).

The works of the British school authors, the most influential of whom are Robert Cox and Susan Strange, are more difficult to place within a single coherent perspective. The borrowings from Marxism, structuralism, and poststructuralism are obvious, as is the influence of world-systems and dependency theories. These works are described as critical because the major authors in the field do not agree to include their works within a constituted perspective such as liberalism or realism, but rather see them as a reaction to the dominant approaches in American orthodox IPE.

The typology proposed by Cohen is both important and useful. But it poses certain problems. It defines the framework of the division lines of IPE as it appears at the time of publication. Cohen's typology reflects the young generation of IPE researchers, specifically in the American school. Even though these young researchers are important authors, they are not (yet) the most important. In the American school, the principal founding fathers—Robert Gilpin, Stephen Krasner, Robert Keohane, Joseph Nye, and Peter Katzenstein—are not greatly drawn to quantitative methods and formal modelling. In their case, qualitative and even historical analyses are more important. In other words, Cohen's portrayal of the field has not always been true and even nowadays it is largely imperfect. These founding fathers, whom Cohen considers the most important, only very imperfectly match his typology. Furthermore, this typology tends to underestimate the divisions within schools. It does not reveal the theoretical diversity of the field's evolution since its foundation. In the American school, for example, different theoretical perspectives are both fundamental and incommensurable.

According to a team of professors working on the Teaching, Research, and International Policy (TRIP) project who conducted several studies on teaching, research, and international politics and policy making, the great majority of American IPE researchers (73 per cent) identify with one of the four key perspectives in international relations: liberal, realist, Marxist, and constructivist (compared to only 45 per cent of researchers in the wider international relations discipline). IPE in the United States has thus been built more firmly around paradigmatic debates than has the wider international relations discipline (Maliniak and Tierney, 2009: 19–22). To these three paradigms must be added that of domestic politics (including the Open

Economy Politics paradigm), which is essential in IPE but is not represented in the survey. This paradigm focuses on the domestic determinants of international political economy. To say the least, it is curious that while the paradigmatic debates are fundamental, even more so than in IR in general, they have been minimized by Cohen to the point of practically disappearing from his *Advanced Introduction to International Political Economy* (2014).

Since the 1970s, the debates in American IPE have essentially been between the liberal and realist perspectives. According to the TRIP project researchers, as of 2009, the overwhelming majority of IPE authors identify with the liberal paradigm. From 1995 to 2006, between 45 per cent and 70 per cent of the articles published in the 12 leading journals, as selected by the TRIP project, belonged to this category. Marxism is the paradigm that has declined the most in the United States since the 1980s. Although it was probably the most important in 1980, with 39 per cent of the articles published, it fell to 11 per cent in 1986, and since 1990 it has never exceeded 10 per cent of the articles appearing in the leading scientific journals (Maliniak and Tierney, 2009: 19–22).

Long presented as the dominant paradigm in the international relations research field, realism remains marginal in IPE, as does the constructivist paradigm. According to Daniel Maliniak, Amy Oakes, Susan Peterson, and Michael J. Tierney (2011), the importance of realism has always been overestimated. The realist paradigm was, even in the 1980s, far behind the liberal paradigm in the broad field of international relations. Since 1980, realism and constructivism have never exceeded 11 per cent of the articles published. These paradigms declined further between 1996 and 2006, representing only 8 per cent of articles published in the IPE field (Maliniak and Tierney, 2009: 19–22).

The contrast is significant when compared with the international relations discipline in general. Since 2011, constructivism has been the most popular paradigm in the United States, very close to the liberal approach. In fact, in 2011 and for the first time, more international relations researchers confirmed they had adopted a constructivist approach at the expense of a liberal or realist approach: 22 per cent identified with constructivism versus 21 per cent for liberalism, 16 per cent for realism, and only 2 per cent for Marxism (Avey et al., 2012: 92). Hence, unlike the situation in international relations, orthodox IPE has not experienced an ideational turn.

Rawi Abdelal, Mark Blyth, and Craig Parsons also suggest that constructivism is marginal in IPE. In a collective work published 2010, in which they sought to introduce constructivism in IPE, they argue that constructivism is progressing everywhere "except in the mainstream of international political economy, which has remained resistant to this trend. As used to be the case elsewhere, the view of the world that still informs much political economy scholarship is materialist and rationalist" (2010: 3).

Although it is still marginal and is regressing, the realist paradigm remains important in IPE, as the debates that most structured the discipline have often been between liberals and realists. Realist authors have served as a punching bag for liberal authors who systematically criticize the former's works. As well, when researchers who identify IPE as their first or second research field are asked which international relations authors have had the most influence on their own work, they name a number of realist authors among the first 25, including Robert Gilpin (second) and Stephen Krasner (tenth) (Maliniak and Tierney, 2009: 21).

In the case of the British school, because Susan Strange was a professor at the London School of Economics and Political Science, Cohen uses the expression "the British school of IPE." For him, the expression should not be understood in a strictly territorial sense. Rather, it unites all those associated with the fundamental postulates of this school. The problem with Cohen's proposal lies in the fact that it underestimates the differences that exist between the IPE of Susan Strange and that of Robert Cox and the neo-Gramscian school. As we will see in this book, these differences are important.

Furthermore, this label is somewhat surprising as we know that Robert Cox is not British, but Canadian (and a Quebecer) and that, in the final analysis, he has had more influence on the development of the heterodox school than Susan Strange. Even though Strange's spirit is still present, few researchers today subscribe to her theoretical proposals. When the community of international relations researchers from Canada and Great Britain is asked to name the researchers who most influenced the international relations field in the last 20 years, Robert Cox is in fourth place with 21 per cent of the votes in the two countries, (but just 3 per cent in United States). With 9 per cent of the votes in Canada and 8 per cent in Great Britain, Strange is less popular than Cox. Furthermore, she gets no more than 2 per cent in the United States, the same as Hedley Bull and Barry Buzan (Jordan et al., 2009: 43).

What is more, Cohen himself admits that the majority of the world's IPE specialists are closer to his typology of the British school than of the American school, including those working in the United States and whom Craig Murphy (2009) calls "America's left-out." For this reason, in the framework of this book, we prefer to borrow from economics debates the terms *orthodox school* and *heterodox school*. Several theoretical perspectives (liberal, realist, neo-Gramscian, feminist, etc.) cut across each of these schools. It is true, as Cohen contends, that, as of the 1980s and 1990s, the IPE developed in the United States took a major turn and increasingly came to resemble the neoclassical economists, the group it sought to oppose in the early 1970s. Most of the IPE works published in the United States are now characterized by the same type of mathematical and statistical techniques found in specialized economics journals. Instead of criticizing the orthodoxy of neoclassical economists as it did in its infancy, orthodox IPE (concentrated mainly in the United States, with a small following in Canada and only marginal support in the rest of the world) has come to adopt neoclassical economists' codes and scientific culture. This shift has led to the appearance of important dividing lines between the orthodox US school and the heterodox school dominant in Great Britain, which also has a strong presence in Canada and around the world.

The Dividing Lines between the Orthodox and Heterodox Schools

The development of the new IPE research field in the early 1970s raised a multitude of questions: What should be included in this new area of enquiry? What object should we study? Who are the major actors? What are the key institutions? What distinguishes IPE from the fields of international economics and international relations? In short, what is the identity of this new research field? All these questions are ontological in nature.

Ontology is a special area in the study of the philosophy of science that focuses its attention on the nature of being and existence. According to Steve Smith, ontology is "what the world is like," or what aspect needs to be explained (2011: 5). For Milja Kurki and Colin Wight, ontology represents a "theory of being: what is the world made of? What objects do we study?" (2011: 19). According to Lene Hansen, ontology is "what is in the world" (2011: 168). Ontology thus calls for a definition of the object studied, its framework, its content, its various fundamental concepts, theories, and approaches, and the diverse elements that constitute the discipline being studied.

To illustrate what ontology is, imagine a political scientist, an economist, and an architect who enter a factory and describe what they see. Their visions of this factory will be relevant and probably accurate but fundamentally different because their ontology is not the same. The debate does not stop there. If we asked three IPE specialists to perform the same exercise, we might also obtain three different visions because, within the same field of research, conceptions of the world vary. This is the case, for example, between the liberals, the realists, and the neo-Gramscians in IPE, or between the orthodox and the heterodox (Macleod and O'Meara, 2007: 7).

In other words, when researchers are working in the same school or within the same perspective, it is unnecessary to talk at length about ontology. However, when the differences between schools or perspectives are substantial, ontological questions rise to the surface. These questions are fundamental because, if there is disagreement about them, dialogue is difficult, if not impossible.

Ontologically speaking, the orthodox and heterodox schools share several points in common. As we saw previously, their definitions of IPE and their descriptions of its historical origins are relatively similar and compatible. Debate on these matters is not critical and the differences are minor. The two schools basically agree on what the field of IPE is.

However, the ontological differences among the major actors in IPE are much more obvious. The orthodox generally conceive of IPE as a discipline related to international relations, but they also share with the political sciences an active concern with public policies and state intervention. The orthodox school remains fundamentally state-centric, meaning that the state is the pre-eminent object of study, the favoured focus of research. The main themes that have structured orthodox research are the effects of globalization on state capacities and public policies, hegemonic stability theory in which the American state has the leading role, regime theory, and the interactions between international political economy and domestic politics. The NGOs and transnational actors that were present in the beginning are today largely cast aside. Even Keohane does not pay much attention to non-state actors nowadays (Cohen, 2008, 2014). In the United States, the boundaries between IPE, comparative political economy, and US politics have become very blurred. Several professors, such as Helen Milner and Jeffry Frieden, are specialists in all three areas (Milner, 1998).

The coherence of the objects of study for heterodox researchers is less obvious. As the heterodox come from diverse horizons, they produce studies on a very wide variety of subjects. Strange, for example, published a number of books and articles on international finance, monetary policies, multinationals, American structural power, and the retreat of the state in favour of the market. For his part, Cox has conducted several studies on international organizations, labour and markets, international relations theories, American hegemony, and world order.

As a general rule, heterodox authors propose research studies that are not state-centric. Thus, unlike the orthodox, they perceive the state as one actor among others. The state is admittedly an important actor, but for Strange and Cox, it is not the only actor and it does not always even play a dominant role in IPE. For heterodox authors, social forces, production factors, power structures, markets, and international finance are major actors in IPE. The very large majority of the heterodox can be considered radical transnationalists or hyperglobalists in the sense that the state is no longer the principal actor in international relations. Their objects of study are more diversified and remain open to several currents of thought. In the heterodox view, the capacity of the state is very perceptibly in decline.

Coxian ontology places "modes of production" rather than states at the centre of the analysis. Cox's emphasis on the "state/society complex" does not mix well with the state-centric tradition of the dominant orthodox approach in the United States. Strange's work as well is marked by this desire to contest the assumption that the state is the only entity that should be taken into account in IPE. For the heterodox, the state-centric approach of the orthodox is too simplistic and does not enable us to understand the human condition. Strange maintained that, depending on the issues, it is possible for banks or oil companies or Colombian drug lords or multinational corporations to be just as important in the question of *cui bono* (who benefits), the question that has always been central in the study of politics (Strange, 1996). In short, the state-centric approach does not take into account a number of actors that exercise significant economic and political power. The most neglected actors, according to Strange, are those of the finance, credit, and technology worlds. In her last article, published posthumously, Strange invited researchers to escape and resist the state-centrism inherent in the analysis of conventional international relations and IPE. The study of globalization should embrace the study of the behaviour of multinational firms just as it does the other forms of political authority (Strange, 1999).

Another important difference has to do with what the *problématique* in world politics should be. To accept the primacy of the state as an international actor only makes sense if we believe that questions of war and peace are the main issues on the international scene. Heterodox specialists, like Strange, do not accept this premise. Security issues are not the only crucial problems in world politics. According to Strange, who gets rich and who remains poor, who has access to health care, medicine, and hospitals and who does not, the protection of forests or the ozone layer are also important *problématiques* (Strange, 1996). Furthermore, violence against individuals or private property damage can have causes other than wars between states. Agents of the state can be responsible for these acts. According to Strange, Chinese dissidents have more to fear from their own government than from possible invasions by foreign countries. Thus, it is imperative that we broaden our notion of what constitutes subject matter and that we multiply the levels of analysis.

The difference between the orthodox and the heterodox in their selection of important actors in IPE influences the levels of analysis of the two schools. When the key actors in IPE are individuals and their collective representations, like states and international organizations, researchers turn more easily towards methodological individualism. On the other hand, when social forces, structural power, production, or markets are the key actors, researchers are more naturally prone to adopt holistic approaches.

While it is not an absolute, orthodox theorists lean towards methodological individualism, rationalism, and even rational choice theory, while heterodox researchers more naturally tend towards holist explanations (Palan, 2009). These two approaches are irreconcilable. The opposition between holism and methodological individualism is rooted in the question of the level of analysis of the international system. The difference between the levels of analysis is highly significant. It lies mainly at the ontological level, but it also has a strong impact at the epistemological and methodological levels (Waltz, 1959; Singer, 1961; Buzan, 1995).

Methodological individualism postulates that social phenomena can be explained based on an aggregation of individual actions. This approach emphasizes the role of the actors or of constituting units in the functioning of the system. A system is thus the sum of its parts. Holism, on the other hand, considers that social phenomena are totalities irreducible to individuals. According to this approach, the system possesses an existence of its own and acts according to its own operating rules.

Orthodox IPE is also rationalist, as opposed to reflectivist or constructivist. The division between rationalism and reflectivism was first outlined in a speech given by Robert Keohane at the International Studies Association (ISA) in 1988. In his presidential address, Keohane remarked on the appearance of numerous theories (such as critical theories, constructivism, feminism, poststructuralism, etc.) that were very critical of the dominant approach. Keohane called these approaches "reflectivist" because they all rejected the positivist causal theories and because they stressed reflectivity and the non-neutral nature of the social and political explanation. In short, the common thread in these new theoretical approaches was their negation of the separation between the researcher and the object observed, the researcher being an integral part of the object studied. These approaches remain skeptical about the possibility of formulating a causal theory and instead stress the interpretation of phenomena.

In their research, a number of orthodox IPE researchers adopt rational choice theory, a variant of methodological individualism. Political scientists first imported this theory from neoclassical economists in the 1950s. To the fundamental postulates of methodological individualism, rational choice theory adds the idea that individuals are egoists, that any action includes a cost and a benefit, and that actors seek to maximize their benefits (Milner, 1997). Keohane argued, for example, that actors are rational, utilitarian, and egotistic, and that they act so as to maximize their interest. The rational choice approach does not focus only on actors' interests; it also allows researchers to integrate in their analyses the interactions between "strategic" actors. Actor interactions refers to the notion that, in calculating their preferences, individuals include the anticipated behaviours of other actors that are also rational (Lake and Powell, 1999). As well, orthodox theorists are increasingly using extremely sophisticated quantitative models to analyze IPE. They believe that these models enable them to explain, for example, the complexity of interstate relations or the incentives to international cooperation.

For the orthodox, the identity and the interests of the actors are exogenous and represent a fact rather than a social construction. Although values and perceptions are important, they remain secondary, as do many aspects of social life. In taking this approach, it becomes possible to create causal theories. Keohane recognizes the limitations of this approach, but he believes that it is very effective for making predictions. It is deductive, contrary to the first forms of positivism, and it is based on empirical observation, measurement, and the possibility of creating causal theories.

When orthodox theorists focus on ideas, as Judith Goldstein and Robert Keohane (1993) have done, ideas are considered as causal factors that are exchanged by already constituted actors. Paul Sabatier and Edella Schlager describe Goldstein and Keohane's approach as "cognitive minimalist" because the latter examined all the possible reasonable explanations before concluding that ideas played an important role (Sabatier and Schlager, 2000: 234). As John Ruggie points out, "For the individuals featured in the Goldstein-Keohane story are not born into a system of social relationships that helps shape who they become. When we first encounter them, they are already fully constituted and poised in a problem-solving mode" (1998: 866).

The heterodox approaches reject *en bloc* the orthodox approach, but also generally reject the rational choice approach. Heterodox theorists do not accept the idea that individuals consistently seek to maximize their choice. Strange criticized the adoption of rationality imported from the works of economists by orthodox IPE specialists. For her, it was a failed attempt to gain in theoretical precision and scientific legitimacy to the detriment of realism. Strange referenced Herbert Simon who proposed the concept of "bounded rationality," the concept that won him the Nobel Prize. For Simon, the rationality of individuals is limited by a number of things, such as the information available, cognitive limitations, and time. Moreover, governments, like enterprises, have multiple objectives in mind when they make decisions. They do not necessarily seek the best solution, but a solution that is satisfactory because it fulfils many objectives, as best as possible. Simon invented the hybrid concept of "satisficing" to describe a decision that, while not optimal, would suffice (Strange, 1996: 20–1).

Nevertheless, according to Strange, even the concept of bounded rationality must be used with caution because it implies that an actor's motivations can be satisfied, that they are stable over time, which means, for example, that a negotiation between governments or firms can fulfil an expectation while, in fact, priorities change too quickly. Besides which, situations being so complex, information is imperfect: there is too much of it, it is contradictory, and government negotiators are not always aware of the priorities and objectives of their governments.

The heterodox believe it is a mistake to affirm the existence of a rationality and a system of thought shared by all the world's actors, regardless of the era and the culture. That reasoning, they say, does not take into account important cultural variations and divergences in representations that exist between the actors. The world of the orthodox is a world in which identities and values are relatively similar (Badie and Smouts, 1999).

More and more, in orthodox IPE, "methodology has replaced theory" according to Ronen Palan (2009: 391). Contrary to the arguments of orthodox researchers, the rational choice approach is profoundly non-empirical. It is based not on observations but on theoretical presuppositions. Rational choice theorists postulate the rationality of actors because it facilitates building a parsimonious theory with a high predictive capacity. In other words, says Palan, the true empirical school is the British (or heterodox) school.

The heterodox lean more naturally towards holistic explanations of IPE. A number of authors, including Barry Gills, Ronen Palan, Barry Jones, and Aukie Hoogvelt, maintain that the theories developed by Cox and Strange belong to the category of neo-structuralist approaches. Structuralism proposes a holistic explanation of the world. Cox's "historical structures" can only be understood by the systematic linkages between them. In Strange's theory of structural power and in Cox's theory of neo-Gramscian hegemony, the nature of power is not relational but structural. These approaches have a kinship with the most well-known structuralist approach, that of Immanuel Wallerstein's world-system theory, but also with that of dependency theorists in the 1960s and 1970s (Palan and Gills 1994; Jones, 1995; Pinter and Hoogvelt, 1997; Gill, 1990b).

Conclusion

This polarization between the orthodox and heterodox schools has sparked a huge debate among specialists. For Benjamin Cohen, the orthodox school (which he calls the American school) has lost its ambitions and is no longer interested in major world issues. Moreover, the articles published in orthodox IPE journals have become "boring" (Cohen, 2010). Nicola Phillips denounces the slow death of pluralism while Kathleen R. McNamara describes the American orthodox school as a "monoculture" (Phillips, 2009; McNamara, 2009). The situation has become so extreme that the pioneers of IPE in the United States, whether Robert Keohane, Joseph Nye, Robert Gilpin, or Peter Katzenstein, would have a hard time finding a job in IPE in a major American university. Even Keynes, Hirschman, and Polanyi no longer fit the profile.

The resulting academic training, career path, and scientific culture to a large extent explain the divergences between the orthodox school and the heterodox school. The years at university and then the socialization in the career of a professor create different scientific cultures—different systems of meaning that the members of an IPE community use in their interactions (Geertz, 1973; Badie, 1993). The members of the two communities have established codes, references, and ways of doing things that are becoming more and more differentiated. The orthodox authors have become insensitive to what is published outside the United States, and the professors of major US universities have their students read very few authors educated outside of US universities. As a result, orthodox and heterodox IPE specialists often have the impression they are not working in the same research field. As we will see in the next chapter, the differences in the scientific culture of the two schools has led to very different conception of what is a legitimate theory in IPE.

Note

1   For Gilpin, these perspectives are ideologies rather than theoretical perspectives. In Gilpin's view, an ideology is a system of thought and belief by which individuals or groups explain how their social system operates and what principles it exemplifies (Gilpin, 1987: 25).

Questions

1. Why and where was international political economy (IPE) invented as a discipline in the 1970s?
2. Why did Susan Strange think that international economics and international relations were a case of mutual neglect?
3. What does transnational relations mean to Joseph Nye and Robert Keohane?
4. What are the founding debates in IPE?
5. What is IPE? Is it more about the economic dimension of international relations or the political determinants of international economic relations?
6. Are IPE specialists "economists" working in political science departments?
7. What are the key debates between the various theoretical perspectives?
8. What are the critical points dividing the American and the British schools, according to Benjamin Cohen?
9. What are the key perspectives in international relations that are also present in IPE?
10. What are the key differences between the orthodox and the heterodox schools?

Further Reading

For a historical perspective:

Frieden, Jeffry A. Global Capitalism: *Its Fall and Rise in the Twentieth Century.*
New York: W.W. Norton & Company, 2006.

Eichengreen, Barry. *Globalizing Capital: A History of the International Monetary System.* 2nd ed. Princeton: Princeton University Press, 2008.

For excellent IPE textbooks:

Cohn, Theodore. *Global Political Economy: Theory and Practice.* 6th ed. New York: Longman, 2011.

Gilpin, Robert. *The Political Economy of International Relations.* Princeton: Princeton University Press, 1987.

Gilpin, Robert. *Global Political Economy: Understanding the International Economic Order.* Princeton: Princeton University Press, 2001.

Oatley, Thomas. *International Political Economy.* 5th ed. New York: Pearson, 2011.

Ravenhill, John, ed. *Global Political Economy.* 4th ed. New York: Oxford University Press, 2014.

For analysis and debate on the International Political Economy discipline and the growing division between the orthodox and heterodox schools:

Blyth, Mark, ed. *Routledge Handbook of International Political Economy (IPE): IPE As a Global Conversation.* London: Routledge, 2009.

Cohen, Benjamin. "The Transatlantic Divide: Why Are American and British IPE So Different?" *Review of International Political Economy* 14.2 (2007): 197–219.

Cohen, Benjamin. *International Political Economy: An Intellectual History.* Princeton: Princeton University Press, 2008.

Cohen, Benjamin. *Advanced Introduction to International Political Economy.* Northampton, MA: Edward Elgar Publishing, 2014.

Dickins, Amanda. "The Evolution of International Political Economy." *International Affairs* 82.3 (2006): 479–92.

Krasner, Stephen D. "International Political Economy: Abiding Discord." *Review of International Political Economy* 1.1 (1994): 13–19.

Maliniak, Daniel, and Michael J. Tierney. "The American School of IPE." *Review of International Political Economy* 16.1 (2009): 6–33.

Murphy, Craig N., and Douglas R. Nelson. "International Political Economy: A Tale of Two Heterodoxies." *British Journal of Politics and International Relations* 3.3 (2001): 394–412.

Palan, Ronen, ed. *Global Political Economy.* London: Routledge, 2000.

Phillips, Nicola, and Catherine Weaver. *International Political Economy: Debating the Past, Present and Future of IPE.* London: Routledge, 2010.

Strange, Susan. "Wake up, Krasner! The World Has Changed." *Review of International Political Economy* 1.2 (1994): 209–19.

Underhill, Geoffrey R.D. "State, Market, and Global Political Economy: Genealogy of and (Inter-?) Discipline." *International Affairs* 76.4 (2000): 805–24.

For US analysis that ignores the heterodox school:

Frieden, Jeffry A., and Lisa L. Martin. "International Political Economy: Global and Domestic Interactions." In *Political Science: State of the Discipline*, edited by Ira Katznelson and Helen V. Milner, 118–46. New York: W.W. Norton & Company, 2002.

Katzenstein, Peter J., Robert O. Keohane, and Stephen D. Krasner, eds. "*International Organization* and the Study of World Politics." *International Organization* 52.4 (1998): 645–85.

Krasner, Stephen D. "The Accomplishments of International Political Economy." In *International Theory: Positivism and Beyond*, edited by Steve Smith, Ken Booth, and Marisya Zalewski, 108–27. Cambridge: Cambridge University Press, 1996.

Lake, David A. "International Political Economy: A Maturing Discipline." In *The Oxford Handbook of Political Economy*, edited by Barry R. Weingast and Donald Wittman, 757–77. New York: Oxford University Press, 2008.

2 Theorizing International Political Economy

Chapter Contents

- Epistemology in IPE
- What Is Positivism in Orthodox IPE?
- Types of Theory
- Theorizing According to the Orthodox Approach
- Theorizing According to the Heterodox Approach
- Theorizing among the Neo-Gramscians
- Theorizing According to Susan Strange
- Conclusion

Reader's Guide

The orthodox and the heterodox have diverging conceptions of a "good" theory in IPE. As positivists, orthodox theorists generally believe in the possibility of creating causal IPE theories. Heterodox theorists, on the other hand, do not adhere to the principles of positivism. Consequently, they say, we cannot use the same tools or the same conceptions of science to explain and understand the world. These debates are fundamental, as they represent the epistemological and methodological dividing lines between the orthodox and heterodox schools. The goal of this chapter is to explain how the scientific cultures of the orthodox school and the heterodox school have led to diverging conceptions of what counts as legitimate theory in IPE. This chapter begins with the general epistemological differences between the two approaches: the orthodox school's adherence to, and the heterodox school's rejection of, the principles of positivism. It concludes by presenting the differences in the theorization processes of the two approaches.

It would be fortunate if a book dealing with IPE theories could provide a simple and widely accepted definition of what a theory is, but in reality there is not "one" definition; there are several, and there are two main reasons for this. First, the social sciences encompass several types of theories.

Second, authors who adhere to the principles of positivism, as orthodox IPE researchers do, base their conception of a theory on what natural scientists say it is; postpositivist authors, who are the majority in heterodox IPE, reject that conception (Sutton and Staw, 1995; Weick, 1995).

As positivists, orthodox theorists generally believe in the possibility of creating causal IPE theories. Heterodox theorists, on the other hand, do not adhere to the principles of positivism and are essentially united in their perception that the world of the social sciences is not that of the natural sciences. Consequently, they say, we cannot use the same tools or the same conceptions of science to explain and understand the world. These debates are fundamental, as they represent the epistemological and methodological dividing lines between the orthodox and heterodox schools.

As a result, while the orthodox and the heterodox can agree on the need to theorize IPE, the two schools have diverging conceptions of what constitutes a "good" theory in IPE. The goal of this chapter is to explain how the scientific cultures of the orthodox school and the heterodox school have led to diverging conceptions of a legitimate theory in IPE. This chapter begins with the general epistemological differences between the two approaches: the orthodox school's adherence to, and the heterodox school's rejection of, the principles of positivism. It concludes by presenting the differences in the theorization processes of the two approaches.

Epistemology in IPE

According to Steve Smith, the underlying cause of the great cleavage between American and non-American researchers in international relations is essentially an epistemological divergence (Smith, 2002). In Smith's words, it is a "US versus the rest phenomenon." He contends that in the rest of the world, international relations specialists remain skeptical about the merits of positivism and the associated belief that a standard exists by which to measure the quality of academic research studies. The studies by Daniel Maliniak and his collaborators largely confirm Smith's assertions: in the United States, the research published in international relations is almost entirely positivist. That is not the case in most of the rest of the world.

This assertion is also true for the works in IPE. At the epistemological level, the IPE orthodox are notoriously positivist. In 1983, approximately 67 per cent of the articles published in the 12 leading journals (those journals that are the most quoted and influential in the discipline) fit into the positivist category versus an incredible 98 per cent in 1985.[1] From 1980 to 2006, the articles that subscribed to the principles of positivism represented 91 per cent of the total! IPE researchers are very positivist (79 per cent), as are security issues specialists (78 per cent) (Maliniak et al., 2011: 445, 461; Maliniak and Tierney, 2009).

In the United States, it is the young researchers who most tend to consider themselves positivists. Among the professors who obtained their doctorate prior to 1980, 65 per cent described themselves as positivists. This number rose to 71 per cent for those who obtained their doctorate after 2000. The renewal of the professorial body in the United States should therefore reinforce this trend (Maliniak et al., 2011: 445).

At the methodological level, orthodox IPE specialists have seen a very marked evolution towards the more frequent use of quantitative methods. According to Maliniak and Tierney (2009), in the 1980s and 1990s, IPE articles made more use of qualitative methods than did international relations articles in general. In fact, at that time, most of the works published in the 12 leading journals were qualitative in nature. The situation is completely different nowadays. In 2006, the final year of Maliniak and Tierney's analysis, an astonishing total of 90 per cent of orthodox IPE works used quantitative methods.

In orthodox IPE, we also see a significant increase in formal modelling in the articles published. According to an analysis performed by Benjamin Cohen, of the 170 articles that appeared in the *International Organization* journal between 1975 and 1979, less than 10 per cent proposed a formal modelling. From 1980 to 1984, this percentage dropped slightly to 7.4 per cent, but in the second half of the 1990s, the average soared to 26 per cent, while from 2000 to 2004 the proportion reached almost 50 per cent. In comparison, of the 161 articles published in the *Review of International Political Economy* between 1994 (the date of the journal's creation) and 1998, only six proposed a formal modelling, or 3.7 per cent of the total. Between 1999 and 2003, this proportion practically doubled, but remained at a very low 5.6 per cent (Cohen, 2008: 42, 55). According to Cohen,

> over time American orthodox IPE has been standardized and it has come to resemble nothing so much as the methodology of neoclassical economics, featuring the same penchant for positivist analysis, formal modeling, and, where possible, systematic collection and evaluation of empirical data. More and more, what gets published in the United States features the same sorts of mathematical and statistical techniques that we have come to expect in economics journals. (Cohen, 2007: 206)

As Cohen sees it, this situation in the United States is due to the fact that political scientists have an inferiority complex when they compare themselves to economists (and a superiority complex when they compare themselves to sociologists). It is the economists who seem to have created the standards of what passes for professionalism among social scientists in the United States. Peter Katzenstein, Robert Keohane, and Stephen Krasner even describe the economics discipline as "the reigning king of the social sciences" (1998: 645). The works of the orthodox IPE school thus tend to imitate economists and their models inspired by the "exact" sciences. This situation is perhaps also attributable to the fact that IPE is a young discipline that wants to demonstrate its rigour. Cohen concludes, "Specialists in IPE want respect, too" (Cohen, 2007: 206). A generational effect may also in part explain these changes. Indeed, those who obtained their doctorate after 2000 are more likely to use quantitative methods (37 per cent) than are their peers who graduated in the 1990s (27 per cent) or 1980s (18 per cent). University training therefore reinforces the trend (Maliniak et al., 2011: 445).

What Is Positivism in Orthodox IPE?

As positivism holds such importance in IPE theories, it is imperative to explain what positivism refers to and what meaning it has for the IPE orthodox. Nowadays, according to Steve Smith, there are four generally accepted positivist postulates in the broad field of international relations in the United States (2008: 16–17). This situation is even more true in orthodox IPE, as the latter borrows a lot methodologically from economics and the mathematical sciences. These postulates are as follows:

1. There is a unity in science; that is, there is no fundamental difference between the natural sciences and the social sciences. Thus, the tools and methods necessary to understand the world of physics or chemistry can be used to explain international relations or IPE.
2. There is a distinction between "facts" and "values." Furthermore, in its hard version, this means that "facts" are neutral from the point of view of theory and independent of the values of the researcher. We can therefore separate the researcher or the observer from the object of research. One of the consequences is that the researcher must avoid passing "normative" judgment on the world.
3. There are regularities in the social world just as in the natural world. It is therefore possible to develop causal theories of IPE.
4. There is no valid scientific research without empirical validation. The conception of science has its roots in empiricist epistemology, which contends that knowledge cannot be based on facts that cannot be experienced by the senses. To be considered true, knowledge must be built on empirical testing. Positivism in the social sciences is therefore predominantly a methodological commitment attached to empiricist epistemology that claims that knowledge can only be based on experience and observation. One must observe the facts and put aside anything that is not observable (Smith, 2008: 16–17).

These conceptions of positivism and empiricism tied in especially well with behaviourists' race for quantification in the 1950s and 1960s. In international relations theory, these issues were part of what is usually called the second great debate between realists and behaviourists. This debate pitted the partisans of a more philosophical, normative, and historical methodology, the first realist theorists, against behaviourist researchers, such as David Singer and Morton Kaplan, who wanted to inject more methodological "rigour" in the discipline. Without calling into question the fundamental postulates or the ontology of the realists, behaviourists reproached realists for their methodology, saying that it was not rigorous enough to be described as "scientific." For behaviourists, some of the fundamental concepts of realists, concepts such as "power" or "national interest," were difficult to measure.

According to behaviourists, international relations could only advance or evolve if researchers adopted positivism. Positivism became a synonym for "scientific" in the behaviourists' perspective. In international relations, they considered that scientific knowledge could only emerge with the accumulation of observable data. With sufficient data, they thought it would be possible for researchers to observe regularities that, in turn, would enable them to formulate laws. Their position is simplified in the inscription on the facade of the University of Chicago Social Science Research Building: "If you cannot measure it, your knowledge is meagre and unsatisfactory" (quoted in Kurki and Wight, 2011: 18). Anything that could not be measured had to be excluded from the international relations research field. Behaviourists especially stressed the importance of introducing quantitative methods in the study of international relations, and encouraged researchers to import methods developed in mathematics and economics departments.

This positivist shift in the American political sciences, which also affects theorists of international relations and international political economy, is of vital importance. It is impossible to understand the works and debates, or even to publish in a reputable scientific journal in the United States, if one ignores the dominant positivism. According to Gabriel Almond and Stephen Genco, in the late 1960s, a person could obtain a Ph.D. in political science with very little or no knowledge in political theory, political history, comparative political systems, international relations, and even in American politics and the US government (Almond and Genco, 1977). William Riker says this situation can be explained by the fact that training graduate students in quantitative methods leaves less time to introduce them to the traditionally taught subjects in politics. In an editorial comment that appeared back in 1974, Riker was proud to announce that two-thirds of the publications of the *American Political Science Review* used a quantitative and statistical analysis.

The choice of positivism has had a decisive impact on research methodology. The methodology no longer adjusts to the object studied; in fact, quite the opposite is true. For Steve Smith, positivism did not so much give international relations theories a method, but "its empiricist epistemology has determined what could be studied because it has determined what kinds of things existed in international relations" (Smith, 2008: 11). Thus, because of positivism, empiricist epistemology, and quantitative methods, it is largely the object that adjusts to the method. Anything that cannot be quantified, anything that is normative, anything that has to do with identity, nationalism, the social construction of reality, or the decision-making process has been largely ignored by positivists.

The hard version of positivism is, however, unsustainable in IPE and has been somewhat softened. According to Milja Kurki and Colin Wight (2011), the austere version of the science advocated by behaviourists has been diluted with the passage of time; nevertheless, the fundamental positivist principles that were derived from the principles of hard science still dominate orthodox IPE. This continues to have lasting effects on the methodological techniques taught in universities, with the hypothesis testing, statistical analysis, and data manipulation that are the indispensable prerequisites of any methodological training.

Orthodox IPE specialists today consider that knowledge accumulation is only possible through objective observation and systematic testing of hypotheses. Deductive logic and the development of parsimonious theories are promoted. As Stephen Krasner, one of the pioneers of the orthodox approach, points out,

> International political economy is deeply embedded in the standard epistemological methodology of the social sciences which, stripped to its bare bones, simply means stating a proposition and testing it against external evidence. Students of IPE have implicitly rejected the sceptical or anti-foundational post-modernist position which claims . . . that "each society has its own regime of truth, its general politics of truth." (Krasner, 2008: 108–9)

According to Jeffry Frieden and Lisa L. Martin, "After a period of internecine paradigmatic conflict, most scholars in the field have accepted a general, positivist approach to investigating issues in the politics of international economics" (2002: 145).

This conception of science and this dominant scientific culture in the United States are very widely contested among heterodox IPE theorists. Consequently and contrary to the orthodox school, heterodox IPE specialists accept a larger ontological and epistemological diversity (Blyth, 2009; Cohen, 2014). In British academia, for example, according to Ben Clift and Ben Rosamond, relations between the disciplines have never been closed off. Clift and Rosamond contend that the IPE practised in Great Britain has been able to exploit the potential of a much greater epistemological and ontological diversity than has the orthodox approach. The influence of sociology, economic sociology, economic history, and heterodox economics, in particular Marxist, evolutionary, and institutional economics, can be added to that of political studies (Clift and Rosamond, 2009: 98).

According to these two authors, British university students do not have to choose to specialize in comparative politics, IPE, or international relations, and doctoral research is not defined in disciplinary terms. The academic order is much more relaxed in the British system than in the American. In the British system, it is easier to produce multidisciplinary research that draws its sources, concepts, and theoretical frameworks from a number of perspectives. British academia is thus less marked by disciplinary boundaries, which leaves more margin in terms of standards of what is admissible as research in IPE.

In addition, the behaviourist revolution never integrated the practices of British political sciences, as it did in the United States. The borrowings from economists were significant but were not necessarily from the works of neoclassical economists, contrary to what occurred more generally in the United States. In Great Britain, *political science* was a contested term and several researchers preferred to use the term *political studies*, as the conception of political science widely accepted in the United States was just one among several conceptions of the political sciences in the UK. This context was more favourable for fertilization between disciplines. While Cohen stated that the Marxist approaches were outside what was acceptable for academic works in the United States, that was not the case in Great Britain (Cohen, 2007, 2008). According to Clift and Rosamond, Marxism was a much more important intellectual tradition in British social sciences than in the United States (Clift and Rosamond, 2009: 99).

Types of Theory

When referring to the term *theory*, most orthodox IPE researchers are thinking about so-called explanatory or causal theories. This conceptualization of theories is hegemonic in economics departments and increasingly in the political science departments of major American universities. Researchers with heterodox leanings generally have in mind more the so-called comprehensive theories, as well as constitutive, normative, and critical theories.

The distinction between an explanatory or causal theory and a comprehensive theory (sometimes also called "interpretive") was introduced in the international relations debates by Martin Hollis and Steve Smith in 1990 (Hollis and Smith, 1990). These two authors drew on the works of Max Weber who made a distinction between the concepts *erklären* and *verstehen*. An explanatory theory (*erklären*) aims to explain IPE in the same way as the natural sciences explain natural phenomena. Explanatory theory originates in the demonstration of a relationship between cause and effect. If this causal relationship can be applied in comparable situations with the same results, we have a theory, say the orthodox. Explanatory theories thus focus on the regularities that enable us to explain the world. This kind of theory normally allows us to explain the present and the past, but also to predict the future and to prescribe policies (even though very few authors do so). Explanatory theories basically ask questions about the "why."

For fundamentally positivist authors, a theory must be supported by a logical justification that permits the researcher to predict something. In its simplest form, we should be able to find a causal relationship: if A, then B. If we cannot find or explain the relationship between A and B in a convincing manner, we do not have a valid theory. In this positivist logic, Cohen writes that a

> theory is best defined as a set of general statements combining the features of logical truth and predictive accuracy. Logical truth means that some of the statements (the assumptions or premises) logically imply the other statements (the theorems). Predictive accuracy means that the statements can be cast in the form of falsifiable propositions about the real world. (2009b: 29)

Katzenstein, Keohane, and Krasner also propose a definition that emphasizes causality. They write, "General theoretical orientations provide heuristics— they suggest relevant variables and causal patterns that provide guidelines for developing specific research programs" (1998: 646).

According to Krasner, the study of IPE in the United States has been guided almost exclusively by the canons that John Searle called the "Western Rationalistic Tradition," which is characterized by the assumption that reality exists independently of the representation that humans make of it. For Searle, this tradition contends that the truth or the falsity of a statement is totally independent of the motives, the morality, or even the gender, race, or ethnicity of the maker (Krasner, 2008: 108).

For their part, comprehensive theories (*verstehen*) disagree that social science can be studied in the same way as natural science. According to the tenets of this type of theory, we can only interpret IPE based on the meaning given to it by the actors themselves. For those working on comprehensive theories, social meaning, language, and beliefs constitute the most important aspects of existence in society. To understand and interpret societies and the actions of actors, we must study them. As one author of the heterodox school said to Cohen, "I don't do findings. I do interpretation" (Cohen, 2014: 64).

While the orthodox school is foundationalist because it claims the world can be judged true or false, this is not necessarily the case for those who favour comprehensive and even constitutive and normative theories. These theories can be anti-foundationalist because they maintain that "truth claims" cannot be so judged, as it is impossible to agree on a neutral ground.

Think, for example, of a debate between a feminist and an Islamic funda-
mentalist expounding their views on the true status of woman (Smith and
Owens, 2008: 274).

Putting it another way, explanatory theory favours causal analysis and
the scientific approach derived from the natural sciences, while comprehensive theory emphasizes the interpretation or the hermeneutic of phenomena.
Explanatory theories rely on the tools and procedure of the natural sciences
and seek to find causal relations, while comprehensive theories focus on
internal logics, motivations, and the meanings that actors give to their
actions. Comprehensive theories therefore require historical perspective and
interpretive sociology.

In short, for tenets of the explanatory approach, comprehensive theories are on the fringes of science. For comprehensive theorists, explanatory
theories merely imitate the natural sciences and depend on assumptions that
are too simplistic for a very complex world in which there are far too many
explanatory variables for the approach to be meaningful.

The so-called constitutive theories, for their part, do not attempt to
explain the world with causal theories or to find causal mechanisms over
time. Constitutive theories instead seek to understand how a social object is
constituted. These theories take many forms. At the most fundamental level,
constitutive theorists seek to understand what an object is. Typical research
questions posed in the creation of constitutive theories include, what functions does the state have in international society? And what is hegemony?
Comprehensive theories fundamentally ask questions about the "how."

The term *constitutive theory* is also used in another sense: for postpositivist authors, the theory co-constructs the reality. This form of theorization
holds that rules, norms, and ideas constitute social objects. For these theorists, the social world is co-constructed through our ideas and our theories.
In sum, we cannot separate the researcher from the theory, and researchers
cannot truly detach themselves from the world they are observing. In this
sense, "It becomes important to theorize the act of theorizing" (Kurki and
Wight, 2011: 29).

Normative theory is a theory of the world as it should be. It is about the
moral dimension of IPE. When a researcher tries to change the world, or describe the world as it could be, that is normative theory. Normative theories
purposively look for ethical judgment criteria on IPE. John Rawls's theory of
justice, for example, is a normative theory, as the author not only explains
what justice is (constitutive theory), but he also defines what it should or
could be (normative theory). His reflections about international justice
with regards to the obligation of rich states towards poorer ones are clearly
normative (Rawls, 1971). Michael Walzer also proposes normative theories
in his attempt to distinguish between just and unjust wars using a moral
empiricism rationale (2006). In IPE, since the 2008 financial crisis and the

rise of the top 1 per cent, normative questions have become more "policy relevant" (see, for example, Piketty, 2014; Blyth, 2013).

Many heterodox IPE authors, starting with Robert Cox, have developed clearly normative theories. That said, even orthodox theorists have developed causal theories with a number of normative elements. The normative objective of liberalism, for example, is to promote peace and prosperity. Realist theorists are implicitly favourable to the stability of the international system and are therefore more conservative, while liberals are favourable to cooperation through the strengthening of law and the creation of international institutions. Critical theorists instead want to explicitly change the system (Reus-Smit and Snidal, 2008).

Critical theory has different meanings in different disciplines, but, in IPE, when we refer to this type of theory, we are referring to the definition by Robert Cox. Cox believes that a theory is situated in time and space, and, most importantly, that it is not neutral. Cox maintains that explanatory or causal theories are "problem-solving theories" as opposed to the critical theories with which he identifies. In an article that helped secure his reputation, Cox explains, "Theory is always for someone and for some purpose" (1981: 129–30). A problem-solving theory accepts the world as it is, with its social relations based on domination and the various institutions that organize it, like a framework for action. The objective of problem-solving theories is to ensure that these relations and institutions work by explaining their functioning and by dealing with the sources of the problems.

According to Cox, critical theories instead seek to understand how the existing order was constituted and how it works. Critical theorists do not take the world as a given or as a fact but rather seek to understand how a social situation, and its transformations, were produced (Leysens, 2008). Critical theories consider the world as a whole rather than focusing on specific problems with limited parameters. Critical theory therefore seeks to "critique" a situation or a social arrangement. A theory can be described as critical when it seeks to identify injustices and show how they were produced. In the title of a 2008 article, Cox is even more explicit: "The point is not just to explain the world but to change it."

For Cox, critical theories are not necessarily incompatible with explanatory or causal theories. In his view, regularities in human activity can indeed be observed. The positivist approach can thus be fruitful but within defined historical limits (Cox, 1986: 244). Cox maintains that the structural approach he advocates is not an alternative to the actor-interactions approach; it is a logical priority to it. In certain cases, Cox even agrees that it is appropriate to combine the two approaches (Cox, 1997; Leysens, 2008: 9). In an interview with Randall Germain for the *New Political Economy* journal, Cox confirmed that he is not opposed to problem-solving theory. These theories are useful but they present obvious limitations during periods of major structural changes (Cox, 1999). In 1996, Timothy Sinclair, in an article discussing Cox's contribution to the theory of international relations, wrote,

> Problem solving and critical theory are not necessarily mutually exclusive. They may be understood to address different concerns of levels within one overall story. However, as Cox argues, the salience of each approach to international relations will vary in relation to each other depending on historical conditions. In conditions of relative stability in the fundamental structures and relationships that constitute international relations, problem-solving work is likely to be more salient. There will be more of a fit between the explanations offered by various theoretical approaches that make up the problem-solving mainstream and scholarly and public perceptions of international relations phenomena. As Cox observes . . . "the Cold war was one such a period." [But when major changes occur, the] utility of problem solving theory breaks down and scholars, the general public and policy makers become more receptive as communities to new ideas that challenge conventional dogmas and received understanding about the limits of the system. (1996: 6)

The criteria that separate the various types of theories are not very clear. For example, a researcher may advance several types of theories at the same time. Critical theories, according to Cox's definition, are also normative. Explanatory or causal, comprehensive, and constitutive theories, however, are so different in their foundations that it becomes difficult, if not impossible, to compare them with one another. They do not present the same logic and are not fundamentally concerned with the same thing. In other words, they are incommensurable. We cannot compare apples and oranges.

Theorizing According to the Orthodox Approach

Explanatory or causal theories seek mainly to "explain the world." The construction of this type of theory generally proceeds from falsifiable hypotheses subjected to empirical testing. This approach promotes the accumulation of knowledge. Orthodox IPE theorists believe that knowledge accumulation is only possible through objective observation and the systematic testing of hypotheses.

For supporters of explanatory theory, a good theory can be judged on the basis of several criteria, such as its accuracy or its generalizability, but the most important criteria are its simplicity and its falsifiability, that is, the possibility of refuting it.

A theory must be as simple as possible and must maximally reduce the number of explanatory factors. The goal of theorizing is to develop a parsimonious theory. The emphasis placed on parsimonious theories by many orthodox IPE researchers tells us a lot about their conception of the nature of the world: even though the world is complex, which makes theorizing necessary, it is simple enough that we can identify stable causal relations over time. It is fair to say, however, that this insistence on parsimony, which dominates US economics departments in particular, is not unanimously agreed upon among American political scientists. But if two theories explain the same phenomenon, the simplest, the easiest to understand will be favoured. A simple theory requires fewer explanatory factors, it is easier to use, and it focuses attention on the genuine explanatory factors. By this logic, a good theory explains a maximum of things with a minimum of variables (King, Keohane, and Verba, 1994: 20).

Falsifiability is another important factor in a good theory. Researchers must test theories or hypotheses that are refutable or falsifiable. As Gary King, Robert Keohane, and Sidney Verba say in their book on qualitative methodology (the most widely used textbook on this topic in American universities and often cited in IPE course plans in the United States), researchers must choose a theory that can be shown to be wrong. Theorists must enhance the possibility of a theory being refuted by formulating it as precisely as possible and by making predictions that are as clear as possible. The more precise a theory is, the easier it will be to invalidate it. Invalidating a theory advances knowledge and science. It is also important to increase the possibility of refutation by choosing theories that maximize the observable implications of those theories (King, Keohane, and Verba, 1994: 19–20).

This insistence on falsification has its roots in the work of Karl Popper. According to Popper, researchers cannot state with certainty that a theory is true, as the truth remains inaccessible to them, but they can state that a theory is the best one available, that it surpasses all the others at a given moment. To distinguish science from non-science, Popper introduced the concept of falsification or refutation. For him, any hypothesis or theory must satisfy the criterion of falsifiability to acquire the status of scientific theory. In short, although in the social sciences we cannot access the truth, we do know when a procedure is incorrect.

According to Popper, researchers must present their hypotheses in such a way as to make it possible to invalidate it, quash it, refute it. A theory that works all the time, regardless of the results of the observation, has no scientific value. A procedure is scientific when it enables researchers to divide the set of conceivable hypotheses into two groups: those with which the hypothesis is compatible and those with which it is not. A social science research study is not a description of the real world but an interpretation conditioned by the selection of explanatory paradigms, the choice of concepts, and the hypotheses testing techniques used. The accumulation of scientific knowledge proceeds by trial and error, by conjecture and refutation (Popper, 1963).

The criticism that can be made of the extreme interpretation of Popper's proposals has to do with the fact that a theory is always accepted with a degree of uncertainty (as it can never be considered true), while the rejection of a theory is a definitive act not open to review. In IPE (and in the social sciences), no theory would have withstood such treatment. Even democratic peace theory, which today is one of the most solid in international relations, would have been rejected in its infancy. Unlike Popper, Imre Lakatos does not believe that scientists are willing to abandon their paradigm because crucial experiments refute or falsify their theory. Lakatos instead contends that scientists work within the framework of scientific research programs that include a hard core of assumptions, a protective belt of secondary hypotheses, initial conditions, and so on (1978). The hard core of the theory is not subject to refutation; only the secondary hypotheses are. For example, in Marxist theory, the hard core is constituted of the hypothesis that social change can be explained by class struggle. The hard core is unfalsifiable because the theory's protagonists have made the methodological decision that this is so. If a researcher chooses to falsify the hard core, he or she changes the research program.

According to Lakatos, research programs become structures. They can be progressive, if they generate new knowledge, if they are able to predict new facts, absorb anomalies, and win over supporters in the scientific community. They can also be regressive, if they have become unable to predict new facts and if they lose influence and followers in the scientific community. Unlike Kuhn's episodic model of scientific revolutions, Lakatos's model conforms more to the evolution of IPE theory, as several concurrent research programs can coexist for a long time and thus contribute to the vitality and the rivalry of scientific debates. Contrary to Popper's approach, Lakatos contends that what is of paramount importance for researchers is not so much the apparent falsifications as the confirmations (1978; see also Chalmers, 2013: 121–37). The concept of falsification is nevertheless central in the teaching of research methodology, particularly in the United States, even though its application is more flexible than that proposed by Popper.

Finally, for King, Keohane, and Verba, the objective of the scientific process is to produce inference. Inference is the use of data to draw broader conclusions about concepts and hypotheses that are the focus of the research. Inference is the process of using facts that we know in order to learn something about facts that we do not know (King, Keohane, and Verba, 1994). This approach and this conception of theory are hegemonic among researchers with orthodox leanings. Figure 2.1 depicts the different steps in theorizing for orthodox IPE researchers.

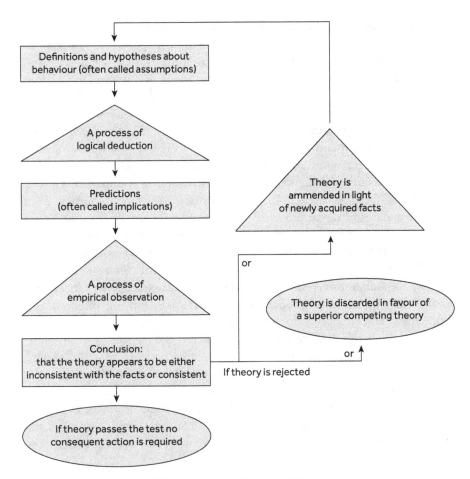

Figure 2.1 Orthodox IPE Researchers' Steps in Theorizing

Reproduced from Hollis and Smith, 1991: 51 by permission of Oxford University Press.

Theorizing According to the Heterodox Approach

Given the methodological eclecticism of heterodox authors, it is difficult to identify what unites them, apart from their criticism of the works of researchers in the orthodox IPE school. The leading authors of the heterodox approach generally present their analyses as "critical theories," or as Christopher Brown describes it, an "oppositional frame of mind" (2001: 192). As we saw previously, critical theories, as opposed to problem-solving theories, do not think of institutions, social relations, and the world order as being self-evident. They question these theories and reflect on how to change them. Heterodox authors are less inclined to develop highly sophisticated scientific models and often have broader research programs.

Since the behaviourist revolution, political science in the United States has taken a resolutely positivist turn. This trend is particularly apparent in international relations and is definitely preponderant in orthodox IPE. It is here that the fracture line between the social sciences in the United States and elsewhere is at its widest. The authors associated with the heterodox IPE school, like those in international relations, have never really adhered to the positivism dominant in the discipline (Smith, 2008; Cohen, 2014). This may explain why certain leading authors in the British School of international relations, such as Hedley Bull, were "skeptical of the possibility of a scientific study of International Relations" (quoted in Cohen, 2007: 212). British researchers in general contested the models derived from natural science and de-emphasized formal methodology. Instead, as Roger Tooze noted, the milieu encouraged the use of the "historical-relativist paradigm . . . drawn from an eclectic mix of factors" (quoted in Cohen, 2007: 212). The anti-Americanism latent in British universities (and we might add in many Canadian universities) has meant that the researchers in these universities do not imitate orthodox political scientists, but, on the contrary, define themselves in opposition to the American approach. Thus, unlike the orthodox, the heterodox are very skeptical about the possibility of developing explanatory or causal theories of IPE. Some propose that IPE should develop along more historical bases (Amin and Palan, 1996; Amoore et al., 2000). Others argue for works of a non-rationalist nature in IPE (Amin and Palan, 2001). Among the most influential authors in heterodox IPE, Robert Cox and the neo-Gramscian school as well as Susan Strange, who is often called the founder of the discipline, are particularly worthy of mention.

Theorizing among the Neo-Gramscians

In the social sciences, the neo-Gramscian approach, advocated by Robert Cox, does not envisage the possibility of the existence of a general or universal law (Cox, 1996b: 53). It is a historicist approach that takes certain elements from Marxism but does not subscribe to the determinism of historical materialism. For Cox, historicism contends that human nature and the structures that frame human interaction change, albeit very slowly.[2] History is the process of their transformation. Therefore, says Cox, we cannot speak of a "law" that would transcend history in any valid sense (Cox, 1996b: 53).

As we said earlier, Cox believed that it is possible to identify regularities in human activity. The positivist approach regarding causal theories can make some sense, but only within certain historical limits. Causal theories are therefore not "universal," as is sometimes claimed. In other words, critical theories and problem-solving theories are not necessarily mutually exclusive. We can envisage them as theories dealing with different subjects within the same encompassing history. The relevance of using the critical approach or the problem-solving approach is determined by historical conditions. When historical structures are relatively stable, the problem-solving approach will probably give better results. In this context, the problem-solving approach will be closer to the perception of things, citizens, and policy makers. For Cox, the Cold War period was one such time of stability. But when historical structures are in transformation, when the world is gradually losing its accustomed bearings, as was the case after the end of the Cold War when the globalization of the economy accelerated, the critical theories approach becomes more relevant.

Stephen Gill, like Cox, maintains that there are different forms of states and world orders, for which the conditions of existence, constitutive principles, and norms vary over time (Gill, 1993: 29). In short, for the neo-Gramscian school, the social science theories that claim to be universalist are not acceptable, except in a specific historical context. Positivist approaches can be useful, but only within the framework of defined historical limits. According to Cox, the objective of the historicist approach is to reveal the characteristics of historical structures.

For Cox, the historicist research program aims to reveal the specific historical structures of a historical moment in which regularities can be identified. This approach, which seeks to expose the historical transformations from one historical structure to another, is thus very different from the approach favoured by orthodox theorists. As Cox puts it, "If elegance is what Robert Keohane writes of as 'spare, logically tight' theory then the historicist approach does not lead to elegance. It may, however, lead to better appraisal of historically specific conjunctures. One person's elegance is another's oversimplification" (Cox, 1996b: 53).

Neo-Gramscians share with the Marxist tradition the idea that theory cannot be separated from practice. The neo-Gramscian approach breaks with positivism because it claims that research, in the social sciences, is not content to merely explain the world through causal theories; it also produces effects on the world. For Cox, the notion of the separation between researcher and theory does not take into account the fact that the analyst is an integral part of the social world observed and inseparable from it. The analyst's subjectivity determines what questions are asked, what kind of data is examined, and what role the analysis plays in restoring balance to the existing order. These implications cannot be dismissed as being irrelevant for this type of knowledge, the purpose of which is to correct dysfunctions and maintain order in a system (Cox, 2002: xxii).

Explanatory or problem-solving theories accept the world as it is as a framework for action, which results in theories that are favourable, at the normative level, to the status quo. Critical theories, for their part, explicitly seek to change the world. The objective of critical theories is to raise the "true" level of people's consciousness. According to neo-Gramscians, this is a necessary, though insufficient, step to changing the world.

Neo-Gramscians argue that orthodox IPE theorists propose reflective theories without knowing it; in other words, even if they claim objectivity, their theories are not neutral. There are not some theories that are normative and others that are not. Theories, when they are circulated, participate in the production of meaning about overall policy; thus, they inevitably produce normative effects on the world. For example, realist IPE theorists are essentially favourable to the status quo. In Cox's view, the American version of realism has become a science in the service of the major powers to manage the international system.

Neo-Gramscians believe that theories and concepts arise from a specific social and historical context characterized by relations between classes, genders, and cultures; this context leads the researcher to adopt a certain point of view about the world, a point of view that is necessarily biased. Hence, theories and concepts are not culturally neutral. For Cox,

> positivism is synchronic: the social world is given. Enquiry about its meaning is pointless: it is just there. The historical method is diachronic: the social world is meaningful—it is good for some, bad for others and conflict over its preservation or change evoke strong passions—and it is "made" by collective action over time. (2002: xxii)

In the neo-Gramscian perspective, it is important to understand and analyze one's own biases and, as far as possible, to explain them. This reflexivity also influences the ontology, epistemology, and process of theorizing. Researchers who produce theories must ask the question, what social interest does the theory consolidate? Is it favourable to preserving the existing order, or does it call for the change of this order?

Furthermore, the concepts used by orthodox theorists, such as national interest, security, or balance of power, are not neutral concepts. Rather, they represent the interests of the dominant classes or of a particular coalition of forces seeking to preserve their social status and their hegemonic structure in the society as a whole. As Cox would say, theories are always for someone or for something. The question to ask then, as Susan Strange did, is *Cui bono*? Who benefits from the situation? Who wins with the preservation of the social order? But also, who is the loser? What is maintained in the structure of domination? Who has the capacity to promote the national interest (which for neo-Gramscians means the interest of the dominant class)?

In terms of epistemology, neo-Gramscians are united in their rejection of positivism. In addition, they are very critical of the use of quantitative methods. Cox also rejects the use of game theory to understand international questions. Game theory assumes that actors are linked by a shared rationality. This view further reinforces the ahistorical way of thinking. Cox and the neo-Gramscians criticize positivism because its models excessively reify the world without seeking to resituate the objects of research in the context of their historical emergence—in their historical structure, to use neo-Gramscian terminology (Cox, 1981).

The social sciences are so fundamentally different from the natural sciences that adopting the latter's tools makes no sense. This theoretical approach maintains there is a duality between the social world and the natural world. The social world is the product of historical power relationships or even hegemony, not of natural or mechanical phenomena. While historical processes are not completely a matter of chance, neither are they random; they are the product of a particular power relationship to be analyzed and resituated in its historical context. Hence, the world is in constant transformation, even though certain periods may constitute "historic blocs"—that is, a particular configuration of forces, relatively stable for a certain time (Bakker and Gill, 2003: 17–20).

Because neo-Gramscian theorists are very critical of positivists, their analyses tend to be more empirical and descriptive. Neo-Gramscians think that the theory normatively guides researchers in their selection of case studies and in their empirical material, as much for what the theory chooses to emphasize as for what it considers secondary and marginal. This does not mean that the facts brought to the forefront by the theory do not exist but that they are used and selected to comply with a certain perspective. Neither does this imply that neo-Gramscians reject empirical analysis, but they do maintain a good critical distance, a certain skepticism regarding approaches that claim to have direct access to the facts.

Neo-Gramscians criticize orthodox IPE theorists because the latter's theories are fundamentally static and ahistorical. They are very critical of the approach of Kenneth Waltz, for example, stating that his theory of international politics does not explain change in international relations. For neo-Gramscians, no historical structures last indefinitely. According to Cox, structures are socially constructed; they become an objective component of the world by their very existence in "the intersubjectivity of relevant groups of people" (1996c: 149). In this context, what is a good theory for neo-Gramscians? According to Stephen Gill, the criteria of a good theory are "scope, consistency, and reflexivity" (Gill, 1990a: 10).

Theorizing According to Susan Strange

Susan Strange's reflection on the exercise of theorizing was less complete than that of the neo-Gramscians. In her book *States and Markets*, she begins the first chapter by formulating four negative and three positive assumptions about what a theory is (Strange, 1988c). Generally speaking, Strange maintained that there was a lot of confusion regarding the nature of theories about the international system and this confusion led to numerous works of theorizing that were not really theories.

Among her negative assumptions (what is not theory), she argued that many so-called theories are very often no more than descriptions of known phenomena with new concepts, but without any real attempts to theorize. Theories may frequently be hiding in this type of study, but they are only rarely made explicit. Again according to Strange, certain "theories" of international politics just rearrange and describe known facts or propose a new taxonomy; taxonomy, or the classification of various elements in a field of studies, in itself does not constitute a theory (Strange, 1988c: 10).

Furthermore, said Strange, the fact of importing from another discipline (such as economics or mathematics) tools or concepts (such as the prisoner's dilemma or a demand curve) does not constitute a theory as such, even if it may prove to be very useful pedagogically. None of these imports in themselves explain the paradoxes or the enigmas of world politics. They are simplification tools and not theories of social behaviour. These tools do not help IPE researchers explain the action of multinationals, political parties, or the state (1988c).

Finally, the development of quantitative methods in the field of international relations does not contribute to advancing theory, according to Strange. She writes,

> The choice of what is to be counted is too arbitrary and the determination of what is causal and what is coincidental is too subjective to provide a basis for explanation. For the most part such methods have been used only to substantiate platitudes and to reinforce conventional wisdom concerning the historical patterns of state behaviour in relation to other states. (Strange, 1988c: 10)

In her positive assumptions (what is theory), Strange argued that a theory must seek to explain one or several aspects of the international system that cannot easily be explained by common sense. A theory must resolve an enigma or a paradox about an important aspect of the behaviour of individuals, groups, or institutions when a simple explanation is not enough. As Strange noted, it is not necessary to develop a theory to explain why people try to leave a burning building. It is necessary to understand why they frequent a store on one side of the street rather than on the other. Therefore, for her, the purpose of studying international relations is to answer baffling questions such as why states continue to go to war when it is already evident that the economic gains will never exceed the costs of the conflict. Several theories have in fact been proposed. IPE also asks some disconcerting questions such as, why do states not manage to regulate and stabilize the international financial system when this system is a vital necessity and experts both within and outside the government agree that the system is dangerously in need of more regulation for its own safety? Once again, theory is the outcome of attempts to answer the question (Strange, 1988c: 11).

According to Strange, theories must not necessarily aspire to predict or prescribe. It is on this point that social science diverges from natural science. The latter may aspire to predict, even if it does not always do so. For Strange, many sciences, from astronomy to microbiology, enrich our understanding of a phenomenon without being able to offer a conclusive explanation of the reasons it occurs. Social science can never make a prediction with any confidence because the irrational or unpredictable factors involved in human relations are too numerous, as are the permutations and combinations of these relations. The social science that has most attempted to predict is economics, but, according to Strange, its actual successes are so mediocre that imitating economists is not to be recommended. Economists are particularly bad when it comes to making predictions about the world-economy because many international trade and exchange rate theories are based on assumptions that no longer hold up in such an integrated world-economy. With regard to prescribing public policies, Strange considered it a matter of choice for the theorist. She believed, however, that as public policies involve value judgments and risk assessments that are exogenous to theory, prescriptions are better made by practical policy makers than by "irresponsible academic theorists" (Strange, 1988c: 12).

For Strange, theories are scientific only in the sense that they respect the scientific virtues of rationality and impartiality and aspire to formulate systematic explanations. The term *social science* is only justifiable, she wrote, to remind us that although our research subjects are more closely tied to our emotions than are the origin of rocks or the composition of molecules, and although these subjects propose subjectively important questions concerning power and wealth, we must in spite of that maintain a "scientific" attitude towards our research. In Strange's view, many problems related to theory and social science ultimately derive from social scientists' inferiority complex regarding natural scientists and, more specifically in our case, the inferiority complex of IPE specialists towards the apparent rigour of economic "science" (Strange, 1988c).

Strange believed that the formulation of a general theory of international political economy is a pointless exercise. For her, the social science ambition to imitate natural science, to discover and elaborate "laws" of the international system, laws so regular that they govern the social, the political, and the economic is—and always has been—a wild goose chase. The time and effort spent on this exercise would have been better employed relearning some of the basic axioms about human vice and human folly, about the perversity of politics and the arbitrary nature of coincidences. This does not mean that social scientists should not also be as uncompromising in their search for the truth as biologists or geologists. But it is a different kind of truth, which is not well served by the aspiration to attain the unattainable or to promise something that, given the nature of the world, cannot be delivered (Strange, 1988c: 16).

As we have just seen, Strange was very critical and sometimes even irreverent regarding the practice of orthodox IPE. She was not a positivist, or even a behaviourist; she rejected the use of quantitative methods and, even more, the works of economists due to their countless normative biases. She did not express very great enthusiasm for the conservatism of American IPE theories. For her, orthodox IPE specialists suffered from myopia when it came to the world around them: "These theories belong to a more stable and orderly world than the one we live in. It was one in which the territorial borders of states really meant something. But it has been swept away by a pace of changes more rapid than human society had ever before experienced" (Strange, 1988c: 3).

Strange rejected Robert Gilpin's idea that nothing had fundamentally changed in the nature of international relations since Thucydides. As Strange wrote, "[orthodox theorists] would rather fit the facts of life into international relations theories than question the validity of the theories to explain the nature, the causes and consequences of change in the world" (Strange, 1994: 209). Also according to her, the changes in the political world were so important and fundamental that they required a revision of existing theories and even the introduction of a new field of research: international political economy. In a scathing response to an article by Stephen Krasner, Strange wrote about international relations theories:

> Once upon a time, there was a professor of international relations who insisted, every year, on teaching the course on theory—and nothing else. One day, a colleague asked him why. "Easy, dear boy. If I teach theory I don't have to read the newspapers or bother about current events. Last year's notes are good enough." By that time, of course, the notes were yellow with age, and although the students dutifully took the course—it was examined, after all—they found it excruciatingly dull. (Strange, 1994: 209)

Strange confided to certain colleagues that she did not consider herself a theorist, but rather an essentially empirical and analytic researcher (Cohen, 2007: 208). Her objective was not to develop a comprehensive theory of IPE but to propose a way of thinking, an analytic framework for thinking (Tooze and May, 2002: 15). For Strange, any reflection on world politics and the world-economy should begin by analyzing the human condition. In 1984 she wrote that IPE should be about "justice, as well as efficiency: about order and national identity and cohesion, even self-respect, as well as about cost and price" (Strange, 1984: x). Strange thus developed an IPE that focused chiefly on society rather than on the state. She was also a committed researcher. To her, the meaning of research was to separate the good from the bad. We can only judge works on their usefulness, she believed. Contrary to many authors, she did not hesitate to pass judgments on ethics or equity; being a researcher was inseparable from values and ethics.

Conclusion

The leading lights of the orthodox approach claim that they develop more rigorous theoretical frameworks that better meet the demanding principles of positivism and empiricism. This process, they believe, makes it easier to generalize and accumulate knowledge. In their eyes, the heterodox approach is too eclectic, even eccentric, to be of value. The heterodox approach is sometimes described as unscientific. It abandons new radical ideas and methods in favour of a methodology largely borrowed from economics and natural science. History, culture, and social context are less important than the parsimonious approach and deductive logic.

It is important to note that the majority of IPE theorists (even the orthodox) admit that it is impossible to elaborate a law of IPE. They are aware of the limitations of the capacity to theorize in the social sciences. According to Stephen Krasner, "The theories are rarely good enough to provide concrete guidance for policy makers" (Krasner, 2008: 124).

The heterodox approach is multidisciplinary, more normative, and very critical of orthodoxy. The methodology of the key authors is based on sociological history and comparative analyses that complexify generalization and knowledge accumulation. Their works are very often far removed from the concerns of practitioners of international relations and political science in general.

This opposition between positivism and postpositivism represents a key point of distinction between the orthodox and heterodox approaches. It has a fundamental impact on the conception of what is a "good" theory in IPE. That said, it is important to qualify this statement. Not everyone agrees with the positivism dominant in the United States, as evidenced by the formation of the perestroika movement in 2000. This movement promotes the idea of greater methodological pluralism and criticizes the domination of positivism, rational choice theorists, and the insistence on formal modelling and the quantitative method on US campuses. It claims that the generalist political science journals in the United States have a bias against international relations research.

Political scientists are not the only ones to criticize the dominant positivist approach. Since the 1970s, several economists, such as Gunnar Myrdal, John K. Galbraith, and Wassily Leontief, have been very critical of the works of economists who have not produced relevant knowledge due to their blind use of the overly simple method of the natural sciences (Myrdal, 1972; Galbraith, 1973; Leontief, 1971). Galbraith rejected what he called "imitative science" (quoted in Dunn, 2011: 83). These economists shared the viewpoint of Albert Hirschman, who believed the problem with economics theories was not that they were too complicated, but that they were much too simplistic!

Notes

1   The 12 leading journals in IR are *International Organization*; *World Politics*; *International Security*; *International Studies Quarterly*; *Journal of Conflict Resolution*; *Journal of Peace Research*; *Security Studies*; *European Journal of International Relations*; *Journal of Politics*; *American Political Science Review*; *American Journal of Political Science*; and *British Journal of Political Science*.

2   The meaning Cox gives to the word *historicism* is very different from the definition given by Popper, for whom historicism represents attempts to find laws of history.

Questions

1. Why is positivism so important in IPE?
2. What are the key postulates of positivism in IPE?
3. What is the dominant scientific culture of IPE in the United States?
4. What is an explanatory or a causal theory?
5. What is a comprehensive theory?
6. What is a constitutive theory?
7. What is a normative theory?
8. What is a critical theory according to Robert Cox?
9. What is a "good" theory according to the orthodox school?
10. What is a "good" theory according to the neo-Gramscians?

Further Reading

For important accounts of the metatheoretical debates over the various types of theories in IR and IPE:

Hollis, Martin, and Steve Smith. *Explaining and Understanding International Relations*. Oxford: Clarendon Press, 1991.

Kurki, Milja, and Colin Wight. "International Relations and Social Science." In *International Relations Theories: Discipline and Diversity*, 2nd ed., edited by Tim Dunne, Milja Kurki, and Steve Smith, 14–35. New York: Oxford University Press, 2011.

For useful sources on positivism in US academia:

Maliniak, Daniel, and Michael J. Tierney. "The American School of IPE." *Review of International Political Economy* 16.1 (2009): 6–33.

Maliniak, Daniel, Amy Oakes, Susan Peterson, and Michael J. Tierney. "International Relations in the US Academy." *International Studies Quarterly* 55.2 (2011): 437–64.

Maliniak, Daniel, Susan Peterson, and Michael J. Tierney. *TRIP around the World: Teaching, Research, and Policy Views of International Relations Faculty in 20 Countries*. Williamsburg, VA: Teaching, Research, and International Policy (TRIP) Project, 2012.

Smith, Steve. "The United States and the Discipline of International Relations: 'Hegemonic Country, Hegemonic Discipline.'" *International Studies Review* 4 (2002): 68–85.

Smith, Steve. "Positivism and Beyond." In *International Theory: Positivism and Beyond*, edited by Steve Smith, Ken Booth, and Marysia Zalewski, 11–43. Cambridge: Cambridge University Press, 2008.

For very influential works of the orthodox school:

Keohane, Robert O., and Stephen D. Krasner. "International Organization and the Study of World Politics." *International Organization* 52.4 (1998): 645–85.

King, Gary, Robert O. Keohane, and Sidney Verba. *Designing Social Inquiry: Scientific Inference in Qualitative Research*. Princeton: Princeton University Press, 1994.

For very influential works of the heterodox school:

Cox, Robert W. "Social Forces, States and World Order: Beyond International Relations Theory." *Millennium: Journal of International Studies* 10.2 (1981): 126–55.

Strange, Susan. *States and Markets: An Introduction to International Political Economy*. London: Pinter Publishers, 1988.

3 The Realist Perspective in IPE

Chapter Contents

- Basic Assumptions of the Realist Perspective in IPE
- The Myth of Globalization
- Globalization, War, and Peace
- Power and Hegemonic Stability Theory
- Power and Interstate Relations
- Conclusion

Reader's Guide

Very little separates realist theorists in international relations from those in IPE, as they share many basic assumptions. The essential difference is that realist theorists in international relations focus exclusively on security issues, while those in IPE add key global economic and financial affairs to their analyses. Realist theorists in IPE are more open to the idea that it is the accumulation of wealth that gives states the means to wage war. For IPE realists, the fundamental variable in IPE is the distribution of power between states. In a bipolar system, for example, the two main powers are destined to be rivals. In a unipolar system, the hegemonic power can promote the opening of markets and the system's stability because it is in its national interest to do so. Realism may not be the most influential perspective in IPE but it remains relevant, as, from the beginning, liberal authors have developed their theory largely in reaction to it.

As we have seen, the vast majority of American IPE researchers (73 per cent) subscribe to one of the four most important perspectives in international relations theory, compared to only 45 per cent whose first field of study is international relations in general (Maliniak and Tierney, 2009). Thus, IPE was built more around these major perspectives than was the wider field of international relations. The liberal perspective is the dominant, or even hegemonic, perspective. The realist perspective, although more marginal, remains essential, as it was built and structured largely in reaction to the liberal perspective and vice versa. These two perspectives are the most important, along with a third that is not mentioned in the previously cited TRIP Project—the domestic politics perspective. The constructivist paradigm, now the leading perspective in international relations theory in the United States, is largely absent from IPE debates, as is the Marxist perspective nowadays.

The debates in American orthodox IPE are therefore essentially between the liberal, realist, and domestic politics perspectives. We shall begin with the presentation of the realist perspective. It may not be the most influential or the most important but it remains relevant, as, from the beginning, liberal authors have developed their theory largely in reaction to it (Maliniak et al., 2011).

Basic Assumptions of the Realist Perspective in IPE

Very little separates realist theorists in international relations from those in IPE, as they share many basic assumptions. The essential difference is ontological: realist theorists in international relations focus exclusively on security issues, while those in IPE add key global economic and financial affairs to their analyses. Realist theorists in IPE are more open to the idea that it is the accumulation of wealth that gives states the means to wage war. International economic and financial affairs spark major distributional issues—some countries gain much more than others. As the accumulation of wealth goes hand in hand with the accumulation of power, IPE realists are more aware that economic and political affairs are inseparable (Gilpin, 1987; Spiro, 1999).

Like realists in international relations, realists in IPE place nation-states at the centre of the analysis of international affairs. According to IPE realists, nation-states are the constitutive actors of the international system. They create the rules of the game, and all other key actors in IPE must operate or develop their strategies within the framework of state-defined rules (Krasner, 2008: 115). This does not mean, however, that states are the only actors that count in IPE, as multinationals, international organizations, and NGOs also play significant roles. But for IPE realists, nation-states always determine the fundamental game rules of the international system, including those regarding economic and financial questions. Nation-states establish the rules within which other actors evolve, and they always wield considerable power over the economy and finance. For realist authors, given that the state is at the centre of international life and determines the rules of the game for all actors, including those of the private sector, it is politics that determines economics, not the other way around as in the Marxist tradition (Gilpin, 2001: 18).

Realists in international relations generally believe that states are independent from society or social pressure. For IR realists, the state does not collectively represent individual interests, as liberals believe, or the interests of the bourgeoisie, as Marxists believe (Kirshner, 2009: 36). Since neorealism was introduced in the debates in international relations theory at the end of the 1970s, most realists have accepted the general idea that states act as unitary and rational actors in their international actions. Domestic policy debates, social pressures, and bureaucratic logics have but a marginal effect on final outcomes (Waltz, 1979; Krasner, 2008). What is crucial for understanding the international game is the distribution of power between states, the anarchy of the international system, and the external constraints. Contrary to neorealists in international relations, those in IPE recognize the importance of domestic factors or domestic politics (we will come back to this in Chapter 5).

For realists in international relations, as well as in IPE, the international system is anarchic, meaning that there is no legitimate political authority above the nation-state. In this context, anarchic does not mean that world politics are characterized by a permanent state of war. As Robert Gilpin points out, states cooperate and create many international organizations in several sectors of international life (Gilpin, 2001: 17). The concept of anarchy means that there is no authority superior to that of states to which a body can appeal in the event of a dispute. In the words of Raymond Aron, international politics unfold "*à l'ombre de la guerre*" (in the shadow of war) (Aron, 1984: 18).

This situation is particularly problematic for realists, as they believe that states are egoists in their international behaviour. Consequently, they cannot count on one another to ensure their long-term security. They must develop their own defence and security strategies; they cannot delegate their security and the protection of their borders to other states. This is what realists call *self-help* (Waltz, 1979: 105–7).

Thus, in their international actions, states pursue their national interest, which is determined by the idea of survival. For realists, security represents a common good, and, as the common good tends not to be ensured properly by the private sector, the state must fulfil this role by creating its own means of survival (Kirshner, 2009). This situation leads to a security dilemma because when a state arms itself to guarantee its security, it spurs insecurity in other states, which opens the way to an arms race. For some IPE authors, including Gilpin, political autonomy or independence is also crucial. In other words, states must avoid being in a situation of economic or financial interdependence in order to maximize their freedom of action. States must strive to be self-sufficient.

States must be attentive to changes in power relationships and to distributional issues during international negotiations. Here, the debate between relative gains and absolute gains is crucial (Baldwin, 1993; Grieco, 1993; Powell, 1991, 1994). While most IPE realists believe that international trade can promote gains for all actors—in other words, that everyone can profit from it—they worry more about the effects of the asymmetrical distribution of these gains. For realists, relative gains (i.e., what one country gains in comparison to another) are a major concern (Gowa, 1986). Given that wealth is what supports military power, what one country gains in respect to another is singularly important. Thus, when mutual gains are possible, wary states must ask themselves how the gains will be shared. They will not be interested in whether both will gain but rather in who will gain the most. If the gains anticipated are too asymmetrical, the privileged state may use these disproportionate gains to implement policies aiming to damage or destroy the other (Waltz, 1979: 105).

For realists, therefore, a state will prefer not to make any gains at all rather than see an enemy make more, as these additional gains will enable the enemy state to strengthen its military capability and its power (Waltz, 1979; Mastanduno, 1998). Not even the possibility of substantial gains will foster cooperation if one of the two players gains much more than the other (Grieco, 1988). States must take relative gains into consideration, as, in certain situations, changes in power relationships may put their security and survival at risk.

Realists believe that the fundamental variable in IPE is the distribution of power between states. This central argument is based on the idea that the characteristics of the international system and the behaviour of states can be explained by how power is distributed. In a bipolar system, for example, the two main powers are destined to be rivals. In a unipolar system, the hegemonic power can promote the opening of markets and the system's stability because it is in its national interest to do so. Power, according to realists, is measured by certain attributes, such as the size of the army, the total or per capita GDP, and the state's ability to make credible threats. A change in the distribution of power between actors destabilizes the system. For example, a number of realists seem to be very pessimistic about China's rise in power. In 2001, John Mearsheimer argued that the United States needed to reverse the trend and do everything it could to slow China's growth (401–2).

As we can see, realists have developed a pessimistic perception of human nature and generally do not believe that humans can learn from their mistakes. This does not mean that ethical and moral issues in the conduct of states' foreign policies are not important to certain realist authors, particularly those of the first generation, but, on the whole, realists do not believe that humanity is moving slowly towards a better world.

While liberal theorists focus their analysis of international organizations and regimes on the cooperation between actors that aims to solve communication problems, realist theorists suggest that international organizations

Box 3.1   Mercantilism and the Realist Perspective

For Robert Gilpin (1987, 2001), the realist IPE perspective is closely related ideologically to mercantilism, also called the "nationalist perspective," according to which a nation's economy must augment its power. A nation's economy serves its politics and ensures its wealth, thereby increasing its political and military power.

The term *mercantilism*, first introduced by Mirabeau in 1764, was popularized by Adam Smith, a Scottish philosopher and economist. For Smith, mercantilism referred to many of the economic practices and much of the economic ideology practised in Europe between the sixteenth and eighteenth centuries. Mercantilists believe that a state's power is measured by the number of gold and silver bars in its coffers. With this wealth, a state is able to maintain a vast army. Mercantilism is defined by at least the two following characteristics: the state seeks to reduce its imports to a minimum; and it seeks to promote its exports in order to clear a trade surplus. Given that it is impossible for all states to have a trade surplus, mercantilists believe that conflicts and wars are inevitable. The international economy is thus a conflict zone of opposing divergent national economic interests.

This economic rivalry between states may take one of two forms. Mercantilism can be defensive or benign, or it can be aggressive or malevolent (Gilpin, 1987: 31–2). In the first form, states take care to safeguard their national interests on the economic front because these interests are deemed to be essential for national security. This type of benign mercantilism may involve preventing foreign investments in certain sensitive sectors of the economy such as defence and energy, or protecting national markets from international competition to promote the consolidation of national industrial sectors.

Malevolent or offensive mercantilism is practised by nationalists who see the international economy as an arena in which to engage in imperial expansion or national territorial expansion. Examples include the expansionist policies of Hjalmar Schacht, Nazi minister of economics, toward Eastern Europe during the 1930s; the imperialism of European powers in Asia and Africa; and Japanese expansion in China in the 1930s.

and regimes reflect the power relations between the great powers. According to Stephen Krasner, regimes represent "implicit or explicit principles, norms, rules and decision-making procedures around which actors' expectations converge in a given area of international relations" (Krasner, 1983: 2). The regime concept was introduced to explain the international governance of

One of the thinkers who adapted mercantilist theses during the industrial era was one of America's founding fathers, Alexander Hamilton. In his 1791 *Report on Manufactures*, Hamilton developed the theoretical foundations of what today we call nationalism or economic patriotism. In his report, Hamilton provided a classic defence of protectionism. He believed that strengthening the American economy and promoting economic development were essential to preserving national independence and security. His political prescription included the following: developing industry rather than agriculture, striving for economic self-sufficiency in order to limit American dependence, engaging in state intervention, and practising protectionism with regard to trade. While Hamilton realized the importance of agriculture, he maintained that it was more important to diversify the American economy in order to end dependence on external forces.

As Hamilton wrote in his report,

Not only the wealth; but the independence and security of a Country, appear to be materially connected with the prosperity of manufactures. Every nation, with a view to those great objects, ought to endeavour to possess within itself all the essentials of national supply. These comprise the means of Subsistence habitation clothing and defence.

The possession of these is necessary to the perfection of the body politic, to the safety as well as to the welfare of the society; the want of either, is the want of an important organ of political life and Motion; and in the various crises which await a state, it must severely feel the effects of any such deficiency. The extreme embarrassments of the United States during the late War, from an incapacity of supplying themselves, are still matter of keen recollection. (Hamilton, 1791)

Hamilton's ideas were very influential. After visiting the United States, German economist Friedrich List was inspired by Hamilton's works to introduce the concept in Germany's territories. In his *National Political Economy System*, published in 1841, the *Nationalökonomie*, or national economy, became a way for German states to enter the future. If the German territories and the United States wanted to catch up to Great Britain one day, pleaded List, they had to protect their infant industry. But for List, protectionism must be the teacher. A nation's wealth is not measured by what it possesses but by what it can produce.

issues such as nuclear proliferation, transnational pollution, telecommunications, transportation, and humanitarian aid, where principles, norms, rules, and decision-making procedures are connected. When an international regime exists, it provides a focal point, a centre of gravity around which actors' expectations converge. Regimes also provide norms and a more or less formal decision-making process. A regime is associated with a particular issue and is characterized by the relationship it establishes between its constitutive elements.

From the realist point of view, relative gains and the distribution of power are important issues that have a strong impact on negotiations and on the creation of international regimes. According to Krasner, states compete for influence in order to define the terms and the operating rules of international regimes, as these regimes have significant distributional effects between the actors (1991). In Krasner's view, powers intervene in various ways in the formation of international regimes: they may select who can participate in the regime, determine the rules of the game, or intervene to modify the distribution of gains. The nature of the institutional arrangements of international regimes is better explained by the distribution of power between the actors than by the communication problems those arrangements are supposed to solve. International organizations and regimes are able to increase or reduce the power of states. According to Mearsheimer, international organizations and regimes reflect the distribution of power between actors in the international system and, more generally, are instruments of the great powers (1994–95: 13).

For realists, these regimes and organizations do not foster cooperation. Rather, world powers use these institutions to maintain their power and even to increase it. While realists recognize that the international system has seen a significant increase in the number of international organizations and regimes, they believe their importance and their effects on international politics have been exaggerated.

According to Krasner, IPE realists discuss essentially two types of issues. The first pertains to the distribution of power in the international system and includes, notably, the hegemonic structure of the international system and its effects on the creation of international regimes. The second pertains to national power and its effects on the relations between states. This chapter will present some major works that are representative of these debates.

Before examining these issues, however it is important to explain how realists perceive globalization, as this phenomenon is central to the discussions. We will also discuss how realists analyze economic interdependence and war. For most realists, globalization is essentially a myth and does not involve important changes in terms of how the international system operates. Gilpin wrote the following in 1981: "The basic assumption of this study has been that the nature of international relations has not changed fundamentally over the millennia. . . . One must suspect that if Thucydides were placed in our midst, he would (following an appropriate short course in geography, economics and modern technology) have little trouble in understanding the power struggle of our age" (Gilpin, 1981: 211). Most realists would agree with this statement today.

The Myth of Globalization

Most realist IPE authors do not believe that globalization represents a truly new phenomenon that is fundamentally transforming international politics. They do not deny its existence or exclude it from the analysis, contrary to certain specialists who concentrate only on security issues. Rather, they try to show that globalization does not fundamentally alter the nature of inter-state relations or challenge realist assumptions. Realists are also very critical of liberal authors who posit that globalization and interdependence significantly affect states' intervention capability (Krasner, 2008; Gilpin, 2001).

For realists such as Krasner, Gilpin, and Waltz, the effects and extensive nature of globalization have been exaggerated, be it in the media or among specialists. Given that globalization is not a new phenomenon, world politics and the international system have not actually changed (Gilpin, 2001; Krasner, 1999). The consequences on public policy and the transformation of the international scene have been overstated.

Krasner responded with sarcasm to the inaugural editorial of the *Review of International Political Economy*, the flagship journal of the heterodox approach: "Change, globalization, transnationalism, the erosion of the state, the transformation of political life. New, new, change, change. Academic reflections about international political economy are beginning to sound more and more like American political campaigns" (1994: 3). For him, as globalization is not a new phenomenon, the effects of globalization on the authority of states are not anything new. Krasner concedes that international finance clearly affects monetary policy and that this phenomenon is relatively new. However, he believes that while states may lose their capabilities regarding certain issues, they may gain influence regarding others, notably military security issues.

According to Krasner, transnational flows, though sometimes presented as a recent phenomenon, have existed for a very long time. Historically, there have been many examples of world economic centres, such as northern Italy, the Netherlands, and Great Britain, that were exporting powers and that invested abroad. Even the spread of viruses is not a recent example. The AIDS epidemic, Krasner reminds us, has not been as destructive as the Black Death of the fourteenth century, which decimated a third of the population in certain parts of Europe (Krasner, 1994).

For Krasner, given that the major issues of world politics are not new, it is not necessary to revise the analytical perspectives in order to examine and explain these issues. According to him, despite the fact that analytical tools have become more sophisticated, neither a theoretical upheaval nor a paradigm change has occurred. The most important conceptual approaches available for contemporary analyses are only the most recent articulations of perspectives that have long existed. In his eyes, the realist perspective remains the most pertinent (Krasner, 1994).

Gilpin is another realist scholar who believes that globalization is not a new phenomenon:

The extent and significance of economic globalization have been greatly exaggerated and misunderstood in both public and professional discussions; globalization in fact is not nearly as extensive nor as sweeping in its

---

Box 3.2   Do Multinationals Have a Nationality?

Charles Wilson, former CEO of General Motors, stated before the senate committee studying his nomination for secretary of defence, "what was good for our country was good for General Motors, and vice versa." Wilson did not see a conflict of interest between his former position, his many GM shares, and the position of secretary of defence, as the growth of the United States and of General Motors naturally went hand in hand. With the globalization of large corporations around the world, does this statement still make sense?

The number of multinationals has been growing rapidly for the past 40 years. According to United Nations Conference on Trade and Development (UNCTAD), while there were some 7,000 multinationals in the late 1960s, in 2011, there were over 82,000 from over 47 countries, controlling 790,000 subsidiaries in 175 countries. These subsidiaries employed over 69 million workers around the world and produced annual revenues far exceeding total global trade in goods and services (UNCTAD, 2012).

In this new context, can we still think like Robert Gilpin that multinationals are in fact national corporations operating in several markets, or, conversely, like Robert Reich (1991), that national origin is no longer so important? According to Reich, a country has nothing more to gain from promoting growth and development by subsidizing, protecting, or promoting the high profit margins of "national corporations."

The multinational concept causes confusion. It encompasses a very heterogeneous group of corporations. As Wladimir Andreff (2003) explains, this concept covers three types of corporations. The first type of multinational is the "mini-multinational," which is found in just a few countries, where it adapts to the local conditions. We also find "banal" multinationals that invest abroad to delocalize part of their production to reduce their costs and have easier access to other markets and less expensive supplies. Evidently, most mini-multinationals and banal multinationals concentrate their most important activities (head office, design, research, marketing, etc.) in their country of origin. The final type comprises multinationals that believe the market is now global, and so they develop strategies that are coordinated worldwide. These global multinationals represent only a few thousand companies. In their case, national bases are less important.

consequences (negative or positive) as many contemporary observers be-lieve. This is still a world where national policies and domestic economies are the determinants of economic affairs. Globalization and increasing economic interdependence among national economies are indeed very important; yet, as Vincent Cable of the Royal Institute of International Affairs has pointed out, the major economic achievement of the post–World War II

On average, the 40 largest multinationals in the world employ 55 per cent of their workers and generate 60 per cent of their revenues in foreign countries. In the United States, foreign sales represent only 25 per cent of the total for companies on the S&P 500. But when we examine only the 40 largest S&P companies, the percentage climbs to 40 per cent. Thus, what is good for General Motors is not necessarily good for America. Around 30 per cent of GM's employees work outside the United States (Paquin, 2008).

The UNCTAD transnationality index confirms this trend. According to the index, Thomson Corporation (a media firm), for example, was the world's most transnational company in 2008. Based on the company's shares and sales and on the number of its employees abroad, UNCTAD estimated that its transnational index exceeded 96 per cent. In other words, 96 per cent of its shares, sales, and employees were located outside Canada. Liberty Global's index was over 95 per cent. The Roche Group slightly exceeded 90 per cent, and the Lafarge transnationality index exceeded 80 per cent. In these cases, can it be said that these companies have a nationality and that this national identity is critical in corporate strategies—namely, their decisions regarding where to locate the head office, where to create jobs, and where to pay taxes?

For most large multinationals, this is even truer in small countries like Canada, where the domestic market no longer dominates economic activity. Global multinationals were formed in vast global networks, bypassing borders. It is increasingly difficult, even impossible, to refer to a national production, as the products of large companies are assembled abroad. Moreover, global network multinationals play national, regional, and local legislatures off one another in order to localize their manufacturing and finance on the most convenient territory. Global multinationals produce within the network and in several territories; therefore, they can no longer be perceived as a reliable indicator of a country's competitiveness.

Realists are skeptical about the power of multinationals and tend to base their analysis on the first two types of multinationals. But that is a bit like using Denmark and Portugal rather than the United States and China to illustrate the power of states. Heterodox theorists, on the other hand, are interested in global multinationals, as these global firms are the ones that have acquired power over governments and over their environment. They represent a central force behind contemporary globalization.

era has been to restore the level of international economic integration that
existed prior to World War I. (Gilpin, 2001: 3)

Like Gilpin, several realist authors argue that it was not until the 1990s that
the global economy was characterized by a degree of economic integration
comparable to that which prevailed between 1870 and 1914. The gold standard era at the end of the nineteenth century, the first globalization, constituted the golden age of the movement of capital, goods, and labour between
countries. This system collapsed with the First World War, and a similar
degree of openness and integration did not exist again until the 1990s.

Gilpin questions the idea that globalization is the cause of most global
and national economic, political, and social problems. He believes that the
unemployment and growth problems countries experience have very little
to do with globalization. These problems are more generally caused by the
development of robotization, by the emergence of new information technologies, and by harmful public policies on a national level. These elements
explain many problems facing Western countries better than globalization.
Criticisms of globalization are often inappropriate, and the problems that
are blamed on the phenomenon often have very little or even nothing to do
with it (Gilpin, 2001: 10).

According to Gilpin, while globalization represents a real phenomenon
that has effectively transformed IPE, it is not as intrusive, extensive, or significant as most authors believe. He points out that national economies are
essentially independent and that globalization is restricted to only a small
number of economic sectors, even though that number is growing. For him,
the extent of globalization has also been exaggerated. He wrote in 2001
that it occurs essentially between the triad of industrialized countries—the
United States, Western European countries, and Japan—and a few emerging countries in East Asia. The presumed impact of the "technological revolution" is apparently also disproportionate. Gilpin explains, "Although the
computer appears to have accelerated the rate of economic and productivity
growth, it is still too early to know whether or not its ultimate impact will
affect the overall economy on a scale at all equivalent to that produced by the
dynamo" (Gilpin, 2001: 10).

In addition to being excessive, according to Gilpin, criticisms of globalization help increase disillusionment regarding the opening of borders
to trade and foreign investments. These criticisms reinforce the idea that
globalization produces detrimental effects on working conditions, on developing countries, and on the environment.

Furthermore, contrary to what several authors assume, globalization exists only because states want it to. For Gilpin, globalization is a conscious
choice and a product of preferences, of hegemonic power, or of the great
powers. The most powerful states have the ability to facilitate not only the

opening but also the closing of the world-economy. Globalization is a choice of states and not the result of technological progress and market preference. Gilpin maintains that the expansion of world trade since 1945 was made possible only by the alliance between the United States and the allied countries in Europe and Asia on security issues. It was because they were under the protection of the United States that countries such as Germany and Japan could rebuild so rapidly and become world economic powers (Gilpin, 2001: 19).

While states create the conditions favouring globalization, they also allow national corporations to expand their business abroad. For Gilpin, multinationals are important actors in IPE. However, their manoeuvring room and autonomy are limited by their home countries' broad foreign policy objectives. Most multinationals are simply national corporations operating in different markets. Gilpin believes that American multinationals are the product of the US government's willingness to allow the economic expansion of its largest corporations in order to acquire more market shares in the world and of the security structure put in place by the United States after 1945 (Gilpin, 1975b, 2001). Hence, it is owing to the *Pax Americana* that American corporations have been able to expand abroad.

Globalization, War, and Peace

Despite the realities of globalization and complex interdependence, realists in IPE suggest that the world remains a dangerous place. Realist IPE theorists disagree with the statement made by Charles de Montesquieu in 1748: "Peace is the natural effect of trade." Rather, realists believe that international trade, by multiplying contacts between actors, can be a source of disagreement and rivalry, and therefore a force leading to conflicts. The effect of economic interdependence is that external economic shocks impact domestic politics, thereby feeding economic nationalism and populism. Moreover, under certain circumstances, trade between two states may be used to increase the political power of one of the two states. Globalization, therefore, is not a synonym for perpetual or democratic peace.

According to Kenneth Waltz, the idea that globalization and economic interdependence promote peace is a myth. Waltz, the father of neorealism, shared both Krasner's and Gilpin's view that globalization is a fad, and he expressed doubts as to whether countries are really interdependent. He believed that globalization is a negligible factor in terms of war and peace (Waltz, 2000). Economic issues are not important enough a factor to prevent countries from going to war. According to Waltz, the nuclear bomb is more important than economic interdependence as a factor of stability. Post–Cold War events show the political weakness of economic forces. The integration, and not simply the interdependence, of portions of the Soviet Union and

Yugoslavia was not able to prevent disintegration or war, despite their inter-twined economic interests. Governments and local populations agree to sacrifice their well-being and even their security in the pursuit of national, ethnic, and religious objectives (Waltz, 2000).

In Waltz's view, the First World War demonstrated unequivocally that economic interdependence is not a sufficient factor to prevent war between two countries. During the years preceding the war, Germany was the larg-est importer of Italian and Russian products, the second largest of British products, and the third largest of French products; it was also the largest exporter to Russia, Italy, and the Austro-Hungarian Empire and the second largest to France and Great Britain. This trade interdependence was not important enough a condition to prevent the War (Waltz, 1979: 158).

Waltz further argued that economic interdependence might even increase the probability a conflict will occur. Where economic interdepen-dence exists, economic crises are felt in several countries, which may fuel anger and lead to war. In summary, realists believe that globalization is not fundamentally transforming the international system and that the realist perspective remains pertinent for understanding and analyzing relations between states.

David Rowe also uses the example of the First World War to support his claim that globalization can be a source of conflict (1999: 195–231). Rowe's argument goes as follows: when rapid and profound changes take place in international trade flows, they affect prices and increase risks related to the global economy. Thus, these changes represent a source of potential conflict domestically. By affecting the prices of available foreign goods, the interna-tional economy has distributional effects that modify the configuration of interests in domestic politics. This reconfiguration of interests encourages the forming of new coalitions, such as those favouring protectionism and those favouring war. In short, economic interdependence is not a synonym for peace. In a second article, published in 2005, Rowe uses the Heckscher–Ohlin model of trade to link the effects of globalization to "increased constraints on military force." He comes to the conclusion that the effects are important but that, contrary to the liberal theory that globalization brings peace, the first globalization was a major cause of the First World War.

Katherine Barbieri is also a skeptic regarding the peace through trade thesis. Barbieri focuses on "dyadic" relationships, meaning relationships between two countries. The author developed her thesis following a quan-titative analysis of 100,000 dyadic relationships over a period of more than 100 years (between 1879 and 1992). Her findings indicate that interdepen-dent dyads are more likely to engage in militarized conflicts than those with fewer trade ties. While trade ties help countries settle their disputes through negotiation, this reinforcement is insufficient for preventing conflicts from escalating. Rather, the empirical evidence produced by the author indicates that heavily trading dyads have more of a chance to experience the most extreme form of conflict—war (Barbieri, 2002: 121). Furthermore, Barbieri found that states that are heavily dependent on trade for their economies are less belligerent than others. Conversely, states that are strong within the system are more belligerent, which suggests for Barbieri that there is a contradiction between the objective to introduce policies fostering economic growth and the objective of peace.

Gilpin provides a more nuanced reflection. He maintains that it is impossible to make generalizations about the relationship between economic interdependence and political behaviour. Sometimes trade relationships ease political relations, and sometimes they aggravate them. What is certain, according to Gilpin, is that trade and interdependence are not guarantors of peace. From another perspective, the collapse of trade has often led to an international conflict. For Gilpin, international relations and questions of peace are essentially determined by the power configuration in the international system and by the strategic interests between great and small powers in the system (2001: 58).

Furthermore, the peace through economic interdependence approach has not been able to prevent new security threats such as terrorism. For many authors, one myth that collapsed along with the World Trade Center is the idea that globalization represents a new form of "Manifest Destiny" that spreads political freedom and economic growth everywhere in the world.

Democratic peace theory has also not found favour in the eyes of realists. Even though several authors see important qualities in the theory, realists take a more nuanced approach. For David Spiro, for example, while democracies never engage one another in armed conflict, they can be very violent with non-democratic regimes. War is also more frequent between democratic countries and non-democratic countries than between non-democratic countries. Moreover, according to Spiro, we must remember that the great democratic powers practised imperialism and colonialism, invading four-fifths of the planet (Spiro, 1994). The colonial powers also used military force to preserve their colonies after 1945. They adopted immoral policies during the Cold War. The United States even helped topple a democratic regime elected in Chile in 1973. According to some, this can be explained by the fact that being a democratic regime is not enough; the regime must be recognized as such by other countries, which was not the case of Salvador Allende's Chile in the eyes of the United States. Malvin Small and David Singer (1982) have demonstrated that democracies initiated 58 per cent of the conflicts in which they participated. Controversially, according to Edward Mansfield and Jack Snyder (2005), democratic peace works only with older democracies. Democracies in transition are more likely to resort to war than older democracies and even authoritarian regimes. The authors ascribe this situation to the weakness of the state, the desire of certain social groups to delay or modify the transition to democracy, and the intensification of nationalist discourse.[1]

Power and Hegemonic Stability Theory

In their analyses in IPE, realist theorists examine the power distribution between states in the international system and its effects on the nature of international regimes. Since the 1970s, the principal analytical debate in IPE has centred on hegemonic stability theory, of which a liberal variant also exists. Briefly, this theory says that a system of open trade, with rules that are relatively precise and followed, can exist only when power is hegemonically distributed—that is, when one state concentrates much more power than the other states.

The basic assumptions of hegemonic stability theory are the following:

1. An open economic and trade order is more likely to be established when a hegemonic power is on the rise.
2. To ensure the open order works properly, the hegemonic power must bear the responsibility of certain common goods on the international scene (the common goods may vary depending on the author).
3. While all actors benefit from the common goods provided by the hegemonic power, the increase in the number of free riders and in the costs of maintaining the system ends up overloading the hegemonic power, which thus begins to decline.
4. The decline of the hegemonic power entails the decline of the open international order (Keohane, 1980: 132).

Historical economist Charles Kindleberger (1973) was the first to formulate the terms of the debate in his book *The World in Depression, 1929–1939*. He ascribed the depression that followed the 1929 crash to the American government's hesitations to assume the leadership of the world after the First World War, when it seemed evident that the British Empire was in decline and no longer able to fulfil a leadership role. Kindleberger believed that to work properly, the world-economy needs one stabilizer, and only one. In the context of the interwar years, it could only be the United States.

According to Kindleberger's theory, the benevolent leader is a powerful state that assumes responsibility for the common or public goods on the international stage. In his opinion, to avoid prolonging the crisis of 1929, the United States should have shown leadership to keep markets open for distress goods, set itself up as a long-term or countercyclical capital lender, adopted a more stable exchange rate system, coordinated macroeconomic policies, and served as a last resort lender to provide the international financial system with the necessary liquidities.

Kindleberger contended that the problem with world public goods is that the responsibility for them lies essentially in the hands of the country that plays the role of world leader. As all countries can profit from public goods without assuming the costs, the multiplication of free riders overwhelms the benevolent leader, which is no longer able to keep up this responsibility. Thus, for Kindleberger, the problem for the United States in the 1980s was not too much power but not enough, not an excess of dominance but too many clandestine passengers. In his interpretation of the 1929 crisis, Kindleberger opposed both Paul Samuelson's contingency theory regarding the causes of the crisis and Milton Friedman's and Anna Schwartz's monetarist interpretation.

Robert Keohane claims this debate in IPE was initiated by Stephen Krasner in a 1976 article. For Keohane, even though Krasner was not the first to discuss the subject, his article was the one to most clearly set the terms of the debate that has engaged IPE researchers since the 1970s. In this article that appeared in the journal *World Politics*, Krasner maintained that an open economy on the international level is more likely to come about "during periods when a hegemonic state is in its ascendency" (Krasner, 1976: 323).

This article is highly critical of the approach developed by Joseph Nye and Robert Keohane and pertaining to power and interdependence (see Chapter 4). Krasner wrote,

> In recent years, students of international relations have multinationalized, transnationalized, bureaucratized, and transgovernmentalized the state until it has virtually ceased to exist as an analytic construct. Nowhere is that trend more apparent than in the study of the politics of international economics relations. The basic conventional assumptions have been undermined by assertions that the state is trapped by a transnational society created not by sovereigns, but by nonstate actors. Interdependence is not seen as a reflection of state policies and state choices (the perspective of balance-of-power-theory), but as the result of elements beyond the control of any state or a system created by states. This perspective is at best profoundly misleading. (1976: 317)

While this approach may explain the developments within an international economic structure, said Krasner, it cannot explain how the structure was actually created.

In his article, Krasner aimed to show that the structure of international trade is in fact determined by the interests and power of states acting to maximize their national goals. His article's most important conclusion is that a hegemonic power distribution is conducive to an open trade system. Krasner called this the "state-power" argument (1976).

To demonstrate his thesis, he divided the phases of international trade between 1820 and 1970 into several historical periods. After the analysis, he concluded that the open world-economy cycles correlate 50 per cent of the time with periods when one state is very clearly predominant. Hegemony correctly predicts an open economy in three of the six periods studied—between 1820 and 1879, between 1880 and 1900, and between 1945 and 1960, but not between 1900 and 1913, between 1919 and 1939, or between 1960 and 1975.

Krasner admitted that this correlation between hegemonic power and regimes that are open to trade and investment is far from perfect. The openness continued during the first decades of the twentieth century, when the British Empire was in decline. In addition, an open trade regime was not established until after the Second World War, although the United States was a hegemonic power by the end of the First World War. He conceded that the causal linkages were delayed, or out of phase, and proposed three pages of amendments to correct what was wrong with his theory. Nevertheless, he concluded that economic independence and transnationalism are subordinate to political and economic power. They are a choice of powerful states. States are not the victims, but the creators of interdependence or what we nowadays call globalization.

Krasner's thesis is clearly within the realist paradigm. It is in the hegemonic power's national interest to open up the world trade system in order to procure new markets for its national producers. The hegemonic power is less affected by the shocks of the world-economy than other states; therefore, the opportunity cost of closure is also weaker. The hegemonic power is less vulnerable to changes abroad and can use its power more easily to ensure that its companies continue to access international markets. *A contrario*, if power were more equally distributed among states, in a multipolar system, for example, states would be less inclined to favour an open trade system. Less economically developed states would try to protect themselves from the danger of depending on other states, while the larger, weakening states, fearful of losing some of their power, would be more susceptible to domestic protectionist pressures. Thus, open trade is more likely to occur when a hegemonic power is in the ascending phase.

In this article, Krasner rejected the idea that states always prioritize the pursuit of wealth above all other issues. Security, political power, independent decision making, and social stability are also essential aspects, but states do keep a sharp eye on how gains are distributed between them. In summary, it is not because free trade is theoretically good for all players, as David Ricardo maintains, that it is perceived as such by each state taken individually. The distribution of power between states is a key factor.

A second author who has contributed significantly to the realist version of hegemonic stability theory is Robert Gilpin of Princeton. Just like Kindleberger and Krasner, Gilpin says in his book *U.S. Power and the*

Multinational Corporation, published in 1975, that hegemonic states such as Great Britain at the end of the nineteenth century and the United States after 1945 have historically supported open trade regimes for investments and trade. Given that these countries were the most advanced economically and technologically and possessed a great deal of capital to invest, this open international market policy was a matter of national interest. Countries with more limited resources might prefer more restrictive regimes, which would permit them to favour national corporations and to gain a competitive advantage (Gilpin, 1975b).

For Gilpin, therefore, when power is distributed hegemonically within the international system, an open trade regime is more likely. The hegemonic power prefers this system because it provides it with economic growth, wealth, and political power, enabling it to convince or even to force other states to participate in this open regime. In return, the hegemonic power provides the essential public goods the system needs to work properly.

Contrary to transnationalists, Gilpin maintains that multinationals expand abroad because powerful states want them to. In Gilpin's view, the success of American multinationals abroad speaks to how political relations are configured. US multinationals have been able to play a key role in world affairs because it has been in the interest of the hegemonic power, the United States (Gilpin, 1975b: 9). Over the long term, however, Gilpin believes that US multinationals spread technological and economic innovation, and, in so doing, undermine the very source of the hegemon's power.

In 1981, Gilpin continued his development of hegemonic stability theory in his book *War and Change in World Politics.* One objective of this book was to adapt Kindleberger's thesis to the realist perspective. But Gilpin's greater ambition was to explain the growth and decline of hegemonic power and to explain change in IPE (Gilpin, 1981: 10–11). Gilpin devised the theory of hegemonic power cycles. He divided growth and decline into phases and sought to predict the economic and security consequences of these changes for the international system.

Gilpin's general thesis is implicitly rationalist and utilitarian. He argues that an international system is built because social actors (states) enter into relationships and create structures while at the same time pushing for their own self-interests. The system's structure reflects the distribution of power within the international system. As power and interests are not static factors, the system transforms and forces actors to re-examine their strategies. The system is in equilibrium when no player can hope to gain from a change in the system. When a state believes it can gain—that is, when the benefits of the change outweigh the costs—the system can change.

The central point of Gilpin's book is that when equilibrium is achieved, it probably will not last, as the costs of maintaining the system outweigh the benefits. If the dominant power(s) cannot restore equilibrium, the new system will reflect the new distribution of power.

Gilpin's thesis is in keeping with Kindleberger's idea, especially regarding the necessity for the hegemonic power to assume responsibility for the international public goods. Furthermore, the hegemonic power must add order and security to its responsibilities (Gilpin, 1981: 10–11). Unlike Kindleberger, Gilpin does not think of the hegemonic power as a benevolent leader whose role is to stabilize the system and be responsible for the international system. For him, the hegemonic power acts on the international stage in its own national interest.

At the end of the nineteenth century, it was in the interest of the hegemonic power, the British Empire, to promote free trade, but also to protect the world trade system. The United States was in a similar situation following the Second World War. Gilpin disagrees with the liberal interpretation that claims free trade is better for everybody. He believes that the United States was motivated only by its national interest and security objectives. Given that the Allies depended on American aid for their reconstruction and that the US economy represented approximately 50 per cent of the world-economy in 1945, American superiority was evident. As the United States was clearly in a hegemonic position, it was in its interest to create an open trade system allowing American businesses and capital holders to expand abroad. This situation enabled the United States to establish an international system that was clearly in its interest initially.

In Gilpin's theory, the sequence begins with the ascension of the hegemonic power on the military, economic, technological, and organizational fronts. This phase is very profitable for the hegemonic power, as strong economic growth enables it to consolidate its economic and military presence in the world.

Subsequently, the period of decline sets in. Both foreign and domestic factors are at the root of this regression. At the foreign level, the costs of maintaining the country's hegemonic position in the world increase more rapidly than the benefits, and the available resources are more difficult to obtain. Moreover, the hegemonic power's technologies, technical skills, and economic capabilities are copied by other rising states.

Domestically, the hegemonic power's economy suffers the effects of the law of diminishing returns. This situation is compounded by the law of the rising cost of war. As well, private and public consumption increase more rapidly than the economy in an affluent society. The transition from a manufacturing economy to a service economy tends to decrease the growth of productivity. Finally, the population becomes increasingly demanding of the hegemonic power's government. People will favour consumption over production and economic development, and resist changes that may be necessary for maintaining the hegemonic power in the world.

The combination of these factors results in an increasingly difficult financial situation that culminates in a serious financial crisis. When this occurs, options are limited. The hegemonic power may confront domestic obstacles, which is arduous, or it may seek to restrain the growth of the rising powers before they become a real threat. The hegemonic state may also unilaterally refuse to bear the cost of certain international public goods, or it may seek to work with other states in a balance of power system against the new, emerging hegemonic power. If the imbalance is not resolved peacefully, the only way to transition from one hegemonic power to another seems to be through war. And this risks plunging the world into a new global conflict.

In 1987, Gilpin published his major synthesis *The Political Economy of International Relations*, the most widely used reference work in IPE courses in American universities during the years following its publication. In it, Gilpin discussed various IPE paradigms but also argued that American hegemony in the international system had been in decline since the 1970s, and that this was affecting the liberal order formed after 1945. Gilpin saw two reasons for this decline: first, the exporting of American technologies to other countries in the world, which accelerated the reconstruction of Western Europe and Japan; and second, the dramatic rise in the costs of containing the USSR. In this context, the American government was no longer able to impose its supremacy or retain its competitive advantages in the world.

The first event to herald the transformation of America's hegemonic position in the international system took place in 1973. That year, the United States lost control of the world monetary system with the end of the Bretton Woods Agreement and the turn toward a floating exchange rate system. The second event that same year was the oil crisis that shook the energy market (Gilpin, 1987: 345). The first event was caused by Germany's refusal to share part of the cost of the international monetary system, and OPEC caused the second. According to Gilpin, for the first time after the Second World War, foreign governments had taken actions that directly reduced Americans' economic well-being.

In this increasingly difficult economic context, which began with the Vietnam War and continued into the Reagan administration, Americans were more and more reticent to bear the cost of the international public good, as a number of countries profited from the system put in place by the Americans after 1945, increasing their own wealth and power by free-riding on the back of America. Consequently, the United States, guided by their national interest, no longer acted as Kindleberger's benevolent leader but as a "predatory hegemon," to use John Conybeare's expression (quoted in Gilpin, 1987: 345). For Gilpin, this meant that the United States was less disposed to subordinate its own interests to those of its allies, and that, in its international actions, it tended to exploit its hegemonic status to reap advantages in keeping with its national interests, which it defined increasingly narrowly. This situation prompted a new era of neomercantilism.

This transformation had critical consequences for the international system. It signalled, first, the return of protectionism and mercantilist policies on the part of the declining hegemonic power and, subsequently, the return of regionalism and aggressive bilateralism (Gilpin, 1987: 363). This type of behaviour garnered sanctions from the other members of GATT (General Agreement on Tariffs and Trade, now the World Trade Organization or WTO), risking further deterioration of the situation. These transformations posed a serious threat for the international trade system and for the survival of the liberal order. The exacerbation of rivalries complicated post-hegemonic cooperation. In the new edition of his book in 2001, Gilpin uses the same type of analysis but targets China as the new potential rival of the United States. For Gilpin and realist theorists, these changes are not good news, especially due to the fear of a hegemonic transition war.

Gilpin's version of hegemonic stability theory is compatible with realist theorists' general assumptions regarding international relations. According to realists, states cannot cooperate in an anarchic environment that makes them egoists. While, for classical realist theorists, peace depends on a balance of powers, for hegemonic stability theorists, it is rather the existence of a hegemonic power that ensures the pacification of the system and that gradually liberalizes world trade. In this model, politics creates the conditions for a liberal economy. Therefore, politics takes precedence over the economy. But there is also a liberal element in this thesis as, once free trade is implemented, it is profitable for all. In this case, the hegemonic power remains attentive to relative gains in order to ensure its supremacy and the system's survival. When the hegemonic power begins to decline, the international liberal order runs the risk of collapsing along with it.

Power and Interstate Relations

For realist IPE theorists, Albert Hirschman's book *National Power and the Structure of Foreign Trade*, published in 1945, constitutes a landmark study on how power influences economic relations between states. In this study, Hirschman examined how states use bilateral trade to increase their power. The basic idea is simple: Two countries trading with each other do not obtain the same benefits; therefore, the trade relationship is asymmetrical. In this relationship, the country less dependent on trade can exploit this situation in order to enhance its power.

Hirschman claimed that there are two ways to use a trade relationship to alter a state's capability or its public policies. First, a state may seek to limit the availability of some very important products or technologies with the aim of restricting access to strategic resources. According to Krasner, the policies of Western countries during the Cold War are a good illustration of this strategy. By limiting the trading of goods, the lending of information, and the convertibility of currencies, Western countries isolated the Eastern Bloc countries. The latter were excluded from the world economic order, including the International Monetary Fund (IMF), the World Bank, and the GATT (Krasner, 2008; Mastanduno, 1991, 1992).

Second, trade relations may be used to force changes in a country's foreign policy. If one of the two states makes a credible threat to modify the trade system, the other state must yield if the cost of the threat exceeds the benefits of trade. For the state more dependent on the trade relationship, it is preferable to agree to the preferences of the stronger state rather than suffer the economic consequences of the threat. But what is a credible threat? For Hirschman, a threat is credible when the relative opportunity costs are asymmetrical. If one of the two actors modifies the system without bearing major costs while the costs are considerable for the second, the threat is credible. If the relative opportunity costs are identical or comparable for both partners, or if they are higher for the one making the threat, the threat is not credible. Thus, the relative opportunity cost is a way to operationalize the concept of power, a concept that has always been problematic for international political economy theorists. In his analysis, Hirschman drew on the example of Germany, which used its trade policy to expand its influence in Eastern Europe during the interwar years, even though its policies were ineffective economically. Realists therefore expect a powerful state to sacrifice economic gains in order to enhance its political power.

Realist theorists pay close attention to transformations of states' power on the international scene, as these transformations have repercussions for interstate relations. One state's rise in power forces others to reassess their relations with it, regardless of the type of political regime (democratic or authoritarian). According to Krasner, realists presume that, in the event of a change in the distribution of power, there will be tensions between states despite economic interdependence. These tensions will not necessarily lead to war between the major powers but will decidedly influence their relations.

In the 1970s and 1980s, for example, Japan broke through as a world power, and this emergence came with sharp tensions with the United States. As Michael Mastanduno demonstrated, on certain issues American decision makers were increasingly worried about relative gains and became more attentive to the bilateral arrangements between the two countries, notably when they involved technological and military transfers (Mastanduno, 1991). American foreign policy regarding Japan differed markedly from that regarding its other allies. American representatives pressured Japan to modify some of its policies on government procurement, medical equipment, automobile parts, portable telephones, and rice. The US government wanted to modify trade terms in order to balance the gains between the two countries. The success of this undertaking was limited, as the opportunity costs were high on both sides.

Another line of argument in the realist perspective pertains to the connections between alliances, security, and free trade. While liberal authors suggest that countries with significant trade relations are less likely to go to war against each other, Joanne Gowa asks whether the anticipation of war influences the choice of trading partners. She maintains that in an anarchic international system, states must monitor every development and the relative gains that may weaken their security. States are thus more inclined to engage in open free trade regimes with allies than with rivals or enemies, not only because openness creates wealth but also because wealth is the condition for increasing military capability (Gowa, 1994).

Distributional issues or relative gains may influence other more specific aspects of international regimes. In his 1990 book, Joseph Grieco poses the following question: "How does the anarchical nature of the international system inhibit the willingness of states to work together even when they share common interests?" According to Grieco, the Tokyo Round of GATT negotiations, which ended in 1979, pertained to an array of subjects, such as non-tariff trade barriers, subsidies, customs valuation, government procurement, and dumping. He maintains that customs valuation was linked to American expectations regarding absolute and relative gains. The Customs Valuation Code[2] was very effective, while the code covering government procurement had much less impact. In the former case, Europe and the United States hoped for equal gains. In the latter case, Europe expected to lose. This situation may be explained thus: States are loath to yield to one another; therefore, they adopt strategies to defend against such an eventuality. Grieco describes these states as "defensive positionalists" (1990). In short, states may refuse to cooperate because they are afraid that the joint undertaking, even though it will procure advantages for all participants, might also create disparities in how the gains are distributed. According to Grieco, the question of relative and absolute gains is central and systematically influences international negotiations.

For Krasner, power relations are also reflected on issues other than those linked to trade. When the IMF was established, for example, American and British conceptions of what the IMF should be were starkly different. The British conception, advanced by John Maynard Keynes, favoured a fund with more autonomy and lending capability. The United States wanted a smaller IMF with a more restricted lending capability. In the end, the American preference was written into the articles of the IMF's constitution. In 1945, the British were debtors, while the Americans were creditors.

A second example pertains to the telecommunications and satellite development sector. Satellites, a new technology controlled largely by the Americans, gave rise to the International Telecommunications Satellite

Organization (INTELSAT), created in 1964 to regulate satellite communication. Normally, this new sector could have been governed by the International Telecommunication Union (ITU), founded in Paris in 1865. However, as the ITU granted one vote to each country, it was not in the interest of the United States for the institution to control satellite regulation. The US proposed the establishment of INTELSAT, where votes would be proportional to usage, thereby providing the largest share to the United States. In essence, according to the realist explanation, a change in power relations led to changes in the rules of the game. The United States wanted a new institution because the existing one, the ITU, did not grant it enough power. A new institution could better reflect the importance of the United States in this area (Krasner, 1991).

Conclusion

Until the 1990s, most specialists thought realism was the leading paradigm among international relations experts. Michael Doyle, for example, maintained that realism was the dominant theory (1997). Similarly, Jeffrey Legro and Andrew Moravcsik (1999) stated that realism was the oldest and most prominent international relations paradigm. For many specialists, realism was at its apogee during the Cold War, before it relinquished its leading position to the liberal paradigm.

According to David Maliniak and his collaborators, this perception was false. Even in the 1980s, the realist paradigm was far behind the liberal paradigm. Today, it is edged out by the constructivist and liberal paradigms. In 2006, only 6 per cent of articles published in the 12 leading journals adopted the realist perspective. In short, realism in international relations and in IPE is a degenerative research program, to use Lakatos's expression. There are fewer and fewer advocates of this approach, and recent studies confirm the growing marginalization of this paradigm. Several factors may explain this decline.

First, the predictive capability of realist theories is a considerable failure. That no one saw the collapse of the USSR coming in 1991 (only 12 years after Kenneth Waltz's landmark book was published) and that, even more surprisingly, this collapse occurred peacefully is simply inexplicable for realist and neorealist theorists. Furthermore, it must be noted that the number of wars has been decreasing for a rather long time. Since 1945, the trend has been even more evident, as formerly belligerent regions such as Europe have been mostly pacified, making war in the region unthinkable today.

The realist conception of globalization also defies common sense, to the extent that it affects how their theses, most of which seem to belong to another century, are received. For several realist authors, such as Waltz, Gilpin, and Krasner, globalization is not a new phenomenon, as European countries were very globalized by the eve of the First World War. Trade interdependence did not prevent the war.

It would be wrong, however, to bury the realist theory in IPE. Perhaps the rise of China represents an occasion for the realist paradigm to renew itself. The prospect of seeing a hegemonic transition occur in a context where China is not a democratic regime lends credibility to realist theses, notably on the importance of relative gains. It is also possible that, in the future, conflicts and wars will not stem from the United States or China having too much power but from the lack of power of many collapsed states that are incapable of participating in international regulation. They represent the black hole of the international system.

Moreover, if IPE realists agreed to revisit their conception of globalization, perhaps they would conclude that the phenomenon is conflict-prone. For example, instability and financial crises may plunge a group of countries into a deep recession, thus inflaming passions and precipitating the return of populism. Furthermore, external shocks, such as severe acute respiratory syndrome, the food crisis, resource scarcity, and oil price increases, are more easily exported around the world, increasing the risk of conflict, even war. The consequences of climate change, notably climate refugees and limited access to drinkable water for certain populations, are most certainly causes for worry. Cyberterrorism is also a growing problem for several countries and multinationals.

Notes

1   Narang and Nelson (2009) re-evaluated Mansfield and Snyder's widely accepted thesis using their database. Narang and Nelson found very different results: only six wars, of the 398 observations or cases, between 1816 and 1992 involved the participation of "incomplete democracies." Of these six wars, only one was initiated by an "incomplete democracy." Furthermore, no "incomplete democracy" had initiated, or even participated in, an external war since the First World War. The findings were only influenced by the participation of the Ottoman Empire in four wars (1877, 1911, 1912, and 1913), and three of these four wars could be counted as just one war (1911–13). Narang and Nelson concluded not only that "weak democracies" are not the problem, but also that they are involved only extremely rarely in wars. The authors write, "there is simply no empirical basis to think, or adopt policies predicated on the fear, that incomplete democratizers will be more belligerent members of the international system" (Narang and Nelson, 2009: 364).

2   On their website under "Technical Information on Customs Valuation," the WTO defines customs valuation as a "customs procedure applied to determine the customs value of imported goods. If the rate of duty is ad valorem, the customs value is essential to determine the duty to be paid on an imported good."

Questions

1. What separates realist theorists in international relations from those in IPE?
2. What is mercantilism?
3. Why do realists in IPE believe that the fundamental variable is the distribution of power between states?
4. What is the difference between relative and absolute gains?
5. Why do we say that realists have developed a pessimistic perception of human nature?
6. Why is globalization a myth according to the realists in IPE?
7. What is the impact of globalization on war and peace according to the realists?
8. What are the basic assumptions of hegemonic stability theory?
9. Do Kindleberger, Gilpin, and Krasner have the same conception of hegemonic stability?
10. Why do realists pay close attention to the transformation of states' power?

Further Reading

The foundations of the orthodox school's realist international political economy:

Guzzini, Stefano. *Realism in International Relations and International Political Economy: The Continuing Story of a Death Foretold.* London: Routledge, 1998.

Kirshner, Jonathan. "Realist Political Economy: Traditional Themes and Contemporary Challenges." In *Routledge Handbook of International Political Economy (IPE): IPE As a Global Conversation,* edited by Mark Blyth, 36–47. New York: Routledge, 2009.

The author most associated with the realist orthodox school is Robert Gilpin. Here are his most important publications:

Gilpin, Robert. "Three Models of the Future." *International Organization* 29.1 (1975): 37–60.

Gilpin, Robert. *U.S. Power and the Multinational Corporation: The Political Economy of Direct Foreign Investment.* New York: Basic Books, 1975.

Gilpin, Robert. *War and Change in World Politics.* Cambridge: Cambridge University Press, 1981.

Gilpin, Robert. *The Political Economy of International Relations.* Princeton: Princeton University Press, 1987.

Gilpin, Robert. *Global Political Economy: Understanding the International Economic Order.* Princeton: Princeton University Press, 2001.

The following works by Stephen Krasner are fundamental:

Krasner, Stephen D. "State Power and the Structure of International Trade." *World Politics* 28.4 (1976): 317–47.

Krasner, Stephen D. *Defending the National Interest: Raw Materials Investments and U.S. Foreign Policy.* Princeton: Princeton University Press, 1978.

Krasner, Stephen D. "United States Commercial and Monetary Policy: Unraveling the Paradox of External Strength and Internal Weakness." In *Between Power and Plenty: Foreign Economic Policies of Advanced Industrial States,* edited by Peter J. Katzenstein, 51–87. Madison: University of Wisconsin Press, 1978.

Krasner, Stephen D. "Global Communications and National Power: Life on the Pareto Frontier." *World Politics* 43.3 (1991): 336–66.

Krasner, Stephen D., ed. *International Regimes.* Ithaca, NY: Cornell University Press, 1983.

4 The Liberal Perspective

Chapter Contents

- Basic Assumptions of the Liberal Perspective in IPE
- Globalization, War, and Peace
- Peace through Democracy
- Peace through International Institutions
- Economic Interdependence as a Factor of Peace
- Globalization and Transnationalism
- Liberal Institutionalism
- The Rational Design of Institutions
- The Debate on Compliance
- Conclusion

Reader's Guide

It was in the 1970s, with the works of Robert Keohane and Joseph Nye on transnationalism and complex interdependence, and the 1980s, with the emergence of liberal institutionalism, that liberalism became the most important perspective in IPE. The liberal perspective in IPE is very similar to the liberal perspective in international relations, except that there is much more emphasis on economic and financial issues. The most important debates have to do with transnationalism, the conception of globalization, and liberal institutionalism. In this chapter we will examine the basic assumptions of the liberal perspective in IPE and the broad outlines of the effects of globalization on questions of war and peace, as the diverse republican peace and commercial peace theories constitute a bridge between liberal theories in international relations and those in IPE. We will then look at the conception of globalization derived from the works of Keohane and Nye and explain the theoretical debates between liberal neo-institutionalism and neoliberalism. The final section will deal with liberal institutionalism. Its main objective is to explain interstate cooperation in an anarchic international system. At first, the institutional approach sought to explain why international institutions promote cooperation. The objective of later studies was to explain how institutions influence states' behaviour and international relations. Today, the debates generally have more to do with the rational design of international institutions and with the issue of states' compliance with their international commitments.

....

It was not until the 1970s, with the works of Robert Keohane and Joseph Nye on transnationalism and complex interdependence, and the 1980s, with the emergence of liberal institutionalism, that liberalism made a comeback in the debates in international relations theories in the United States. These debates also built the foundations of IPE, and since the 1990s liberalism has been the dominant perspective.

According to David Baldwin, there are several variants of liberalism in international relations theory: sociological, republican, and commercial liberalism as well as liberal institutionalism (Baldwin, 1993). Sociological liberalism refers to the notion of international society and interdependence in a context of globalization. Republican liberalism spotlights the debate on democratic peace. Commercial liberalism is based on the idea that commercial interdependence promotes peace. Liberal institutionalism mainly focuses on the role of international institutions.

In IPE, the debates are essentially the same, but there is much more emphasis on economic and financial issues. The most important debates have to do with transnationalism, the conception of globalization, and liberal institutionalism. In this chapter we will examine the basic assumptions of the liberal perspective in IPE and the broad outlines of the effects of globalization on questions of war and peace, as the diverse republican peace and commercial peace theories constitute a bridge between liberal theories in international relations and those in IPE. We will then look at the conception of globalization derived from the works of Keohane and Nye and explain the theoretical debates between liberal neo-institutionalism and neoliberalism. The final section will deal with the most recent debates on the rational design of international institutions and on the research on compliance with international agreements.

Basic Assumptions of the Liberal Perspective in IPE

For some authors such as Michael Doyle, there is no canonical description of liberalism, while for others, such as Stanley Hoffman (1977), the liberal perspective simply represents the projection on the international scene of the liberal philosophy that originated in the Enlightenment. The central feature of the normative view of the liberal perspective is that it transposes the liberal philosophy (rule of law, representative democracy, protection of private property, free trade, peaceful settlement of disputes, etc.) onto international issues. In international relations and IPE theories, this perspective therefore possesses a long history, the historical roots of which date back to the writings of Grotius, Locke, Kant, Smith, Ricardo, Mill, and Keynes.

The liberal perspective also possesses many different variants. Owing to the serious disagreements among liberal authors, it is more difficult to isolate the basic assumptions of this perspective versus the realist perspective. As a general rule, the liberal perspective is based on the belief that humans are endowed with reason and that they have the capacity to improve their condition and to create a just society. For Scott Burchill (2001: 33), liberals have faith in human reason and in the capacity of humans to realize their individual potential. Liberals are more optimistic than realists about the evolution of world politics. The increase in the number of democratic regimes, the downward trend in wars between states, the multiplication of the number of international organizations and institutions, as well as the economic and financial globalization are indicators of this progress (Zacher and Matthew, 1995).

Liberals are predominantly pluralists but also individualists—pluralists because, for them, states are not the only actors in the international political economy. They are important actors, even fundamental ones, but the international scene comprises a multitude of actors, whether they are international organizations, non-governmental organizations, multinationals, or private foundations. And they are individualists because the liberal perspective believes that people act rationally in the pursuit of their well-being, prosperity, and peace. People are rational and calculating, but they pursue different goals: leaders of state want more wealth and security for their citizen-voters, CEOs of multinationals aspire to more profits or market shares, environmentalists hope to preserve ecosystems and fight climate change, terrorists want to change the existing political order through the use of violence, and so on.

Some authors, such as Andrew Moravcsik, push the argument even further. For him, liberalism places state–society relations at the centre of the explanation of world politics. The fundamental causal factor that influences the behaviour of states in world politics is the relationship between the state and the domestic civil society, and between the state and the transnational society in which the state is embedded. The fundamental actors in international politics are rational individuals or groups that are averse to risk, especially the risk of losing their proprietary rights. These actors interact and exchange with the state's representative institutions to promote their own interests (Moravcsik, 1997: 521). Moravcsik's liberal approach is a bottom-up approach, because it is the demands and the preferences of individuals or social groups that constitute the national interest and that explain the behaviour of states. The institutions representing the state are like transmission belts, carrying the interests and preferences of individuals. These interests and preferences are then translated into public policies (Moravcsik, 2003: 163). According to the liberal conception of domestic politics, the state is not a solitary actor, as it is for realists. Rather, it is an institution that defends the interests of various actors in domestic politics. As Moravcsik writes, "In the liberal conception of domestic politics, the state is not an actor but a representative institution, constantly subject to capture and recapture, construction and reconstruction, by coalitions of social actors" (2003: 163).

This approach recognizes, however, that all actors or groups do not have the same capacity to influence and that the nature of the political regime and the institutions influences the behaviour of states. The nature of the political regime thus becomes very important, as the interests and preferences of the actors are not fundamentally the same in democratic, autocratic, or authoritarian regimes. In an authoritarian regime, few actors influence decisions, so the pressures emanating from the society are less important. Risk aversion would also explain why democratic regimes are more peaceful.

In the liberal perspective, individuals defend their interests and their preferences alone or in a group, but in a competitive environment. This approach contradicts the realist image of the chief executive who acts rationally for the national interest. According to Moravcsik, government action is constrained by the interests, identities, and power relations of the individuals and groups, whether inside or outside the state, that exert pressure on decision makers to make policy choices that conform to the interests of those individuals and groups. This approach has certain similarities to the neo-Gramscian approach (Chapter 6) and the domestic politics paradigm (Chapter 5). In short, liberals analyze a vast array of actors on several analytic levels.

Unlike realists, liberals do not believe that world politics are determined by the distribution of power in the international system. Instead, they are the outcome of a series of decisions and actions taken by individuals and groups to defend their interests and preferences. In a situation of interdependence, states, which are the transmission belt of the interests of individuals in domestic politics, seek to have their preferences adopted in other states that also seek to impose their own.

The nature of the international system is not the result of the distribution of power; nor is it the result of the demands of the dominant classes, as Marxists propose. Rather, it is the outcome of the preferences of states. When a suboptimal outcome in the Pareto sense occurs (the Pareto optimum is reached when the well-being of one individual cannot be improved without worsening that of at least one other individual), one such outcome being protectionism, Moravcsik explains this outcome not by the relative gains and the power distribution in the international system, but by the social preferences of one or several groups in domestic politics (obviously, Moravcsik assumes that free trade creates an optimal outcome). Hence, it is the state–society relationship that has the most impact on choices in world politics. When a conflict emerges, states will try to solve the social problems at the national and transnational levels before focusing on the problems related to cooperation on the international scene.

Liberal theorists' conception of power differs from that of realists. For realists, the reflection on power is always strongly shaped by questions of high politics or military security (Barnett and Duvall, 2005). In the realist perspective, power is not an absolute; it manifests in a relationship, an interaction. According to liberal authors, in particular Keohane and Nye, the major error of many realist theorists in international relations is to consider the attributes of power as fungible. Money, for example, is a fungible resource as it can be exchanged for a product or a service. Some realist authors make the mistake of thinking that power is fungible in the same way that money is; in other words, they treat the attributes of power as though they had the same characteristic as money. Yet the nature of power in international relations is much more complex and even at times paradoxical. In fact, the nature of power permits state A to influence state B in one case, but it also allows state B to influence state A in another area of international action.

For liberals, the conception of power in international relations is also too closely linked to the *problématique* of war and peace. If the military/strategic competition is a zero-sum game, economic competition is not. Realists are a little too quick to assert that the goal of foreign policy for states is to create wealth in order to increase power. But wealth accumulation does not have the sole objective to accumulate power so as to better dominate the international system. Accumulated wealth also permits states to create employment, reduce poverty, and quite simply to benefit from it! The importance of economic issues is so great that international politics have switched from an international situation of a zero-sum game (the Cold War) to a situation in which all the actors can potentially make gains.

For classical realists, power is the prerogative of states. If this statement might at one time have seemed obvious, liberals find it increasingly difficult to support. In today's world, there are states that have no real power and non-state actors that, depending on the issues, wield considerable power. It is important to note that all states do not have the same power. By excessively reifying the state, we put on the same footing the American state, the Chinese state, the French state, and the state of the republic of Nauru, which has no national currency and a population of 10,000 (fewer than the number of people living or working in the Burj Khalifa Tower in Dubai). We can probably affirm that more than a quarter of the states in the world have practically no power, whether they are quasi-states or collapsed states. Can a country that does not have sufficient financial resources to delegate representatives to the UN be considered a power? In many countries, it is Mafia organizations, drug dealers, or multinationals that hold much of the power.

For liberals, the internationalization of the economy and finance broke the link between power and territory. Since the 1960s and 1970s, non-state actors have helped to transform the international scene, which was until then reputed to be dominated by states. As Keohane and Nye maintain, in a world of complex interdependencies, a world composed of a multitude of issues, power is diffuse. Thus, the power of the actors varies depending on the issues. In the oil industry, Saudi Arabia is powerful; in the financial sector, New York and London are important players; in international trade negotiations, the United States and the European Union cannot be ignored. Small countries that use legal standards at the UN to influence procedure are not completely powerless. As the WTO operates by consensus, these small countries are, in this forum, important actors. International organizations, for their part, can mobilize a number of experts to influence the behaviour of states or NGOs (Barnett and Duvall, 2005).

The power of private actors in IPE is also important. Many multinationals will use their resources and their power of influence to guide the direction of state trade policies. As Helen Milner showed, the power of private economic actors can be measured by their ability to influence trade negotiations, for example (1988). Large firms in particular have played an important role in setting environmental standards at the international level. Their influence can be very negative, as with US and Canadian oil companies with regard to the Kyoto protocol; but it can also be positive, as when the chemicals company DuPont and the German firm Hoechst pressured for the adoption of the Montreal Protocol on CFCs. Private actors can also be pressured. It is a fact that transnational activists have used shame campaigns and boycotts to force many multinationals to change their behaviour and show greater respect for human rights (Barnett and Duvall, 2005: 41).

In summary, liberals in IPE do not think of the exercise of power in the same way as realists do. Power can no longer be understood only as a state's desire to impose its will on others through its military superiority. The various actors do not have the same power capabilities. Depending on the issues, they may be more or less influential. For example, ecologists and the military exercise very little influence on decisions related to interest rates, unlike economists and business people (Keohane and Nye, 2012). One thing is certain however: with the unprecedented development of new information technologies, every actor is a potential international actor. A computer specialist can outsmart a national security system or commit an act of cyberterrorism in the comfort of his or her own office!

Using this analytic perspective as his base, Keohane presented one of the most famous criticisms of hegemonic stability theory. According to Keohane, the hegemonic stability approach is too deterministic. It claims that as states are very powerful, they triumph in all areas of international competition. Keohane drew on the thesis he developed with Nye, which proposes that in a world of complex interdependencies, comprising a multitude of issues, power is diffuse. Depending on the issues, one state may be powerful while others may be vulnerable. According to these authors, a more fine-grained analysis of the distribution of power, based on specific issues, is needed. Even the most powerful of states is sometimes vulnerable.

In addition, according to Nye, power can be separated into hard and soft power. Hard power represents the power of constraint, command, and coercion. It is founded on a tangible resource, military force. But, says Nye, in an interdependent international system, the use of force is not as effective as it used to be. Power is not as fungible as in the past. Military power gave states the ability to acquire resources through the use of force. Nowadays, the use of force has become too onerous and too dangerous for the modern great powers (Nye, 1990). Hard power is also less effective, as the nuclear bomb makes the use of force dangerous.

In this context, soft power acquires importance. Soft power is a gentler form of power, non-coercive and less concrete. It is a power of seduction that is founded on intangible resources such as culture, institutions, ideas, and it allows its holder to ensure that other actors want to imitate it. Soft power makes its holder a model that other actors want to copy and it allows the state that holds it to structure a situation in such a way that other countries make choices or define their interests in accordance with its own. The constitutive elements of soft power are less tangible than those of hard power, but its use is by and large less costly than the use of military force. Hence, for Nye, the most powerful state is not so much the one with the greatest military capability, but the one that has the ability to rally around it the largest coalition, to control information, and to decide the agenda, in large international organizations, for example. Power is the ability to achieve the desired result and to be able, if necessary, to change the behaviour of others in order to do so (Nye, 2002).

As the international system encourages multiple interactions between numerous actors and as these actors learn from these interactions, the realist concept of anarchy is put into perspective. Cooperation on the international scene cannot be reduced to questions of power between egotistic states. Power is important, but it is exercised in the framework of rules and international institutions that, by the very fact, make international cooperation possible. Liberals expect the growth of globalization, interdependence, communication networks and knowledge diffusion, and the spread of democracy to encourage even greater cooperation, thereby fostering peace, justice, and prosperity. Thus, without neglecting relative gains, liberal authors believe instead in the importance of absolute gains. For liberals, cooperation is a positive-sum game.

Liberal authors see organizations and international law in a positive light. In the case of international law, even if they admit that this law is less hierarchic and more difficult to enforce than national law, it remains one of the principal instruments for framing and maintaining order in the international system. Without international law, there would be no stability for states or governments; territories and air spaces would not exist; ships might sail the seas, but at their risk and peril; property within and outside of a territory would not be protected from theft or depravity; nationals abroad would have no protection or rights; diplomatic relations would be difficult, as would international trade (Henkin, 1979). States create international organizations in order to facilitate cooperation between states, reduce the risks of conflicts, and govern globalization.

The liberal institutionalist perspective proposes that the imperfections of international society can be corrected by establishing international institutions and by international law. In recent works on institutions, liberal institutionalist authors have examined cooperation in a context of political market failure. The central idea is that states might not succeed in maximizing their usefulness because they adopt an egotistic behaviour that favours their own interests. These approaches are based on game theory and rational choice theory (Cooley, 2009: 48).

Globalization, War, and Peace

This section presents the framework of the debates concerning the effects of globalization, regional integration, and trade on war and peace, as these issues have strongly affected the debates in IPE and represent a bridge between the works in IPE and those on security issues.

For a long time, many authors argued that commerce, free trade, and economic interdependence promote peace between nations. As far back as 1748, Montesquieu stated, "Peace is a natural effect of trade." Many other authors, such as Jeremy Bentham, John Stuart Mill, and Norman Angell, have shared a similar point of view. Liberals generally agree that international trade reduces the incentives to war. However, authors differ about the causal mechanisms that lead them to this conclusion. For some, economic interdependence reduces the risk of war; for others, it is free trade or the coordination of monetary policies; some claim it is the nature of the political regime, as democracies do not wage war with other democracies; and finally there are some who say it is international institutions that promote conflict mediation. As a general rule, liberal authors believe that people want to be free and to prosper, which fosters the expansion of democracy and trade, and, by that fact, also encourages law and international organizations to promote and regulate these processes. This virtuous dynamic promotes peace. The following section briefly presents the debates on peace through democracy, through institutions and then through trade, because these debates have a considerable influence on the contemporary works in IPE.

Peace through Democracy

For some authors, globalization of the economy favours the advent of democracy and it is the nature of the democratic regime that is a driver of peace. Some authors such as Joseph Schumpeter (1950), Seymour Martin Lipset (1959), and Friedrich Hayek (1960) have supported the idea that free trade and capital flows, by encouraging a better allocation of resources, increase personal incomes, which in turn promotes economic growth and feeds the demands for democratic regimes. According to Barry Eichengreen and David Leblanc, there is a correlation between the growth of world trade and the number of democracies. Between 1975 and 2002, the world saw a fourfold increase in the number of democratic regimes while, during the same period, global trade as a percentage of world GDP rose from 7.7 per cent to 19.5 per cent (Eichengreen and Leblanc, 2006: 1).

Democratic peace theory is based on Kant's idea that democracies, or in his case republics, do not go to war with one another. According to Michael Doyle, who is the author most identified with the return of this thesis inspired by the works of Kant,

> When citizens who bear the burdens of war elect their governments, wars become impossible. Furthermore, citizens appreciate that the benefits of trade can be enjoyed only under conditions of peace. Thus, the very existence of liberal states, such as the United States, the European Union and others, makes for peace. And so peace and democracy are two sides of the same coin. (Doyle, 2004)

Several variants of democratic peace theory exist, but in general it is believed that liberal and pluralist political regimes moderate extreme positions and contribute to improving the dissemination of information, thus avoiding misunderstandings. Conflicts between democracies are supposed to be less frequent due to the institutional control that limits a government's ability to make unilateral decisions. Democratic regimes, founded on the separation of powers, make the practice of collective decision making inevitable. The existence of formal decision-making processes that at times even necessitate the sanction of parliament, as well as the need to take the pulse of public opinion when making choices as dramatic as war, tend to slow down decision making and guarantee that decisions are at least minimally supported by a large share of public opinion.

As democracies must marshal public opinion in favour of a war, the undertaking takes more time than in non-democratic regimes. By increasing the delays, democracies make possible attempts at mediation and give more time to calculate the consequences of the choices. Decision-making processes are also more transparent and therefore more predictable. The transparency of the process is perceived from the outside and may ease the fears of the actors in the potential conflict. Hence, it is easier to avoid a preventive offensive or a sudden attack by the enemy. Democracies also share values and are linked by trade interdependence (Doyle, 2004).

Peace through International Institutions

The second argument emphasizes the role of international institutions and integration as promoters of peace. It is the marriage of trade liberalization and the creation of international institutions that bring peace. These institutions permit the emergence of what Karl Deutsch called a "security community" (1957: 5–7)—that is, a group of states in which there is a real assurance that the members of this community will not use violence against one another but will resolve their conflicts peacefully.

The theorist most closely associated with the functionalist approach to international organizations is David Mitrany, through his book *A Working Peace System: An Argument for the Functional Development of International Organization*, published in 1943. After the First World War and the failure of the League of Nations, Mitrany's aim was to imagine an institutional system that would produce peace. Mitrany concurred with the realists' analysis—the 1966 edition of his book is even prefaced by Hans Morgenthau—concerning the omnipotence of states. He proposed that instead of hoping for peace from an improbable political agreement amongst all states, it would be better to understand what unites these states and to use their ties as possibilities to strengthen interdependencies and build a lasting peace.

According to Mitrany, it is futile to set up a large international organization to draw countries closer together because this vast institution would reproduce political cleavages. A preferable action would be to create technical international organizations to meet functional needs. States would accept these organizations because they fulfil a need. Mitrany's approach would be to gradually build an institutional system that would replace power politics with a system of states engaged in a cooperative dynamic based on the organization of joint public services. In Mitrany's system, the growth of economic and social interdependence would lead towards greater integration and promote the adapted institutionalization of organizations. The intertwining of interests would then set the boundaries for power politics and foster peace. By endeavouring to respond to economic and social needs, Mitrany's system of functional peace would push questions of a more politic nature to the background.

The neofunctionalism developed by Ernst Haas, who ultimately theorized the Jean Monnet method, borrowed from Mitrany's functionalism but with the fundamental difference that it focuses on the continental or regional level, the role of elites, and the economic integration that is deployed in a series of small steps taken towards a goal, which leads to more cooperation and which eventually will spill over into political integration (Haas, 1958). According to Haas, the elites of important social groups in Europe realized that their interests could be better satisfied in expanded political groups. These elites therefore set aside power politics to devote themselves to the construction of a united Europe. The European Coal and Steel Community (ECSC) was the starting point of this integrative logic, as after integrating the coal and steel industries under the High Authority of the ECSC, the elites realized that the success of this policy required even broader integration. Consequently, the convergent demands of the elites to bring about integration created a spillover effect that spread to other sectors. The further the integration extended, the more it underwent gradual politicization and the supranational institution became responsible for functions that are traditionally the responsibility of the nation-state. For Haas, integration ultimately produces a new political community and the bases of a new national conscience.

The empty chair crisis under De Gaulle and the difficulties of European integration in the 1970s forced Haas to write a strong criticism of his own theory, a criticism that today seems quite excessive, as integration subsequently saw significant new developments. Nonetheless, Haas's approach is still useful for understanding the processes of integration (Haas, 1975). European integration is perceived today as being a factor in the pacification of a formerly bellicose Europe.

Economic Interdependence as a Factor of Peace

The modern version of peace through trade is identified with the American political scientist Richard Rosecrance (1999). In 2002, Rosecrance asserted that, after the attacks of 11 September 2001, we are seeing the emergence of a world where the most important resources are also the least tangible, where territory is less important than the level of education of the population, where the reserves of goods, capital, and labour count for less than economic flows, and where regional interests are supplanted by the globalized economy (Rosecrance et al., 2002: 13). According to Rosecrance, during the period of territorial covetousness, exchanges between countries took place through the intermediary of their armies. Nowadays, when technology, people, and information circulate rapidly between countries, states have access to factors of production on a world scale, which replaces the need for geographic expansion (Rosecrance et al., 2002: 14).

It is true, Rosecrance qualifies, that the territorial ambitions of small peripheral states continued to attract a disproportionate amount of attention from media and from many researchers in the 1990s. However, these conflicts all belong to the past, according to Rosecrance. For poor countries, whose development still depends on resources from the land, be it agriculture, oil, or diamonds, the natural resources of neighbouring countries still arouse the desire to covet. But elsewhere, where economic development and growth are achieved through brainpower, countries seek more simply to liberalize trade in order to have stable access to resources and thereby reduce political uncertainty. The possibility for entrepreneurs or governments to have access to factors of production and raw materials throughout the world has replaced, in developed countries, the need for geographic expansion (Rosecrance et al., 2002: 40–68). All this has the effect of reconfiguring international relations and reducing the risk of conflicts. This reconfiguring is driven by the virtualization of firms and states.

According to Rosecrance, the structures and operations of large firms have transformed rapidly since the 1980s. Multinational corporations are becoming virtualized by concentrating more and more of their activities on strategy, design, marketing, and finance rather than on production. They leave production to others. This new business model born in the United States is based on the wager that it is possible to increase a firm's productivity and competitiveness by using the assembly line factories of other firms. In the United States, Nike, for example, is the head of an empire, but does not itself make the products it sells. It concentrates mainly on design and marketing rather than on production, which is located in factories in other parts of the world.

Thus, says Rosecrance, as industries increasingly delocalize their production, and as technology, knowledge, and capital play a more important role than land, the functions of the state are being redefined. The state no longer controls the country's resources as it did in the mercantile era; it prefers to negotiate with capital and with labour forces in order to draw them into its economic sphere and thereby stimulate its own growth. Moreover, the virtual state encourages the delocalization of its production so it can concentrate its efforts on advanced services: research and development, design, financing, marketing, and transportation. The economic strategy of a virtual state is now at least as important as its military strategy; its ambassadors have become the representatives abroad of its trading and financial interests. As Rosecrance sees it, a new reality is appearing in modern international relations, a reality in which developed countries fight less for political domination than to attain a greater share of world production, and gradually abandon their military and territorial ambitions (Rosecrance et al., 2002: 13).

Stephen G. Brooks further develops the thesis proposing that transformations in the structures of multinationals profoundly affect security issues between states. For Brooks, trade is no longer the motor of security between states, as trade is no longer the primary means of organizing international economic transactions. Now, it is the multinationals that act as the integrating force of international trade through the organization of their production. In Brooks's opinion, globalization of production has created a series of transformations at the level of global security. Globalization of production is marked by four fundamental changes: greater geographic dispersion of production, growing importance of intra-firm alliances, increase of foreign direct investments (FDI), and transition to a knowledge economy in developed countries. All of these factors mean that multinationals act as a significant force for peace between the great powers. This transformation is not universal, however, as the internationalization of production does not affect all countries and industrial sectors with the same intensity (Brooks, 2007, 1999).

Patrick McDonald contends that it is not trade between countries but free trade that is a factor of peace. By eliminating certain sovereign functions of the state such as the possibility to erect trade barriers, free trade promotes peace. According to McDonald, the potential to build protective trade barriers enhances the influence in domestic politics of social movements that are the most likely to want to increase the military power of the state and to solve disputes through war. The author's statistical analyses show that the higher the level of free trade, and not just trade per se, the lower the number of military conflicts (McDonald, 2004).

McDonald therefore contradicts the argument of realists, who reject the thesis of commercial peace using the example of the First World War. According to McDonald, historians have demonstrated that the first era of globalization was supported by a reduction of transportation costs and by certain trade liberalization measures. After the rise of protectionism in Europe around 1879, it was evident that the principal European powers were the primary trading partners of the other powers and that they were economically dependent. An analysis in terms of opportunity costs of closure would suggest that this interdependence should have prevented the 1914 war. But when we look towards the increase in tariffs and protectionist policies, we can predict the use of force to resolve problems (McDonald, 2004: 569). Therefore, it is free trade and not just trade that is a factor of peace between countries.

Erik Gartzke, Quan Li, and Charles Boehmer argue that we must instead look towards monetary policies as contributors to peace. According to these authors, establishing a link between international economics and conflicts is limited in two ways (Gartzke, Li, and Boehmer, 2001: 391–438). Cross-border economic relations are a much broader phenomenon that involve more than just trade. As well, states that trade must coordinate, to varying degrees, their monetary policies. According to the authors, capital interdependence contributes to peace, independent of trade, democracy, and various other variables. Monetary coordination and interdependence require states to negotiate compromises. Through these interactions, states create a series of linkages that are mutually economically beneficial. Although the operation of these linkages may cause minor disputes, their principal effect is to foster conflict resolution. Political shocks that threaten to destroy economic linkages generate information, thereby reducing uncertainty when leaders negotiate. Channels of economic interaction thus help states to communicate better (Gartzke, Li, and Boehmer, 2001: 418).

Bruce Russett and John Oneal tested the effects of the aforementioned three variables of peace that are based on the works of Kant. These three variables are democracy, economic interdependence, and being a member of an international governmental organization (IGO). Each of these variables, according to the authors, helps to produce the conditions for the creation of the two others. These three variables create a virtuous circle that produces peace. Russett and Oneal, who conducted an important quantitative study on the relationship between democracies and war, maintain not only that democracies rarely engage in militarized conflict with one another but also that they are generally more peaceful than authoritarian states. The authors' analysis also revealed that economically interdependent states tend to avoid conflict with their trading partners. Furthermore, the more memberships in international organizations a state has, the less it tends to resort to the use of force against other members of these organizations (Russett and Oneal, 2001).

The three variables therefore produce a systemic effect because the more present the three criteria are, the more they correlate with the absence of war. The authors draw on rationalist and constructivist approaches to identify the causal mechanisms that may explain this situation. They assert, for example, based on rationalist arguments, that interdependence can foster peace by creating a joint commercial interest that would be destroyed by war. IGOs can contribute to peace by sanctioning countries that do not respect the norms, proposing mediations between the parties, reducing transaction costs, following up on actions, reducing uncertainty, and so on. From the constructivist point of view, the three factors can foster the development of an international community with a shared sense of identity, modify perceptions and preferences, and foster the dispersal of norms and the development of common values.

According to Russett and Oneal, this order is not unchanging as its evolution is the result of the strategic choices made by the states. States are free to reverse the virtuous circle and plunge into the vicious cycle of war. Nothing is absolute. Moreover, the authors declare, Kantian peace can be severely affected by an economic recession (Russett and Oneal, 2001).

Globalization and Transnationalism

Liberal IPE authors, unlike realist authors, start from the idea that globalization is an important phenomenon that transforms the functioning of the international scene in the sense that it creates an increasingly complex interdependence and an acceleration of transnationalism. In the Preface to the third edition of *Power and Interdependence*, Robert Keohane and Joseph Nye write, "globalization refers to an intensification of what we described as interdependence in 1977 [in the first edition of the book]. Indeed, many aspects of world politics resemble the liberal portrayal of the 1970s more than the realist image of the 1980s" (2012: xxiii). But according to Keohane, globalization is a process that is not completed, as the world is only partially globalized (Keohane, 2002).

Nye and Keohane introduced the debate on transnationalism in the early 1970s. For them, "'transnational interactions' . . . describe the movement of tangible or intangible items across state boundaries when at least one actor is not an agent of a government or an intergovernmental organization" (Nye and Keohane, 1971: 332). Although the authors recognize that the phenomenon is not new, they maintain that governments' control over transnational movements has been weakened by technological changes (notably subsidiaries of large corporations), by the flow of information in the mass media, and by the growing number of government programs that increasingly encroach upon various groups in civil society. According to Nye and Keohane, to effectively manage this more and more transnational world requires greater international cooperation (1971).

The authors continued to develop their thinking, and in 1977 published *Power and Interdependence*. While their first work had introduced the concept of "transnationalism," their book proposed the notion of "complex interdependence." These notions convey new conceptions of the dynamic of international relations and IPE.

Complex interdependence comprises three basic characteristics:

1. "Multiple channels connect society." These channels include the informal ties between government elites and formal diplomatic institutions, as well as the informal ties between non-governmental elites and transnational organizations (such as multinationals). These channels are therefore interstate, transgovernmental, and transnational (Keohane and Nye, 2012: 20).

2. "The agenda of interstate relations consists of multiple issues that are not arranged in a clear or consistent hierarchy" (Keohane and Nye, 2012: 20). According to the authors, this means that military security issues are not always placed at the top of the public agenda. Many international issues have in the past been considered as domestic policy issues and the distinction between what is international and what is not remains unclear. These issues affect several ministries or departments, not just departments of defence or foreign affairs. They also affect other levels of government, such as subnational or local governments, and influence various coalitions within and outside governments.

3.   Military force occupies a less central role and is not used against other interdependent governments within the region. In some cases, the use of military force is irrelevant—for example, in a disagreement over economic issues between the members of an alliance (Keohane and Nye, 2012: 21). That said, military power may be a factor between rival blocs.

With these works, Keohane and Nye attacked head-on the realist school of international relations. In fact, complex interdependence contradicted the conception of classic IR realists that was perceived as being at the height of its fame in the 1970s. For Keohane and Nye, economic interdependence brought together a variety of transnational actors that, through their access to channels of communication, could have a significant influence on world politics. In a world of complex interdependence, comprising a multitude of issues with no clear hierarchy (security, energy, raw materials, international finance, technology, environment), power is diffuse and the use of force is counterproductive or irrelevant.

Power is no longer used in the same way it was during the Second World War, say the authors. Hence, depending on the issues, one state may be powerful while others may be vulnerable. In this context, power is transformed and reflects a state's ability to control outcomes. According to Keohane and Nye, even the most powerful of states is sometimes vulnerable, no matter how large its army.

In this context of growing complex interdependence, it is more and more difficult for a democratic state to develop a coherent foreign policy because it is difficult to hierarchize priorities. The proliferation of non-state actors in the decision-making process complicates the process even more. This phenomenon is exacerbated for the largest countries such as the United States. As a result of their analysis, Keohane and Nye could then claim that a new paradigm of international relations was necessary.

In the 1970s, certain critics claimed that Keohane and Nye's book was interesting but irrelevant (in a context in which the USSR had just invaded Afghanistan and well before the advent of the Internet). It was only later, in the 1980s and even more so in the 1990s, that the world came to resemble more and more clearly the ideal type of complex interdependence. As Keohane and Nye themselves put it,

> The continued relevance of this book can be accounted for in large part by the fact that what is now called "globalization" has brought the world closer to complex interdependence on certain issues—for example, climate change and financial markets—and in certain parts of the world— for example, relations among the advanced democracies. (Keohane and Nye, 2012: xxvii)

However, the criticisms from realist theorists remained severe. Stephen Krasner, for example, asserted that Keohane and Nye's research program had failed. Krasner wrote,

> As a research programme, however, transnational relations failed because in most cases it could not clearly specify *ex ante* actors, their interests, or their capabilities. If all actors are relevant, and actors can have many different interests, and the ability of actors to pursue these interests is not well defined, then any outcome in international politics would be consistent with the theory; that is, after the fact it would be possible to find some group of transnational actors that supported public policy that was ultimately selected. But if a theory can be made consistent with every possible outcome then it explains nothing. (2008: 112)

In response to this type of criticism, Keohane and Nye wrote in the Preface to the fourth edition of their work,

> *Power and Interdependence* never purported to make predictions about the future or to provide a methodology for doing so. Instead, it was designed to provide concepts that would help observers of world politics to understand and interpret what they saw, so that they could fit it into some general patterns and not be surprised by developments that would indeed surprise those with the statist-security framework previously put forward by "realist" political theory. The test of the validity of this framework, therefore, is not whether it predicted these events or would have led its practitioners to do so (it did not), but whether it helps us understand their ramifications: the "shock waves" so to speak, that reverberated after the events. (2012: xxviii)

Keohane and Nye's theory is therefore not an explanatory or causal theory, for which Krasner faults them, but a constitutive theory. These works by Keohane and Nye have been often cited in the United States, particularly in the third debate on international relations theories. Although the concept of "complex interdependence" has been replaced by that of globalization, the phenomenon that these authors sought to identify with this concept is now largely taken for granted.

Liberal Institutionalism

The second major trend of the liberal approach that has been dominating IPE debates since the 1980s is liberal institutionalism. Its main objective is, to paraphrase the title of a book by Kenneth Oye, to explain interstate cooperation in an anarchic international system (1986). During the first few years, the institutional approach sought to explain why international institutions promote cooperation. The objective of later studies was to explain how institutions influence states' behaviour and international relations (Sterling-Folker, 2011). Today, the debates generally have more to do with the rational design of international institutions and with the issue of states' compliance with their international commitments (Simmons and Martin, 2001: 192). This section presents these debates successively.

Initially, liberal institutionalists accepted realist theorists' idea that cooperation is sometimes difficult due to the anarchic nature of the international system. They maintained, however, that institutions can facilitate international cooperation. As Keohane wrote,

> Realist theories that seek to predict international behavior on the basis of interests and power alone are important but insufficient for an understanding of world politics. They need to be supplemented, though not replaced, by theories stressing the importance of international institutions. Even if we fully understand patterns of power and interests, the behavior of states (and of transnational actors as well) may not be fully explicable without understanding the institutional context of action. (1984: 14)

Therefore, Keohane asked the following question: "How can cooperation take place in world politics in the absence of hegemony?" (1984: 14).

Contrary to some realist theorists' predictions, the role of international institutions did not diminish with the decline of American hegemony that began in the 1970s (or even with the end of the Cold War).[1] Rather, these institutions tended to become more important in international affairs. Realism and neorealism were confronted with an "ocean of anomalies," in terms of international cooperation (Keohane and Martin, 2003: 75). This paradox needed to be explained.

Liberal institutionalists believe that international cooperation became increasingly important after the Second World War. It became more institutionalized and extensive, as the following organizations demonstrate: the UN, the GATT (and then the WTO), the IMF, NATO, and, on a regional basis, the European Union, in addition to many international regimes. For Keohane, potential collective gains explain the considerable increase in the number and reach of institutions of multilateral cooperation (2003).

According to Robert Keohane and Lisa Martin, institutions are "persistent and connected sets of rules (formal and informal) that prescribe behavioral roles, constrain activity, and shape expectations" (2003: 78). Institutions establish, to varying degrees, the rules of the game. These international institutions may take several forms: an international or formal non-governmental organization, an international regime, or informal agreements. It is the degree of institutionalization that differentiates institutions.

For Keohane, American politicians' perception of international institutions changed following the monetary crisis and oil shock of the early 1970s. According to Keohane, political leaders and academic analysts in the United States realized that global issues necessitated a systematic coordination of implemented policies and that this coordination could not take place without international institutions (2003). The multiplication of international institutions indicates a growing institutionalization of world politics, which seems to be to everyone's advantage, even that of the superpowers. Keohane believes that superpowers, because they seek to influence events throughout the world, need rules that are generally accepted by other states. Even an uncontested superpower like the United States could not achieve its objectives by exercising its influence only through bilateral relations: a policy of persuasion carried out on such a scale would have too high a cost (Keohane, 2003).

According to Keohane and Martin, liberal institutionalism is a criticism of, and an amendment to, realism. Initially, liberal institutionalism adopted practically all the basic assumptions of neorealists, except that it treated information as a variable (Keohane and Martin, 2003: 81). Liberal institutionalists did this less out of conviction than as a research strategy. As Keohane and Martin write, "this decision was admittedly taken more for analytical convenience and rhetorical effect than out of deep conviction. It was a tactical decision, later reversed, rather than part of institutional theory's hard core" (1995: 43). The objective was to start from the same point as the neorealists in order to modify their axioms. Liberal institutionalism is therefore thought of as the "half-sibling of realism" (Keohane and Martin, 2003: 81).

According to Keohane and Martin, neorealism and liberal institutionalism have four points in common:

1. States are the primary actors in world politics.
2. States behave as if they were rational, in the sense that they assess their strategic situations in light of their environments, and seek to maximize expected gains.
3. States pursue their interests (which prominently include survival), rather than behaving altruistically.
4. States operate in a world of "anarchy," without common government. (2003: 73–4)

States are thus utilitarian and rationalistic and exist in an environment where international agreements cannot be hierarchically enforced. Therefore, institutionalists anticipate that states will cooperate only if they have enough interests in common.

The synthesis of the two approaches is so great that Ole Waever estimates that neorealists and institutionalist neoliberals agree on 90 per cent of the issues, the rest being just empirical divergences (2008: 162–4). It is for this reason that several authors refuse to include liberal institutionalism within the liberal perspective. For others, as liberal institutionalism implicitly subscribes to this idea of cumulative progress in human history and focuses on international institutions and cooperation, it constitutes a liberal approach (Sterling-Folker, 2011: 117). It is consistent with the idea developed by liberal theorists that international institutions can promote peace, prosperity, and justice.

The crucial difference between neorealism and liberal institutionalism is implicit rather than explicit and allows liberal institutionalists to question the validity of neorealist theorists' inferences about the behaviour of states. This fundamental difference pertains to the role of information. Neorealists believe that information about the intentions of states is important but of poor quality. States must therefore assume the worst and act defensively. They may cooperate, but this cooperation is not durable and takes place on an ad hoc basis. Neorealists doubt that it is possible for states to systematically improve the quality of information coming from the international environment. Thus, the lack of information and the impossibility for states to fundamentally change the international system force them to opt for a defensive strategy.

For their part, liberal institutionalists consider information a fundamental variable for explaining interstate cooperation. Information, they say, may be influenced by human actions. While a lack of information may limit cooperation in an anarchic system, nothing prevents states from acting to improve the quality of available information to promote cooperation. Liberal institutional theories, therefore, pertain to the role of international institutions in the production and propagation of information. These institutions may perform this role in many ways. They may help make the behaviour of states understandable by providing information on the intentions of other states, by establishing standards, or by providing reliable causal theories on the relationship between an action and a result. In all cases, they reduce both the costs of the exchange and the uncertainty. They are at once an independent variable and a dependent variable because they change as a result of human actions and transform the processes and expectations, which may profoundly impact the behaviour of states (Keohane and Martin, 1995: 46). According to Lisa Martin, who has conducted studies on economic sanctions, cooperation is greater when sanctions are imposed in an institutionalized environment (1992).

For Keohane, however, cooperation does not mean automatic harmony between states. He maintains that international institutions must be built in order to help governments achieve their mutual goals and to gradually alter the governments' conception of their own particular interests in order to broaden the range of cooperation (Keohane, 1989: 11). In a situation of harmony, the particular policies promoted by the various actors to attain their objectives are compatible, but in a situation of cooperation, policies need to be adjusted. International trade regimes, for example, help appease rivalries, as it is extremely costly for states to renounce cooperation.

The landmark work that structured the neo-neo debate (neo-realism versus neo-liberalism) is *After Hegemony*, by Robert Keohane, published in 1984. This book was a reply to neorealists and realist theorists in IPE regarding hegemonic stability theory. It represents Keohane's attempt to synthesize neorealism and complex interdependence. This combination produced what today we call institutional liberalism.

For Keohane, if hegemonic stability theory is entirely false, then there is no reason to think that the end of American hegemony would be significant in terms of cooperation or international stability. On the other hand, if it is entirely true, then there is cause to be concerned about international stability. In *After Hegemony*, Keohane aims to demonstrate that states can cooperate even when the hegemonic power, after playing an important part in setting up cooperation institutions, has begun a period of relative decline. According to Keohane, repeated attempts at cooperation in the 1970s suggest that the hegemon's decline does not necessarily mean the death of cooperation (1984: 9).

This was a major issue, as many analysts believed that the decline of American hegemony relative to the other powers would destabilize the world-economy with recessions and conflicts. Keohane focused on post–World War II institutions in the areas of money, trade, and oil. According to his argument, the advantages of these institutions and these regimes are maintained independently of the rise or decline of a hegemonic power. Institutions are not conceived as one-time or temporary arrangements; rather, they are a variable intervening between the economic and political powers of the international system and the final result. For Keohane, regimes survive the hegemonic power, as they facilitate cooperation by circulating information and reducing obstacles to trade, thereby reducing uncertainty. States need international regimes. Keohane's book emphasizes the creation of regimes and of international institutions, as well as their persistence.

To demonstrate his thesis, Keohane drew inspiration from economists, importing game theory into IPE theory and adapting market failure theory, in which there are transaction costs associated with uncertainty (Bator, 1958). Keohane discussed cooperation between sovereign states within a *political* market failure context (1984: 85). Political market failure refers to a situation in which a transaction is not correctly carried out because the political market is organized in such a way that an otherwise rational behaviour becomes irrational. This may contribute to suboptimal results in the Pareto sense. In IPE, this might mean that states refuse to cooperate because they are uncertain of other states' motivations. Centred on game theory and on the rational choice approach, market failure theories are often associated with information asymmetry theories (Greenwald and Stiglitz, 1986). The institutionalist trend in economics suggests that market imperfections can be corrected by setting up institutions that promote the exchange of information. Also, in IPE, liberal institutionalists advocate the creation of international institutions in order to correct the failures caused by certain states' refusal to cooperate due to their uncertainty about other states' motivations.

Institutions, which play an intermediary role between states and outcomes, help solve political market failure problems by providing information about how other states behave. States cooperate with international institutions because these institutions provide states with information, ipso facto reducing uncertainty and making the world more predictable.

Contrary to Gilpin and other realist authors, Keohane perceives institutions and international regimes not in terms of power but in terms of interest. As we have seen, the starting point of Keohane's thesis is the same as that of neorealist theorists, but, unlike them, Keohane does not conclude that states must practise self-help. Such a policy, he reasons, risks producing perverse effects or outcomes inferior to those theoretically possible.

The lessons of the prisoner's dilemma led Keohane to conclude that there are situations where it is preferable for actors to choose multilateral actions, as action based on rational self-interest leads to undesirable outcomes. For Keohane, the prisoner's dilemma produces outcomes of this kind because prisoners cannot communicate with one another. If they could, they would

---

Box 4.1   **The Prisoner's Dilemma and International Cooperation According to Robert Keohane**

The prisoner's dilemma, formulated by Canadian mathematician Albert W. Tucker in 1950, derives from game theory and describes a situation in which it would be in the interest of two actors to cooperate but they do not do so because there are strong incentives to betray the other player and because the context prevents the players from communicating with one another. Thomas Schelling calls this situation a "mixed-motive game"—a game characterized by a combination of mutual dependence and conflict, of partnership and competition.

Here is an example of the prisoner's dilemma: two guilty robbers are arrested by the police and incarcerated in two different jail cells, without the possibility to communicate with one another. The prisoners know that the police have only enough evidence to convict them for misdemeanours leading to 30 days in jail for each prisoner. With insufficient evidence to charge

have the leisure to develop an optimal strategy. International institutions are crucial in international relations because they make communication easier, thereby reducing uncertainty caused by the lack of information.

Neorealist authors who are critical of liberal institutionalism suggest that if there were no hegemonic power, no country would follow up on or enforce international agreements and, consequently, none would apply sanctions against free riders. For institutional neoliberals, the question presents itself only when two actors are involved in a single-round situation. In the contemporary international system, however, international cooperation between states takes place on many issues and over a long period. Consequently, as the probability that the actors will meet again is sufficiently high, the issue of the next interaction will be important to them. Therefore, it is in their interest to play the cooperation game.

Robert Axelrod developed the clearest explanation of this thesis by using game theory. According to him, some states win the cooperation game and some states lose, but, over the long term, cooperative behaviour is the best strategy, as a state that cheats or defects harms its reputation and sets precedents that other states may use against it. Violating the rules procures short-term individual gains but represents a long-term collective problem. When there is only one round of play, actors may choose to act like free riders without too many consequences, but when cooperation is an iterative game, meaning a repeated game where other interactions are anticipated, actors are less likely to defect. The incitement to cheat is less enticing due to

them with robbery, the inspector interviews the prisoners one at a time and offers the same deal: "If you admit to the robbery and you implicate your accomplice, and if he still does not confess, we'll let you go free. In this case, your accomplice could be condemned to five years in prison." If both confess, they will each face one year in prison.

Faced with this proposal, the two thieves are confronted with a dilemma: if they cooperate with one another and plead not guilty, they will each do 30 days in jail, but if they betray their accomplice, they might be set free. From the perspective of individual rationality and self-interest, each prisoner has an optimal strategy: to admit to the crime and implicate the accomplice. But if both act this way, both prisoners will be in a less advantageous situation than if they cooperated with each other. In short, they are facing a disjunction between individual rationality, which urges breaking ranks and going it alone, and collective rationality, which favours cooperation. The behaviour that is rational at the individual level is not rational at the collective level. In fact, it is very clearly suboptimal as it produces an outcome inferior to that in which the two prisoners cooperate with each other (Keohane, 1984: 68–9).

the fear of being punished in the future. Players that do not play the game face problems that may outweigh the benefits of defecting. For Axelrod, this is what explains cooperation and the persistence and multiplication of organizations and international regimes (1984).

The political market failure approach has been applied to other issues related to international trade, finance, and the environment (Stein, 1990). A state might, for example, hesitate to conclude a free trade agreement, though economic theory says that all countries signing the agreement will win, even those at a disadvantage in all sectors of production. The best strategy for each state is to apply an optimal tariff, but if all countries behave the same way, they are all at a disadvantage. If one country does not impose a tariff while others do, this country will probably be in an unfavourable situation. These political market failures could be diminished, even eliminated, by the creation of international institutions such as the World Trade Organization. This institution can determine the norms of what is acceptable behaviour for a state, establish and enforce the rules of the game, conduct studies and follow up on important issues, and provide a dispute resolution process.

In the area of finance and banking, for example, it is easy to understand that a state's egotistic and rational behaviour could lead it to want to attract as many banks and international financial institutions as possible to its territory. To do so, it might choose to loosen prudential rules to allow these institutions to grant increasingly risky loans and thus generate higher profits. If all countries adopted this kind of risky behaviour, they would all find themselves in an extremely dangerous situation. When finance is internationalized, the collapse of one country's financial institutions might cause many financial institutions around the world to suffer the same fate. Beginning in 1988, to alleviate the market failure problem, countries adopted Basel Accords I, II, and III, which aim notably to regulate the capital requirements of banks (Kapstein, 1989).

International institutions are thus created to promote trade, reduce risks, and make the world more predictable. They organize regular meetings between heads of state and their advisers so that the actors can get to know one another, listen to one another's discourse and preferences, find commonalities, and try to find collective solutions to common problems. International institutions provide information, standards, and routine procedures; establish reputations; foster interactions; and provide a forum linking issues and facilitating bargaining. They decrease uncertainty related to the anarchic nature of the international system and enable states to focus on their mutual interest.

Liberal institutionalism maintains that states also seek to provide information about their commitments and about themselves in order to strengthen their credibility, and that they seek to accumulate information about others. Thus, states set up international institutions to improve the quality of information about one another. International institutions provide information about actors' intentions, their past (notably about their compliance with past agreements), and their credibility. The transparency and readability of a situation reduce transaction costs.

Another effect international organizations have is to create a centre of gravity for international issues. International institutions thus prevent the over-dispersion of issues in multiple forums and the proliferation of incompatible norms. According to Kenneth Abbott and Duncan Snidal (1998), international organizations centralize collective actions by developing a stable organizational structure that is supported by a bureaucracy. These structures make collective actions more effective and strengthen the organization's ability to influence the understanding, the environment, and the interests of states. By becoming proxies of functions determined within the international system, international organizations become specialized and are able to give precise and technical advice (Goldstein and Martin, 2000).

Moreover, international institutions help to centralize the decision-making process. This centralization also ensures that the circulation of information is improved and enables organizations to demonstrate leadership by proposing compromises and, if necessary, by mediating. The most institutionalized international institutions can play a mediating role regarding distributional issues, gather information about actors' preferences, and attempt to propose fair compromises. When actors agree on the benefits expected from cooperating and on the distribution of gains, it is no longer necessary to renegotiate everything at every meeting. To respond to distributional issues, organizations may also introduce compensatory measures or establish positive incentives. The IMF, for example, provides funds to countries that follow its policy recommendations. Without international organizations, this situation would be difficult. The role of international institutions is to reconcile preferences, promote cooperation, and seek to ensure that states fulfil their international obligations. They set precedents, structure the framework within which bargaining takes place, and increase the cost of failure, as failure discredits the institutions and their member states.

In addition to creating opportunities for states to cooperate, international organizations influence them and impose constraints on them. For example, they may establish the agenda for certain issues, forcing states ipso facto to take a position. That being said, according to Michael Barnett and Martha Finnemore, while these organizations have some autonomy (e.g., they influence the agenda), they are subject to pathologies, as several of them are becoming increasingly bureaucratized (1999).

The Rational Design of Institutions

The liberal institutionalist approach that has dominated the debates in American IPE since the 1980s is now more concerned with international institutions, their inner workings and their rational design. According to David Lake, governments create international institutions in order to reduce the risks of opportunism and the costs of governance (1996). The risks of opportunism are higher with weak levels of hierarchization, while hierarchic institutions cost more in terms of governance. States must choose an institution situated somewhere between these two dynamics.

Barbara Koremenos, Charles Lipson, and Duncan Snidal (2001) refocused attention on the contractualist approach to international institutions. Given that it has now been acknowledged that international institutions promote interstate cooperation, these authors looked more pointedly at the design and diversity of forms that the many international institutions can take. According to them, the missing aspect in the debate is a sustained analysis of how international institutions actually work. They write,

> Our basic presumption, grounded in the broad tradition of rational-choice analysis, is that states use international institutions to further their own goals, and they design institutions accordingly. . . . The most direct implication is that design differences are not random. They are the result of rational, purposive interactions among states and other international actors to solve specific problems. (2001: 762)

As Koremenos, Lipson, and Snidal point out, large international institutions have different types of organization. Some are global and open to all states, while others are regional and comprised of only a few members. Certain institutions operate by consensus, while others confer vetoes upon certain countries. Some institutions are very institutionalized, while others are much less so. According to these authors, five key dimensions allow us to understand the differences between international organizations: (1) membership rules; (2) degree of centralization of tasks; (3) rules for controlling the institution or the ability to constrain members; (4) flexibility of arrangements; and (5) scope of issues covered by the institution.

After evaluating the impact of various independent variables, including, for example, the impacts of distributional issues and of conformity, the number of actors and the distribution of mutual gains, the enforcement of standards, and various types of uncertainty, Koremenos, Lipson, and Snidal proposed 16 conjectures, including the following: "Restrictive membership increases with the severity of the enforcement problem," "centralization increases with uncertainty about behavior," and "flexibility decreases with number" (2001: 797). According to the authors, the 16 conjectures are valid regardless of the issues addressed by the institution or the type of institution.

In another article, Koremenos demonstrated that when states are facing uncertain distributional issues in the long term, they will choose to limit the duration of international agreements. Agreements having to do with economic issues such as exchange rates, finance, investment, and trade tend to have a time clause necessitating new negotiations; this is less often the case with treaties related to the environment, security, and human rights (Koremenos, 2005). According to this analysis, economic issues are not less contentious than security issues. This assessment is consistent with that of Robert Keohane and Lisa Martin, who found that relations between the United States and Japan and between the United States and Germany were more contentious on trade and financial issues than on security issues (Keohane and Martin, 2003: 87).

Several authors have empirically applied the rational design approach. Walter Mattli, for example, examined private international arbitration (i.e., whereby a country appeals to an arbitration system outside its domestic law in order to resolve contractual problems between private actors or between private and public actors). This type of institution is now the norm for arbitration between companies and even between a state and a company that are parties to a treaty or to an arbitration clause (Mattli, 2001). Mattli examines the flexibility and speed of these institutions when settling transnational commercial disputes. These private forums for arbitration and for enforcing contracts are perceived by large multinationals as being more flexible and more efficient than national legal systems.

The Debate on Compliance

Another approach to these issues pertains to the credibility of states' commitments and to the role of international institutions. For liberal institutionalists, the core question is why states respect their agreements in the absence of a central government that can enforce them (Chayes and Chayes, 1993; Downs, Rocke, and Barsoom, 1996). Why do states choose to honour their international agreements rather than not honour them? What tools can international institutions use to compel states to honour international agreements? Thus, without a world government that can guarantee international agreements are implemented, the credibility of states' commitments becomes crucial; if states doubt that other states will fulfil their obligations, cooperation is at risk. The issue of compliance is a conceptual and methodological debate, notably because actors have the possibility to interpret the exact meaning of the rule to be implemented (Simmons, 1998). States are surrounded by many rules and may choose which rules to comply with and to what degree.

Some international organizations are better equipped than others to deal with such questions. The most effective institutions, such as the WTO, boast dispute settlement mechanisms, the role of which is to enforce the organization's rules. Therefore, they are less likely to be victims of free riders than the former GATT, which relied on consensus. The WTO has even rendered decisions that contravened the interests and preferences of the great powers (Drezner, 2007). Certain regional organizations and institutions that do not fulfil a universal vocation, such as the European Union and NAFTA, also have mechanisms that compel states to honour agreements. The European Union, with its Commission and Court of Justice, holds a supranational power to conduct follow ups to assess and, if necessary, call member states to order. A debate also exists regarding the effectiveness of regional institutions compared to that of international institutions (Acharya and Johnson, 2007).

Most international organizations, however, are limited in their capacity to enforce the decisions they make, as these decisions are often only recommendations. Thus, an organization's effectiveness depends largely on members' willingness to fulfil their commitments. Peer pressure, which is widely used in international organizations, may be effective in urging delinquent states to respect their agreements. States seeking to forge or preserve a reputation are sensitive to this pressure. Certain institutions have characteristics facilitating the implementation of agreements. They may, for example, disseminate certain information in reports, such as the WTO's and IMF's national reports. By conducting systematic assessments of members' practices, international institutions foster compliance. By establishing verifiable standards and outcome assessment measures, it is easier for public decision makers to ascertain the intentions of other states. The readability of behaviour heightens the credibility of commitments and increases the cost of defection. When institutions provide financial incentives, arbitration procedures, or legal notices to resolve problems, they also encourage states to comply (Simmons, 2002).

In a world where it is so easy not to fulfil one's international obligations, the question of legalizing obligations becomes paramount (Simmons 2000, 2001). States are tending more and more to rely on legal processes to resolve trade disputes by lodging complaints, where decisions are enforceable, for treaty violations against third parties. Moreover, by becoming members of international organizations such as the WTO or the IMF, governments are formally bound to one another. As a result, the cost of violating international agreements increases, facilitating their implementation. The legalization and harmonization of norms ensures that institutions are stable and that international trade and monetary relations are readable. For example, Frederick Abbott maintains that Mexico wanted to formally join NAFTA, with its constraining arbitration clauses, in order to reduce transaction costs, foster transparency, decrease risks for investors and private exporters, and reassure international investors regarding its commitment to liberalize its economy and pursue its own reforms (2000).

While authors do not agree on this point, several specialists believe that international institutions must be flexible in order to avoid defection. Rules and standards may be established for the purpose of predicting how states will act, but they must not be too restrictive. Organizations must be flexible enough to accommodate significant changes of circumstances. As Keohane asks, "In a world without centralized government, why should states comply with obligations that had become inconvenient?" (2002: 7). According to Peter Rosendorff and Helen Milner, "International institutions that include an escape clause generate more durable and stable cooperative international regimes" (2003: 852). Escape clauses allow countries to deviate temporarily from their obligations, and they make long-term commitments more realistic. Thus, the more organizations allow member states to adjust their obligations to keep up with changing circumstances, the less governments are tempted to reject obligations that no longer apply. Furthermore, it is essential for institutions to be able to reform themselves, if necessary.

The situation is comparable for trade agreements. When two countries negotiate a trade agreement, much uncertainty persists concerning the actual economic consequences for national actors and their reaction to any undesired effects. This question is important for two countries that envisage larger integration. Agreements that allow no room to manoeuvre, or "optimal imperfection," in relation to unanticipated results make long-term cooperation arduous (Downs and Rocke, 1995).

Constructivist arguments are increasingly present in the debates about institutions. For constructivists, institutions are important, as they create social knowledge. They play a role in creating identities and interests that enable actors to agree on common objectives. The GATT and the WTO have been helping to create standards that establish the rules of trade liberalization. These organizations have made free trade theories more socially acceptable. This is why the WTO and the IMF have become symbolic targets of the anti-globalization movement. The protectionist argument no longer has the same impact, and few governments are willing to promote the end of international trade.

Conclusion

Today, the liberal approach is largely dominant in IPE. The international context certainly has a lot to do with that. Close to 70 years after World War II and more than 25 years after the end of the Cold War, the relevance of the realist paradigm is in decline. What is more, the international scene increasingly resembles what Keohane and Nye described in the 1970s. Even the hypotheses of the decline of the American Empire and the proliferation of international organizations and regimes are now for the most part validated, which was far from being the case in the 1970s or 1980s. The most severe criticisms of liberal institutionalism, aside from those made by realists, maintain that in the more contemporary works, NGOs and non-governmental actors are largely absent from the analysis. This is in stark contrast to the works by Nye and Keohane in the 1970s. As well, critics believe that the liberal approach neglects national or domestic politics factors (institutions, interests, and ideas), particularly those that affect international negotiations. These debates will be the topic of the next chapter.

Note

1   In 1990, John Mearsheimer wrote, "it is the Soviet threat that provides the glue that holds NATO together. Take away that offensive threat and the United States is likely to abandon the Continent, whereupon the defensive alliance it has headed for forty years may disintegrate" (1990: 52). He also predicted that the European community would probably get weaker rather than stronger over time. On the general role of institutions, he maintained that institutions have only a minimal influence of the behaviour of states and little chance to promote stability in a post–Cold War environment.

Questions

1. What are the differences between the liberal perspective in IPE and in international relations?
2. Are liberals more optimistic than realists about the evolution of world politics?
3. What is hard and soft power?
4. What is the impact of globalization on war and peace?
5. What is transnationalism and complex interdependence?
6. What is liberal institutionalism and why is it thought of as the "half-sibling of realism"?
7. What is a political market failure according to Robert Keohane?
8. What is the rational design of institutions?
9. Why do states respect their agreements in the absence of a central government that can enforce them?
10. Why are some international organizations more effective than others?

Further Reading

On liberal institutionalism:

Keohane, Robert O., and Lisa L. Martin. "Institutional Theory As a Research Program." In *Progress in International Relations Theory: Appraising the Field*, edited by Colin Elman and Miriam Fendius Elman, 71–109. Cambridge, MA: MIT Press, 2003.

Martin, Lisa L. "Interests, Power and Multilateralism." *International Organization* 46.4 (1992): 765–92.

Oye, Kenneth A. *Cooperation under Anarchy*. Princeton: Princeton University Press, 1986.

Simmons, Beth, and Lisa L. Martin. "International Organizations and Institutions." In *Handbook of International Relations*, edited by Walter Carlsnaes, Thomas Risse, and Beth A. Simmons, 192–211. London: Sage, 2001.

Stein, Arthur A. *Why Nations Cooperate: Circumstance and Choice in International Relations*. Ithaca, NY: Cornell University Press, 1990.

The author most associated with the liberal orthodox school is Robert Keohane. Here are his most important publications:

Keohane, Robert O., and Joseph S. Nye. "Transnational Relations and World Politics: An Introduction." *International Organization* 25.3 (1971): 329–49.

Keohane, Robert O., and Joseph S. Nye. *Power and Interdependence: World Politics in Transition*. 1977. New York: Longman, 2012.

Keohane, Robert O. "The Theory of Hegemonic Stability and Changes in International Economic Regime, 1967–1977." In *Change in the International System*, edited by Ole R. Holsti, Randolph Siverson, and Alexander L. George, 131–62. Boulder, CO: Westview Press, 1980.

Keohane, Robert O. *After Hegemony: Cooperation and Discord in World Political Economy*. Princeton: Princeton University Press, 1984.

Keohane, Robert O. *International Institutions and State Power: Essays in International Relations Theory*. Boulder, CO: Westview Press, 1989.

Keohane, Robert O., and Helen V. Milner, eds. *Internationalization and Domestic Politics*. Cambridge: Cambridge University Press, 1996.

Keohane, Robert O. "Problematic Lucidity: Stephen Krasner's 'State Power and the Structure of International Trade.'" *World Politics* 50.1 (1997): 150–70.

Keohane, Robert O. *Power and Governance in a Partially Globalized World*. New York: Routledge, 2002.

5 Domestic and Open Economy Politics

Chapter Contents

- Interests
- Institutions
- The Second Image Reversed
- Ideas
- Conclusion

Reader's Guide

The domestic politics paradigm is concerned with the interaction between the domestic factors and the global factors that influence the outcomes of a policy. Researchers attempt to decode what affects and motivates state behaviour and preferences. There are two categories of works in this paradigm. The first examines how domestic politics influence IPE. The second reverses the direction of the analysis and studies the effects of the international system on domestic politics; this is the "second image reversed" approach, to use the term coined by Peter Gourevitch. Specialists in this analytic level usually have a dual expertise: in IPE and in comparative political economy. More recently, some researchers have preferred to identify their works with a new paradigm: Open Economy Politics (OEP). OEP is a direct descendant of the domestic politics approach. OEP adopts the general assumptions of neoclassical economists and international trade theory but with the major difference that it also incorporates fundamental political variables into the equation. Even though there is considerable overlap between OEP and the domestic politics approach, OEP focuses mainly on interests and institutions but not on ideas, and it clearly derives from the orthodox school, which means that it is positivist, hypothetical-deductive, and focused on quantitative methods. That said, OEP is nevertheless included in the domestic politics approach. The core of the debates surrounding these approaches may be analyzed with the help of the "three-I" approach, which centres on interests, institutions, and ideas.

In international relations theory, authors traditionally identify three levels of analysis. These levels are taken from a book by Kenneth Waltz published in 1959, *Man, the State and War,* in which Waltz defined three "images" in international relations. The first image is that of individuals or human nature in general; the second is that of the domestic organization of states; and the third represents the international system, in particular its anarchic nature (Waltz, 1959). In the contemporary literature, these three images are used to specify the level of analysis of a study on an international issue. They are useful heuristic tools that enable researchers to bring some order to a complex world.

The neorealist and institutional liberalism approaches in international relations theory correspond to the third image. They are systemic or structural approaches and they focus their attention on the anarchic nature of the international system. The nature of the system determines the preferences of states that are thought of as unitary actors. In addition, these approaches postulate, if only implicitly, a separation between domestic politics issues and international politics issues. To facilitate analysis and prediction, these approaches assume that state preferences are constant and rational. The national interest is a fact rather than a social construct and studies pertain mainly to the constraints and incentives originating in the international system; in the case of realists, for example, these studies concern the distribution of power between the actors. Waltz called this the outside-in approach (Waltz, 1979: 63).

The domestic politics paradigm concentrates its analysis instead on what is situated within a country, or the inside-out approach. According to Jeffry Frieden and Lisa Martin, this approach (which is at the level of Waltz's second image analysis) is concerned with the interaction between the domestic factors and the international factors that influence the outcomes of a policy (Frieden and Martin, 2002). Researchers attempt to decode what affects and motivates state behaviour and preferences. This paradigm is still a largely positivist one in which authors set out to develop middle-range causal theories. There are two categories of works in this paradigm. The first examines how domestic politics influence IPE (Katzenstein, 1976). The second reverses the direction of the analysis and studies the effects of the international system on domestic politics; this is the "second image reversed" approach, to use the term coined by Peter Gourevitch (1978). Specialists in this analytic level usually have a dual expertise: in IPE and in comparative political economy. These two disciplines have influenced one another to such an extent that nowadays it is difficult to differentiate between them (Milner, 1998).

Since the end of the 1990s, some researchers have preferred to identify their works with a new paradigm: Open Economy Politics (OEP). The concept of OEP was first used by Robert Bates in 1997 in a book about the political economy of the world coffee trade. According to David Lake, OEP is a direct descendent of the domestic politics approach. It is a nascent paradigm of IPE that appeared in the 1990s. OEP adopts the general assumptions of neoclassical economists and international trade theory but with the major difference that it also incorporates fundamental political variables into the equation. As in IPE as a whole, OEP is a bridge between political science and economics. Institutions are central in the analysis. According to Lake, "OEP provides a model of how international institutions can be studied and understood from within an integrated theoretical approach" (2009: 221).

Even though there is considerable overlap between OEP and the domestic politics approach, OEP focuses mainly on interests and institutions but not on ideas, and it clearly derives from the orthodox school, which means that it is positivist, hypothetical-deductive, and focused on quantitative methods. This is not always the case with the domestic politics approach, in which the majority of works precedes OEP. That said, OEP is nevertheless included in the domestic politics approach.

The domestic politics paradigm, contrary to OEP, is more open to the role of ideas. It focuses on Waltz's first image; it is concerned with psychological factors and values. Robert Jervis (1976) extended our understanding of the first image with his works on perceptions and misperceptions in international relations. Nowadays, the rise of constructivism in international relations theory, as well as the cognitive analysis in comparative politics and public policy, are starting to attract notice in IPE.

The core of the debates surrounding these approaches may be analyzed with the help of the "three-*I*" approach, which centres on interests, institutions, and ideas. The typical line of questioning in the domestic politics approach examines why, when, and how countries choose to promote trade liberalization. In simpler terms, what are the political determinants of the globalization of the economy? Domestic politics is the independent variable and openness to or adoption of free trade is the dependent variable. While many economists have a favourable bias towards free trade, they believe, somewhat naïvely, that countries will adopt free trade because it is a good public policy. IPE scholars who specialize in the domestic politics paradigm instead believe that political factors are determinant and that openness to international trade is complex because it affects a number of powerful interests in domestic politics. The second line of questioning has to do with how the globalization and liberalization of trade affect the interests of actors, such as unions or industrial sectors, and how in return the latter position themselves in the political debates. In this case, globalization is the independent variable and domestic politics is the dependent variable (Lake, 2009). These two lines of questioning are the essence of Waltz's inside-out and outside-in approach.

Interests

The analyses in IPE that emphasize interests focus basically on the politics of interest groups. This type of analysis starts with a specification of the interests of individuals or of their collective representation as an interest group. According to Gene Grossman and Elhanan Helpman (2002), actors that will be affected by a policy will mobilize resources to defend their interests. If the actor in question believes it can benefit from a public policy, it might, for example, lobby or contribute massively to the funding of a political party, particularly in the American context. If the actor might be harmed by the policy, the actor will mobilize resources to try to prevent the policy's adoption.

The basic idea is that powerful interest groups can influence the outcome of a policy. Large banks, for example, might derail reform of the international financial sector; multinationals would have their preferences written into trade agreements; insurance companies might determine a large part of the content of reforms in the US health system because that is in their interest.

Analysts begin with the assumption that actors have interests. These interests are a given, a fact. The unit of analysis is not always very clear: Is it the individual, the firm, or a particular sector of society (such as manufacturing or class interests)? When a policy affects a group of individuals, analysts consider the group to be relatively homogeneous. As Lake writes, "In other words, when a policy affects a set of individuals in the same way, they are typically treated as if they constitute a homogenous group or, for purposes of analysis, a single actor. In some OEP theories, individuals are primary but in most, firms, sectors, or factors of production are taken to be the relevant units" (2009: 226).

In the OEP approach, the majority of the authors use economic theories to deduce actors' interests and preferences. Some authors use the Heckscher–Ohlin–Samuelson model (HOS), which assumes that all factors are mobile across occupations within countries and, therefore, capital and labour will possess opposing interests. Others use specific factor theory, also known as the Ricardo–Viner model, which is based on the idea that at least one factor of production is assumed to be specific to a particular industry while the other factors are mobile across sectors. Despite these differences, the idea that political actors seek to maximize their interests and that their preferences are stable is widely accepted.

Many analyses begin with the assumption that when an individual or a group is negatively affected by a public policy, the individual or group can be expected to mobilize against that policy. In contrast, if an individual or group will benefit from the outcomes of a policy, the individual or group can be expected to act to promote adoption of the policy. Actors' preferences are essentially determined by the importance of an issue for them. If an issue is important for a group and the effects of the policy are very concentrated, it will motivate the actors concerned to take action to defend their interests (Frieden, 1991). To give an example, workers who possess special skills that are not easily transferable between industries will be more likely to demand employment insurance regimes or good severance pay packages. In another example, firms that invest massively in highly specialized sectors will tend to demand protectionist measures against foreign competition.

The starting point of the research is therefore to determine the interests of the political actors in general and specific terms. The goal is to learn whether an actor's interests are concentrated or diffuse. Most researchers think that concentrated interests will win out over diffuse interests. In the case of firms, their interest will be radically different depending on whether or not their activities are exportable or whether or not their production requires a large quantity of imported products, and so on. This "production profile," as Gourevitch (1986) called it, is often presented as a good predictor of where firms are positioned in relation to trade liberalization.

The diverse industrial and service sectors vary in regards to this type of consideration. For example, to explain the adoption of the Smoot–Hawley Tariff Act in 1930 in the United States, Elmer Schattschneider (1935) began with the premise that the industries favourable to protectionism had a very concentrated interest in the adoption of such measures while the consumers who would benefit from free trade had diffuse interests. Since then, several studies have adopted this analytic perspective according to which electors, for example, have little influence on public policies, not just because their interests are diffuse, but also because the issues are complex and difficult to understand (Gourevitch, 1986).

However, it is not enough to explain things in terms of concentrated and dispersed interests. Frequently, actors from the same sector, who have concentrated interests, are on opposite sides of important issues. According to Helen Milner, global multinationals have a disproportionate influence on trade issues and on the formulation of economic policies (Milner, 1988). Their international positioning makes them very favourable to trade liberalization measures and, in developed countries, these actors will be the central players in the dissemination of the free trade ideology and against protectionism. In the past, they were able to marginalize the influence of other major industry actors favourable to increasing protectionist measures. This is a case of two groups of actors with very concentrated interests but with conflicting positions. It is also possible that very powerful actors with highly concentrated interests can have strong positions on more general public policy issues. The financial sector, for example, generally supports anti-inflationist policies despite their widespread effect.

The emphasis on interests permits IPE analysts to explain a certain number of important phenomena. A vast number of economists, for example, maintain that free trade is very beneficial for domestic economies and that protectionism negatively affects a country's growth and wealth. Given this, how can we explain the persistence of protectionism and the resistance to trade liberalization? The explanation, according to IPE specialists, has to do with interests. While free trade can be beneficial for a country's overall economy, it will have differentiated effects on the various actors. Some groups will invariably lose as a result of the policy. In short, international trade and trade liberalization create winners, but also losers. The nature of the domestic economy will largely determine what group has an interest in promoting trade liberalization and what group has an interest in opposing it. Ultimately, it is the government that decides who wins and who loses.

Economists Wolfgang Stolper and Paul Samuelson were the first to develop a model to understand why some actors are favourable to free trade while others are not. Their particular focus was the effects of free trade on the distribution or allocation of income in a given country. When a country chooses free trade, it increases its specialization in the dominant factor of production in its economy, which results in an increase in wages through the simple law of supply and demand. In contrast, however, abandoning production of a good for which this country has no comparative advantage leads to a downturn in wages and employment in this sector. Although Ricardo argued that countries benefit from specialization and free trade, the Stolper–Samuelson theorem qualifies this claim by concluding that within countries there are winners and losers even if overall the country is a winner. The losers are those who, prior to free trade, benefited by their scarcity. This model has been used in IPE to establish links between trade policies and national coalitions of interests.

Using this type of analysis, Ronald Rogowski (1989, 1987a) demonstrated, in his book *Commerce and Coalitions*, how changes in trade opportunities can affect the power of national interest groups. Rogowski asked, why do countries have such different cleavages and political coalitions? Why are some countries more open to free trade while others are generally more hostile to it? According to Rogowski, the explanation lies in the growth of international trade. He used a three-factor model (land, capital, and labour) to determine the interests of the national actors relative to free trade. Drawing on the Stolper–Samuelson theorem, he affirmed that those who possess abundant resources will be favourable to free trade, while those who have fewer resources will choose defensive strategies such as protectionism. This cleavage represents the lines of the coalitions for and against free trade. The more international trade increases, the more the political power of pro-free-trade coalitions increases while that of the other coalitions decreases. This mechanism, says the author, explains how coalitions are created according to the nature of the country and the three factors.

Hence, in developed countries that have more capital than low-cost labour, trade liberalization has the effect of strengthening the power of those who possess the capital and diminishing the power of the others. If we accept the idea that public policy decisions are the result of the preferences of groups in a society, trade liberalization affects coalitions and weakens the relative power of unions by increasing the relative power of employers (Rogowski, 1987a). This model has been used to explain the opposition of blue-collar workers in Canada and the United States to NAFTA, unlike those in Mexico where there is a larger pool of less qualified labour. It also explains why French or Canadian farmers are opposed to the liberalization of certain agricultural sectors in WTO trade negotiations. That said, Stephen Magee (1978) set out to test the Stolper–Samuelson theorem by examining the "lobbying behaviour" of representatives of capital and labour in the trade bill of 1973 in the United States. He came to the conclusion that capital and labour almost always testified on the same side of the proposed legislation.

Governments may use the strategy of issue linkage to sidestep domestic pressures. This is how Christina Davis explains the progress towards liberalization in the agricultural sector. According to her, liberalization policies in this sector have progressed because international institutions changed the balance of interests within countries in favour of liberalization, despite pressures from very strong agricultural lobbies. By linking several issues, negotiators encourage many lobbies favourable to liberalization to mobilize. In this way, despite strong resistance from national pressure groups, negotiators can use international negotiations to support liberalization. International institutions can enhance the credibility of the commitment (Davis, 2005, 2004).

Originally formulated in the context of trade policy, OEP has been extended to other sectors. Jeffry Frieden published a study that used a similar argument with respect to the financial sector (Frieden, 1991, 1998). Public policies pertaining to money and credit are political choices that have considerable distributional effects. Frieden claims that liberalization in the financial sector has important and predictable distributional effects that will permanently change the interests and preferences of the various groups. Exporting manufacturers and international investors will prefer stable interest rates, as that allows them to better anticipate the costs of their imports and exports. In contrast, entrepreneurs who produce for local markets will tend to favour a more autonomous monetary policy that would allow government to adjust interest rates in response to the local situation—that is, reduce interest rates when consumption is declining.

Institutions

Interests are framed and channelled by political institutions in such a way that these institutions have a considerable impact on the outcome of public policies. Political institutions largely determine the rules of the game and attribute to a group of actors a decisive influence in a decision-making process. Institutions aggregate conflicting social interests, with a certain degree of bias, and establish the bargaining rules between actors. For Lake, "In highly institutionalized settings, like most domestic political systems, established rules and procedures generally reflect group strength over the long term" (2009: 228).

In 1976, Peter Katzenstein introduced in IPE the idea that "domestic structures" influence the international policy of states and the world-economy. For Katzenstein, it is important to analyze these structures as, contrary to the claims of various authors, notably Keohane and Nye, the structures of developed countries are not as similar as is sometimes asserted. Hence, countries confronted with the same issues will produce different outcomes in terms of public policies. States are no longer thought of as black boxes, and Katzenstein was one of the first professors to unlock the box by introducing several levels of analysis in his research (Gourevitch et al., 2008: 893). With this new approach, he brought IPE closer to the studies in comparative politics.

In the 1978 volume *Between Power and Plenty*, which Katzenstein edited, he stressed the variations in the international economic strategies of industrialized countries. According to him, these variations are chiefly explained by the differences in their domestic structures. The volume's contributors analyzed six countries that had experienced the same systemic constraints (the oil shock) from the international system. Their goal was to measure if and how the countries' responses varied (Katzenstein, 1978). Variations in states' actions are an illustration of their autonomy with respect to societal pressures and to the different instruments available to them. The authors' conclusions show that states that are relatively strong in the face of societal pressures, such as France or Japan, were able to act quickly with specific objectives. They set about seeking alternative energies under state control. In both cases, large nuclear power plants were built to ensure more energy independence and therefore more political autonomy from outside pressures. In the United States, where the state is weak and more permeable to societal pressures, the government response to the problem took more time and the result was less coherent. Numerous interest groups, from environmentalists to oil cartels, pressured the government, each proposing its own solution. When the government attempted to satisfy several groups with diverging opinions, the policy became a jumble of reforms with no clear priority.

In the same work, Stephen Krasner looked at the "paradox" of the United States, externally strong but internally weak (Krasner, 1978b). Krasner analyzed the relationship between the state and society and its effects on the decision-making process in IPE. He developed the idea that certain states have more autonomy in the face of societal pressures than others. In countries where the state is strong, decision makers are relatively isolated from these pressures. In countries where the state is weak, the situation is reversed. For Krasner, the United States is a good example of a weak state as the US government is very permeable to the pressures of social actors, notably interest groups that can put pressure on Congress, the president, and his advisers, or resort to legal battles. In the United States, power is divided between the executive branch and the bicameral legislature. Party lines are weak and the judicial system and central bank are relatively independent of political control. Certain bureaucracies also have close ties with social actors, what today we call public policy networks (Krasner, 1978b).

Japan, for its part, is a strong state—a state that is quite autonomous in relation to its society. In Japan, decision making is concentrated in the hands of a few key actors within the executive. The executive is strong enough to implement a public policy and to ensure the support of influential actors from civil society through the introduction of incentive measures or through coercion. In Japan, the Ministry of Economy, Trade and Industry has played an important historical role in the promotion and defence of state interests. As well, the Liberal Democratic Party has dominated national politics since its creation in 1955, holding almost unbroken power until its historic defeat in the 2009 elections.

The works of Michael Mastanduno on the containment policies engaged in by the United States during the Cold War are another example of research that takes the same analytic line. Mastanduno's analysis is concerned with the efforts of Western countries to control the transfer of goods and technologies. It focuses on the roots of cooperation and international alliances in regards to the control of exports in US foreign policy during the Cold War. Drawing on hegemonic stability theory, Mastanduno maintains that these containment policies required a leader, one who would be a benevolent leader within CoCom (Coordinating Committee for Multilateral Export Controls). The members of CoCom roughly correspond to the members of NATO. The need for American leadership stemmed from the fact that the actors' preferences were sometimes divergent and even conflicting. US policy during the Cold War was based on a strict and very wide embargo. As the United States had a very conflicted relationship with the USSR, the US government, which shouldered the responsibility for the defence of Western Europe, hoped to maintain its military superiority over the long term. To do this, it chose to control the export of a long list of "militarily sensitive" goods and technologies and sought to influence Soviet foreign policy by increasing or decreasing the trade of these goods.

In his analysis of the role of the United States in CoCom, Mastanduno concluded that the American leaders were weak and inconsistent. According to him, the explanation for the US attitude was not the relative economic decline of the United States, but rather the institutional fragmentation of the

American state and notably the permeability to contradictory pressures from society and the private sector. The combination of a powerful executive and internal fragmentation produced an incoherent policy (Mastanduno, 1992).

The organization and type of a country's political regime also have an influence on IPE. Several authors have examined the behaviour of democratic regimes. These works, which share some points with democratic peace theory, develop similar lines of reasoning. For example, they share the idea that pairs of democratic regimes are more likely to negotiate a tariff reduction than are a democratic country and a non-democratic country (Mansfield, Milner, and Rosendorff, 2002). Democratic regimes have a greater tendency to proceed with unilateral liberalizations (Rosendorff, 2005a). Democratic regimes obtain more concessions in the form of tariff reductions with their trade partners than do non-democratic countries (Rosendorff, 2005b).

Several studies pertain to the role of the legislative and executive branches in international trade policies. Some authors maintain for example that in the United States, the executive (the president) is by nature more favourable to free trade, while the Congress (legislature) is more protectionist. This situation is explained chiefly by the fact that, following the Smoot–Hawley Tariff Act of 1930, the system was redesigned to grant the president more power in the negotiation of trade agreements. This system evolved into the Fast Track Negotiating Authority (or the Trade Promotion Authority), which allows the president to negotiate a trade agreement that Congress can approve or reject, but cannot amend or obstruct. According to several specialists, this change in the US political system explains the more liberalizing trend of US trade policy since 1945 (Haggard, 1988; Bailey, Goldstein, and Weingast, 1997).

There is even more evidence that institutions impact public policy. According to Rogowski (1987b), the type of institution structurally influences policy outcomes. Rogowski found, for example, that large constituencies (president) favour the promotion of the public interest, while smaller constituencies (Congress) favour protectionism. Short electoral terms (two years for the House of Representatives) lead to opportunistic policies (protectionism), while longer terms foster long-term policies (free trade).

As well, the growing number of checks and balances and vetoes in a political system—that is, actors with the authority to block or delay a policy—favours the lowest common denominator or the status quo (Rogowski, 1999; Cowhey, 1993). This situation also affects a government's ability to respond to external shocks (MacIntyre, 2001).

Rogowski and Katzenstein also developed the idea that proportional representation systems are more favourable to free trade. Katzenstein (1985) wrote of an affinity between the proportional representation of small Northern European countries and openness to international trade. These small countries developed neo-corporatist institutions to facilitate a response to economic shocks—namely, cooperation between capital and labour in order to moderate wage demands—but, in exchange, they provided a compensatory social welfare system to ease the impact of economic shock on workers (Katzenstein, 1985: 150–6). Rogowski maintains that "the more an economically advanced state relies on external trade, the more it will be drawn to the use of [proportional representation], a parliamentary system, and large districts, with (presumably) all that that combination entails" (Rogowski, 1987b: 206).

In general, according to Rogowski, proportional representation systems have more political parties than do countries with majority systems. Their parties are more disciplined, more ideological, and more stable in the face of a sudden change of mood among the electorate. This type of system also encourages higher electoral participation. In the US system, in contrast, the president is elected separately from his party, which affects party discipline. As the election of the president is not dependent on the election of his party in legislative elections, the president is less inclined to respect the party line and less attentive to local distinctiveness. Large constituencies would therefore reduce the influence of interest groups and increase the electoral influence of the average elector, while majority uninominal systems would favour the protectionist. The consequence is that the first type of system would be more favourable to free trade and would rely less on subsidies and sectoral measures than the second type of system.

More recent works examine the variations in the types of democracies and their effects on trade policy outcomes. Grossman and Helpman (2005, 2002) established that first-past-the-post democracies tend to be more protectionist. Doces and Rosendorff have established, for their part, that presidential systems are more protectionist on average than parliamentary systems (Doces and Rosendorff, 2005). Susan Lohmann and Sharyn O'Halloran showed that when the president and the legislature are divided along partisan lines, protectionist measures are fostered (1994). For Michael Laver and Kenneth Shepsle, this situation would have the same type of impact on trade negotiations as a minority government in a parliamentary system (1991). For Fiona McGillivray, the stronger the party discipline is, the weaker the influence of interest groups on government trade policies (1997). Democracies in which party discipline is strong (Canada) lean more readily towards protectionism for widely dispersed industries in safe districts. In contrast, weak party discipline (the United States) gives concentrated industries in marginal districts more lobbying power for protection. Other authors have drawn attention to the financing of political parties. The influence of interest groups is deemed weaker when financing is exclusively public than when contributions from private business are very high (Frieden and Martin, 2002).

Another line of research focuses on the bargaining process in institutions and how it affects the outcome of a negotiation. A relevant and influential contribution was made by Robert Putnam in the 1980s and 1990s. Putnam (1988; Putnam, Evans, and Jacobson, 1993) coined the "two-level game" metaphor to capture the dynamic and complexity of international negotiations. The two-level game metaphor, and subsequent scholarship on double-edged diplomacy, refers to the idea that central government negotiators have to negotiate simultaneously with domestic and international actors to secure a negotiation. According to Putnam,

> The politics of many international negotiations can usefully be conceived as a two-level game. At the national level, domestic groups pursue their interests by pressuring the government to adopt favorable policies, and politicians seek power by constructing coalitions among those groups. At the international level, national governments seek to maximize their own ability to satisfy domestic pressures, while minimizing the adverse consequences of foreign developments. Neither of the two games can be ignored by central decision-makers, so long as their countries remain interdependent, yet sovereign. (Putnam, 1988: 434)

For Putnam, "each national political leader appears at both game boards" (Putnam, 1988: 434).

Since these publications, many authors have commented on Putnam's metaphor. For example, Helen Milner (1997) has argued that the division of power between the executive and the legislative branches, as well as elections, are more important in an international negotiation than Putnam's metaphor gives them credit for.

Applying the two-level game approach and drawing on rational choice theory, Milner proposes that the analyses that treat the state as a unitary actor are fundamentally misleading. She maintains that states are instead polyarchic, as the decision-making process is shared by two or more actors—for example, the legislative and the executive branches. In a polyarchic system, different actors have different preferences but must share the decision-making process. In short, there is no national interest, and decisions are more the result of a compromise between actors than of a hypothetical national consensus. Milner contends that it is the outcome of the national game (and not the fear of relative gains, that another country may gain more, or that it may cheat) that, ultimately, will determine how an international game is played and what the cooperative behaviour will be. Milner pays particular attention to the influence of a country's strategic game on trade negotiations.

In the case of the United States, Milner's model identifies two key actors: the president, who has his own preferences on the degree of liberalization desired, and the legislature, that must ratify all international agreements. To simplify the analysis, Milner posits that the negotiation is taking place between two countries (the domestic politics of the other country are not analyzed in as much detail as those of the United States). At the international level, the actors will assume that the outcome of negotiations will conform to the Nash equilibrium. (In game theory, the Nash equilibrium is reached when none of the actors can change its strategy without weakening its situation, as the reciprocal strategies of the actors are known.) Hence, the analyst's focus will be mainly on what is happening in domestic politics. Two factors attract our attention: the interests of the legislature, particularly the distance that separates its preference from that of the president, and the degree of uncertainty in the negotiation.

This situation gives rise to several conjectures concerning the conditions upon which an agreement is possible and the distribution of benefits between the actors. One of Milner's contributions to the theory is to explain the condition upon which Schelling's conjecture holds true. According to this conjecture, it may be to the negotiator's advantage to have his hands tied, by the legislature, for example, during a free trade negotiation. If the legislature has to ratify an agreement and gives the negotiator only a little room for manoeuvre, the negotiator can use this situation to maximize the country's gains. Thus, rather than being a constraint or an obstacle, national actors can become a strategic advantage for the negotiator. This logic applies often but not in all circumstances. When the legislature is too antagonistic, when it does not want an agreement to be reached despite the president's favourable opinion, the chances that an agreement can be concluded will be severely undermined.

Milner, along with Mansfield and Rosendorff, set out to learn if the situation changed when a democracy negotiated with an autocratic regime in which the legislature is not required to ratify the agreement. Their conclusion, supported by the statistics, is that when two democratic regimes negotiate with one another, they more easily succeed in reducing trade barriers than when a democratic regime negotiates with an autocratic regime (Mansfield, Milner, and Rosendorff, 2000).

Lisa Martin (2000) also challenges the theory of executive dominance advocated by many international negotiation theorists, including Putnam. According to Martin, the legislature in democratic regimes has the ability to block the implementation of an international obligation, even when legislative approval is not required. The legislature may establish its influence through budgetary control, through control procedures in relation to the executive, through the appointment of agents, and through procedures for the implementation of treaties. Thus, an international commitment negotiated without the participation of the legislature may lack credibility. International agreements gain credibility when the legislative branch is included in the negotiations through an institutionalized mechanism. This situation applies in both presidential and parliamentary systems. This way of negotiating reduces uncertainty because the legislature reveals information to national negotiators but also to other states. By participating in the negotiations, it can also reveal its societal preferences concerning what can be implemented. Martin demonstrates that the legislature's presence in negotiations promotes the implementation of international commitments. It thereby strengthens the credibility of international commitments of states, whether in the United States or Europe (Martin, 2000).

While the majority of the works on institutions deal with their effects on negotiations and international trade, other studies, for example, the studies by David Leblang (1999) and Lawrence Broz (2003), tackle different themes. According to these authors, floating exchange rates are more likely to be present in a democracy than in an authoritarian regime. According to Leblang, they are more likely to be seen in a proportional representation regime than in a first-past-the-post system. In a first-past-the-post system governed by a single political party, governments prefer adjustable exchange rates so they can manipulate them for electoral reasons.

The Second Image Reversed

An increasingly important line of research in IPE pertains to the "international sources of domestic politics" or "the second image reversed." One of the most productive areas of debate concerns the effects of globalization of the economy and finance on states and public policies. In the scholarly works in IPE, we find two opposing theses on the effects of globalization on the welfare state: the declinist thesis and the transformationist thesis (Paquin, 2014).

Many works have examined the effects of the globalization of the economy and of finance on nation-states and public policies. Since Richard N. Cooper popularized the concept of economic interdependence in 1968, a substantial number of the works on globalization stress the growing vulnerability of states in relation to globalization. Hence, for a majority of specialists, globalization and public policies are antagonistic. The action of states is conceived in a territorial framework that has become too narrow, while globalization is by definition a phenomenon that occurs across borders. States' capacity for action is therefore diminished, except when they act in coordination with other states on the world stage. The trend is a convergence towards the neoliberal model. As far back as 1969, Charles Kindleberger stated, "the nation-state is just about through as an economic unit" (207). In the 1980s, sociologist Daniel Bell declared, "The nation-state is becoming too small for the big problems of life, and too big for the small problems of life. . . . In short, there is a mismatch of scale" (1987: 14) In 1995, Kenichi Ohmae prophesied the end of the nation-state and the rise of region-states.

A number of authors agree that globalization limits public choices and that it imposes a convergence of public policies towards the neoliberal model. Globalization may, for example, make a public policy unsustainable. According to John Goodman and Louis Pauly, capital control was a relatively simple measure to apply in the years from the end of World War II to the 1970s (1993). The creation of Eurocurrencies and the liberalization of the financial sector fostered the very strong growth of international financial activities in the 1980s and 1990s. This situation made it very difficult for states to maintain control over cross-border investments. In this case, the transformations of the international financial sector forced governments to re-examine their decisions regarding capital control.

The more popular thesis on the effects of globalization, that of the declinists, suggests that globalization of the economy and finance as well as regional integration processes such as NAFTA and the European Union exert very strong pressures on the welfare state. Generally, declinists contend that the globalized economy is more and more competitive, that the glorious era of the welfare state is over and the social-democratic project is drawing to an end, as states are no longer able to ensure strong economic growth or even to effectively intervene to foster the creation of wealth and to redistribute it. As Margaret Thatcher said, "There is no alternative!"

For declinists, the story of globalization and its effects on state intervention goes as follows: after the Second World War, Western states set up welfare states whose essential characteristics were the democratization of education, greater accessibility to health care, benefit plans for the unemployed and more widespread social policies such as pension plans, maternity leaves, and public daycare.

These policies were possible because, in the postwar years, these countries were relatively sheltered from global competition. They could more freely increase taxation levels and create very generous welfare states (Reich, 1991). With the strong demographic growth after the war, the developed world was thus able to enter the "thirty glorious years" period. Even though these countries had different foundations and different trajectories, they all set up sizeable welfare states, even the United States (Scharpf, 2006).

The economic crisis in the 1970s marked the beginning of the end of the interventionist state (Pierson 1994; Gourevitch, 1986). The gradual opening up of world trade, the failure of Keynesian-type stimulatory policies and the arrival of stagflation forced Western countries to adopt policies of the neoliberal and monetarist order (Hall, 1993). It was the start of the *"Trente laborieuses"* (thirty laborious years), a period when developed states began to rethink their role in the economy: they were forced by the globalization of the economy to reduce the size of the state, slash social programs, increase the cost of education, privatize many government corporations, and replace their industrial policies with trade liberalization policies. In return, this trade liberalization strengthened global competition, which added to the pressure on Western states to cut spending in social programs and lower taxation levels even further, according to the race-to-the-bottom hypothesis (Spar and Yoffie, 2010; Castles, 2006). After the 1970s crisis, the Western world entered a period of "permanent austerity," according to Paul Pierson even though, he says, the welfare state was practically unchanged (1998).

Globalization, the astounding growth in the number of multinationals and offshorings as well as in global competition, phenomena that reached their apogee with the exceptional rise of the BRIC (Brazil, Russia, India, China) at the start of the twenty-first century, further accentuated the pressure on developed countries (Friedman, 2006). Among these countries, those with the gloomiest future are the countries that have sizeable social programs, heavy taxation, a high rate of unionization, and a very conciliatory attitude towards workers' rights. The more social-democratic countries, such as Sweden, Finland, and Denmark, are therefore particularly vulnerable.

In contrast to the declinist school of thought, transformationists question the thesis that welfare states are in decline due to globalization. Authors who espouse this approach argue that welfare states are compatible with globalization. In fact, countries that have the highest tax rates, a high unionization rate, and a highly interventionist state manage better, in relative terms, than countries that have destructured their welfare state the most since the 1980s (Paquin, 2014).

For transformationists, empirical data does not confirm the hypotheses of the retreat of the state in economic and social spheres, hypotheses that are largely accepted in the public discourse and in a large part of academic research (Hay, 2008). While globalization and increased global competition are very real and well-documented phenomena, their presumed effects on the retreat of the state in developed countries are greatly exaggerated (Krugman, 1996). Authors who claim that globalization announced the end of the welfare state and even of social democracy often neglect to identify the mechanisms by which globalization affects a state's capability and, in so doing, they exaggerate its effects (Paquin 2011, 2008). A number of hypotheses derived from the deductive logic on the retreat of the state in the face of globalization are quite simply not empirically tested and, most of the time, are based on prejudgments.

Furthermore, many authors maintain that the welfare state and social democracy in the case of the Nordic countries are products of globalization rather than being threatened by it. This thesis, that openness to international trade promotes the construction of the welfare state and of social democracy, is not new or even recent. In 1978, David Cameron established that the best predictor of the increase in the ratio of tax revenues to GDP of OECD-member countries (in 1960 and 1975) was the degree of openness to the global economy—the correlation coefficient was 0.78 (Cameron, 1978). Cameron therefore claimed that economies that are open to international trade tend to have a higher degree of industrial concentration, which favours larger unions. Cameron's thesis goes even further. In his study, the openness of economies to international trade is also correlated to the presence of social democratic governments, with high unionization levels as well as strong labour market regulations. The author's theory is that, in a context of growing international openness, unions put pressure on social democratic parties to set up generous welfare states in order to limit the risk represented by the increased exposure to the global economy. Thus, in these countries, the ratio of public expenditures to GDP is higher than elsewhere because it serves chiefly to reduce the risks of external shocks. Since 1978, this correlation has been validated and built upon by several other researchers (Hay and Wincott, 2012; Hay, 2008; Garrett, 1998; Rodrik, 1998a, 1998b; Bates, Brock, and Tiefenthaler, 1991).

In 1985, for example, Peter Katzenstein argued that "small states" in Europe with open economies had developed corporatist institutions that facilitated economic adjustments and cooperation between capital and labour, notably wage restraint in exchange for a substantial welfare state to protect workers from external shocks. The consequence is that small democratic states in Europe (with the exception of Switzerland) have larger welfare states and economies that are more open to international trade. The explanation for this situation is found in the corporatist institutions that go back to the 1930s and 1940s (Katzenstein, 1985).

Dani Rodrik of Harvard University believes this situation arose because the welfare state was intended to reduce the risks and inequalities inherent to market economies, notably those most open to trade. It is not surprising therefore that the role of domestic governments grew considerably during the postwar period in parallel with the expansion of international trade. It is also not surprising to find that the countries most open to trade (such as Denmark, the Netherlands, and Sweden) saw the most rapid development of the welfare state (Rodrik, 1998a: 557). For Colin Hay, welfare state growth is supported by the marked increase in exports because domestic firms that are present on international markets experience rapid growth, offer good jobs, and pay high taxes, like their employees, which has a very positive effect on state revenues (2008).

According to John Ruggie, this trade-off is the basis of the Keynesian compromise. Ruggie believed that the economic order that emerged after the war was different from those that preceded the war. The distinction between the pre- and post-war orders lay in the adoption of multilateralism and of what is called embedded liberalism. This term refers to the Keynesian compromise established by governments after 1945 that aimed to restore trade and international investments while at the same time safeguarding political and national social goals—by allowing policies favourable to full employment and to state intervention in general. The Keynesian compromise of the liberal international economic order is based on the idea that countries accept the principle of trade liberalization at the international level, while allowing themselves to temporarily withdraw from their international commitments if the opening of international trade endangers a fundamental goal of their domestic politics. The international economic order introduced after 1945 thus recognized the legitimacy of state intervention as a basic principle and set out to protect states' right to maintain social cohesion (Ruggie, 1983).

According to Nathan M. Jensen, there is very little empirical proof supporting the idea that high taxation levels or other forms of fiscal policies significantly affect the foreign direct investments (FDI) that a country receives (Jensen, 2008: xii). He writes,

> There is very little empirical support for claims that taxes or other forms of government fiscal policy seriously affect FDI inflows. Levels of corporate taxation and government spending have almost no impact on FDI flows. Governments that maintain higher levels of government spending and corporate taxation are not punished by international financial markets. (2008: xii; see also Jensen, 2013)

Duane Swank shares this opinion: "contrary to the claims of the international capital mobility thesis . . . the general fiscal capacity of democratic governments to fund a variety of levels and mixes of social protection and services may be relatively resilient in the face of internationalisation of markets" (2002: 276).

The race-to-the-bottom thesis is also a myth according to transformationists. For them, the taxation level of large firms has not significantly decreased in the last 40 years (Drezner, 2010). Even though the recent trend indicates a slight decrease in direct taxes on firms that seems to confirm the race-to-the-bottom thesis, the overall tax burden of firms has, in fact, increased slightly since the mid-1980s (Hay, 2008; Steinmo, 2003; Heichel, Pape, and Sommerer, 2005; Garrett and Mitchell, 2001).

In addition, empirical evidence does not confirm the hypothesis of the neoliberal convergence and the race to the bottom, but instead shows the persistence and even the greater differentiation of capitalism models (Hay and Wincott, 2012; Sapir, 2005; Amable, 2003; Hall and Soskice, 2001). Since the mid-1990s, IPE theorists have been rediscovering the variety of capitalism models. Although the constraints imposed by globalization are important, states' responses to these constraints are very different. Linda Weiss believes, for example, that states' reform strategies are the source of the competitive advantages of nations (1999). Some of the most prosperous economies require significant state intervention. The variety of capitalism models leads to different responses to globalization and, in this context, states play a fundamental role in the creation of wealth.

The American research program on the varieties of capitalism was launched by Peter Hall and David Soskice (2001). Their line of argument is similar to that of France's Michel Albert. Hall and Soskice's varieties of capitalism approach is focused on the major industrial groups and draws a distinction between the capitalism of liberal economies, such as Great Britain and the United States, and the capitalism of coordinated economies such as Germany. American and British firms are shaped by the particular practices of their environment. Their capital derives from the capital-risk market in the start-up phase and then from the stock markets. One of the important effects of this is that the firms tend to concentrate on short-term returns while the relationships between firms tend to be competitive and contractual. The relationships between the workers and the holders of capital depend on market conditions. Professional training is the responsibility of government, individuals, and universities—not of firms. Competencies are secured by hiring new employees and not by providing professional development or retraining. This leads to troubled and more conflicted labour relations. Unionism is discouraged and labour relations are as decentralized as possible. The state promotes the liberal economy and defines the legislative framework that gives a great deal of power to firms over unions. Jobs tend to be less protected and more precarious. These characteristics of the capitalism of liberal market economies enable firms to be more reactive to the transformations of the economy and more competitive in sectors where innovation is the key to developing new markets. This model of capitalism also has many firms in low value-added industries because workers are generally low skilled, poorly trained, and underpaid. These firms are very vulnerable to offshoring.

In countries with coordinated market economies, large firms are less exposed to pressures from financial markets because among the holders of capital there is a higher concentration of share ownership by strategic actors that have developed long-term strategies of return on investment. Shareholders have less influence over corporate strategies. Negotiation between social partners, long-term relationships, and similar diverse mechanisms unconnected to market forces make it possible to resolve key problems. Hall and Soskice claim that firms from these economies have very different strengths and weaknesses. The large German industrial groups are formed in a particular environment where institutions give the labour force an important role in firm management. Wages are relatively higher and employment is more stable over the long term. Consequently, the quality of the relationship between workers and holders of capital is fundamental in the strategy and the development of large industrial groups. Emphasis is also placed on solid professional training, with teaching institutions and firms being urged to cooperate to create a qualified labour force. In this model, the state encourages collaborations between firms and between workers and management. This model of capitalism more easily produces firms in the high value-added advanced engineering sectors that are based on long-term investments and in which workers become highly specialized.

The consequence of the varieties of capitalism approach is that two firms in the same sector, an American and a German, will tend to organize according to different logics due to the institutional constraints of the capitalism models. Hall and Soskice conclude that firms from a variety of capitalism models will not react in the same way to globalization because the institutions present in the various countries do not elicit the same types of behaviour. According to the authors, when firms coming from different contexts enter into competition in the IPE, their behaviour is largely determined by their specific model of capitalism. For example, a German firm in the pharmaceutical industry excels in manufacturing but not in basic research, and because the state heavily regulates biotechnology research, large German firms will move their laboratory to the United States and will have access, in this way, to resources they are lacking in their country. Thus, according to the Hall and Soskice model, globalization, far from creating a neoliberal convergence, strengthens national differences. The historical trajectories of German firms will not follow the same path as those of large American groups. As the large German and American groups must specialize in the area of their strength, globalization will increase divergences. This is the opposite of the convergence hypothesis.

Another example: in countries with coordinated market economies, firms obtain the majority of their resources from their relations with their employees, with bankers, and with the government. Because these resources are not found outside the national territory, these firms are more reluctant to move production abroad. When they do, they tend to create fundamentally different organizations. In Japan, Toyota, for example, offers promotion only to managers who have succeeded in climbing to the top of the corporate ladder. In the United States, this same firm recruits its managers in the marketplace. American firms have worked this way for a long time. In American firms, ties with the institutions in their country are not as strong, which facilitates movement abroad. A number of authors now subscribe to the varieties of capitalism approach.

Ideas

The analyses that focus on the interests of actors clearly possess a strong heuristic value. However, several authors believe that an explanation based solely on interests is incomplete, as interests are neither mechanical nor predetermined. They are shaped by ideas, beliefs, norms, and identity of what IPE is and by the actors' representation of themselves. How actors conceive of their interests necessarily passes through the filter of ideas.

In orthodox IPE, constructivism, a term coined by Nicholas Onuf (1989) and legitimized through the works of John Ruggie (1983), Alexander Wendt (1992, 1999), and Peter Katzenstein (1996), has not had the same effect as it had in international relations theory (as we will see, this is much less true for the heterodox school, notably the neo-Gramscian approach). The constructivist approach in IPE remains relatively marginal. According to Benjamin Cohen, "the debate has barely even begun" (2008: 134). Certain authors or works should nevertheless be mentioned.

In international relations theory, constructivists acknowledge that social reality is socially constructed. As Emanuel Adler points out, "The material world does not come classified. . . . Therefore, the objects of our knowledge are not independent of our interpretation and our language" (2002: 95). In other words, the fact that a political actor has interests does not inform us about the actor's choices. For authors who are interested in the role of ideas, there is no predetermined logic. Final decisions are made after the variable of ideas has intervened, either through a cost-benefit analysis or through a necessarily subjective evaluation of the various scenarios. Ideas have a central role in determining the interests that are then channelled by institutions. Ideas are determinants of the identity of the actors and of their interests.

Ideas and the processes of the social construction of ideas are therefore critical. Keynes wrote, "Practical men . . . are usually the slaves [of the ideas] of some defunct economist" (1936: 383). Keynes was only half right. Ideas favourable to excessive liberalization of the financial sector were thought out by economists, a good number of whom are still living. As Rodrik argues, after the 2008 crisis, many analysts accused the large investment banks such as Goldman Sachs of having too much power over politicians (Rodrik, 2012). These financial institutions exerted far too much influence in Washington. This argument is certainly accurate, but it forgets the fundamental role of the epistemic community in regards to the liberalization of finance. The ideas of some very influential economists from a handful of very large American universities had the effect of legitimizing these financial liberalization policies. It was economists and their ideas that permitted US politicians and senior public servants to think that what is good for Goldman Sachs is also good for the United States.

Peter M. Haas is the author most cited on the influence of "epistemic communities." An epistemic community is a channel through which new ideas circulate from society towards government decision makers, as well as from one country to another (Haas, 1992: 27). An epistemic community is a network of professionals who have authority over certain public policy issues pertaining to their field of expertise. The members of an epistemic community share a set of beliefs about the causes of a phenomenon, about the evaluation criteria, the norms, and the public policies to implement.

For Haas, the dominant ideas, such as Keynesianism in the 1960s, are important determinants in the choice of a policy as well as in the explanation of a policy's persistence. With the creation of the United Nations system, after the Second World War, these epistemic communities were increasingly solicited and became increasingly influential on the international scene. The more technical an issue is, the smaller the epistemic community and the greater the influence of its members.

Haas was able to demonstrate that the presence of an epistemic community in the decision-making process of a country altered a public policy. He gives the example of donor countries that ceased to provide direct food relief because the economists specializing in that issue claimed that this type of policy hindered the development of local production and kept recipient countries in a dependent situation. North African governments also changed their policy towards pollution after they created departments of the environment that employed scientists specializing in these issues.

Other authors, such as Judith Goldstein and Robert Keohane, emphasize the role of ideas in domestic politics in the formulation of foreign policy. They look specifically at how ideas influence the behaviour of states and decision makers. According to Goldstein,

> In most cases, policy makers have incomplete information about their environment and thus must rely on causal models in making policy choices. Here ideas are like road maps, linking policies to a constellation of interests. But ideas also serve other purposes. Even when political entrepreneurs understand the effects of changes in market forces, they still depend on ideas about how to translate these forces into a political and economic program. It is not markets but ideas that establish the rules of the game, that demarcate for policy makers the proper form of new programs, that privilege particular constituencies. (1993: xii)

For Goldstein, ideas are also embedded in institutions, which means that a decision taken at a given moment in a particular context may persist even if the dominant ideas and interests have changed. For example, in the 1930s, the United States opted for an interventionist state in the agricultural industry with a large number of protectionist measures. In the same period, state interventionism in the manufacturing sector failed due largely to decisions rendered by the Supreme Court. This dual situation was institutionalized or entrenched in American legislatures and it was reflected in the US government's economic foreign policy after the Second World War. The US government had agriculture excluded from the GATT despite the fact the US agricultural industry was one of the most productive in the world after 1945 (Goldstein and Keohane, 1993).

Policy choice is also influenced by the popularity of a paradigm. Peter A. Hall (1993) examined the roles of paradigms in public policies and more particularly, paradigm changes. He convincingly explains the passage from the Keynesian paradigm to the neoliberal paradigm using Great Britain as his example. In industrialized countries, the economic turbulence of the 1970s linked to the globalization of the economy and to the appearance of stagflation invalidated the Keynesian paradigm that was no longer able to anticipate the coming changes. Keynesian-inspired economic policies began to be called into question. The erroneous predictions of the specialists resulted in the failure of the macroeconomic public policies of the British government.

The British government then reacted by introducing one-off measures, adjusting Keynesian practices, and, playing in the margins of economic theory, experimenting with new formulas. All were unsuccessful. Hence, Keynesian-inspired policies lost their credibility and their legitimacy among politicians and citizens. Unemployment set in, market sluggishness spread, everyone wanted to escape the crisis, even at the cost of radical solutions. It was then that monetarism and neoliberalism appeared as alternatives to the Keynesian paradigm.

To explain the change, Hall drew on the social learning concept in public policies. This concept has been used in public policy theories since the 1960s, but it is central in several works using the cognitive approach to public policies (Hugh Heclo, Paul Sabatier, and Pierre Muller in particular). The usefulness of the social learning concept is that it allows one to circumvent the approaches that explain public policies based solely on power relationships between actors.

The social learning concept enabled Hall to show that governments change their course of action, their instruments, or even their public policy paradigm because they learn from their mistakes. Paradigm or instruments may change because new ideas have emerged, such as monetarism for example, or because certain policies have shown their ineffectiveness (such as Keynesianism in Great Britain in the 1970s).

According to Hall, there are three levels of change: the first concerns only the level of use of an instrument, the second occurs when other instruments are used, and the third occurs when there is a paradigm change. This is what happened in Great Britain in the 1970s and 1980s, says Hall.

According to him, the changes of the first and second order can be explained chiefly by the concept of social learning as these types of changes are in the domain of specialists and experts, while the third order change, the policy change, came after Margaret Thatcher's rise to power. This policy change was supported by the press and by monetarist thinkers. In the third order case, social learning is not the only factor at play: partisan fights and new actors also had an impact (Hall, 1993). Hall's model is often used to explain the neoliberal turn of the 1970s and 1980s (Blyth, 2003).

Conclusion

The domestic politics and OEP paradigms are traditionally more compatible with the liberal paradigm than with the realist paradigm in IPE. The debates in American IPE oppose systemic approaches, notably the neorealist and neoliberal approaches, and the domestic politics approaches that place more importance on domestic factors and national institutions. That said, constructivist works in international relations theory are beginning to make their appearance in IPE theory, even though they are still very much on the fringes.

The research on domestic institutions still requires considerable work. Very few analyses have focused on federalism, political parties, courts, bureaucracies, or public administrations. The domestic politics paradigm has not yet found its Graham Allison. Most of the analyses have to do with the effects of globalization on public policies and on trade issues while financial and environmental issues are still largely neglected.

Questions

1. What are the three images in IPE and what is the second image reversed?
2. What is Open Economy Politics?
3. What does an "interests"-based analysis in IPE mean?
4. How do "domestic structures" influence international policy according to Peter Katzenstein?
5. How do institutions impact trade policies?
6. What is the "two-level game" metaphor?
7. What is the declinist point of view regarding the effects of globalization on the welfare state?
8. What is the transformationist response to the declinist point of view?
9. Why has constructivism remained relatively marginal in orthodox IPE?
10. Why is the domestic politics approach more compatible with the liberal paradigm?

Further Reading

For a summary of the discussions on the domestic policy paradigm:

Frieden, Jeffry A., and Lisa L. Martin. "International Political Economy: Global and Domestic Interactions." In *Political Science: State of the Discipline*, edited by Ira Katznelson and Helen V. Milner, 118–46. New York: W.W. Norton & Company, 2002.

Gourevitch, Peter. "The Second Image Reversed: The International Sources of Domestic Politics." *International Organization* 32.4 (1978): 881–912.

For interest-based approaches:

Frieden, Jeffry A. "Invested Interests: The Politics of National Economic Policies in a World of Global Finance." *International Organization* 45.4 (1991): 425–51.

Milner, Helen V. *Resisting Protectionism: Global Industries and the Politics of International Trade*. Princeton: Princeton University Press, 1988.

Rogowski, Ronald. "Political Cleavages and Changing Exposure to Trade." *American Political Science Review* 81.4 (1987): 1121–37.

Rogowski, Ronald. *Commerce and Coalitions: How Trade Affects Domestic Political Alignments*. Princeton: Princeton University Press, 1989.

For institution-based approaches:

Katzenstein, Peter J. "International Relations and Domestic Structures: Foreign Economic Policies of Advanced Industrial States." *International Organization* 30.1 (1976): 1–45.

Katzenstein, Peter J., ed. *Between Power and Plenty: Foreign Economic Policies in Advanced Industrial States*. Madison: University of Wisconsin Press, 1978.

Katzenstein, Peter J. *Small States in World Markets: Industrial Policy in Europe*. Ithaca, NY: Cornell University Press, 1985.

Krasner, Stephen D. *Defending the National Interest: Raw Materials Investments and U.S. Foreign Policy*. Princeton: Princeton University Press, 1978.

Krasner, Stephen D. "United States Commercial and Monetary Policy: Unraveling the Paradox of External Strength and Internal Weakness." In *Between Power and Plenty: Foreign Economic Policies in Advanced Industrial States*, edited by Peter J. Katzenstein, 51–87. Madison: University of Wisconsin Press, 1978.

Martin, Lisa L. *Democratic Commitments: Legislatures and International Cooperation*. Princeton: Princeton University Press, 2000.

Putnam, Robert. "Diplomacy and Domestic Politics: The Logic of Two-Level Games." *International Organization* 42.3 (1988): 427–60.

Rogowski, Ronald. "Trade and the Variety of Democratic Institutions." *International Organizations* 41.2 (1987): 202–23.

Rogowski, Ronald. "Institutions as Constraints on Strategic Choice." In *Strategic Choice and International Relations*, edited by David A. Lake and Robert Powell, 112–36. Princeton: Princeton University Press, 1999.

Debates about globalization impact on states:

Garrett, Geoffrey. "Capital Mobility, Trade and the Domestic Politics of Economic Policy." *International Organization* 49.4 (1995): 657–87

Garrett, Geoffrey. "Shrinking States? Globalization and National Autonomy in the OECD." *Oxford Development Studies* 26.1 (1998): 453–78.

Hall, Peter, and David Soskice, eds. *Varieties of Capitalism: The Institutional Foundations of Comparative Advantage*. New York: Oxford University Press, 2001.

Jensen, Nathan M. *Nation-States and the Multinational Corporation: A Political Economy of Foreign Direct Investment*. Princeton: Princeton University Press, 2008.

Swank, Duane. *Global Capital, Political Institutions and Policy Change in Developed Welfare States*. Cambridge: Cambridge University Press, 2002.

Swank, Duane. "Tax Policy in an Era of Internationalization: Explaining the Spread of Neoliberalism." *International Organization* 60.4 (2006): 847–82.

For idea-based approaches:

Abdelal, Rawi, Mark Blyth, and Craig Parsons, eds. *Constructing the International Economy.* New York: Cornell University Press, 2010.

Blyth, Mark. *Great Transformation: Economic Ideas and Institutional Change in the Twentieth Century.* Cambridge: Cambridge University Press, 2003.

Goldstein, Judith L., and Robert O. Keohane, eds. *Ideas and Foreign Policy: Beliefs, Institutions, and Political Change.* Ithaca, NY: Cornell University Press, 1993.

Goldstein, Judith L. "The Impact of Ideas on Trade Policy: The Origins of U.S. Agricultural and Manufacturing Policies." *International Organization* 43.1 (1989): 31–71.

Haas, Peter M. "Introduction: Epistemic Communities and International Policy Coordination." *International Organization* 46.1 (1992): 1–35.

Hall, Peter A. "The Movement from Keynesianism to Monetarism: Institutional Analysis and British Economic Policy in the 1970s." In *Structuring Politics: Historical Institutionalism in Comparative Analysis*, edited by Sven Steinmo, Kathleen Thelen, and Frank Longstreth, 90–113. New York: Cambridge University Press, 1992.

6 From Marxism to Neo-Gramscianism

Chapter Contents

- Marxist Approaches in IPE
- Dependency Theory
- The World-System Approach
- The Neo-Gramscian School
- Robert Cox
- The Rediscovery of Gramsci
- The Structural Power of Capital
- The Politics of Mass Production
- Conclusion

Reader's Guide

The neo-Gramscian school and the British school mainly developed outside of and in opposition to the dominant paradigms in orthodox IPE presented in the previous chapters. Where the neo-Gramscian school and the British school differ is in the greater affiliation between the neo-Gramscian works of Robert Cox and his successors and the Marxist and neo-Marxist approaches. Marxism in IPE comprises a large assortment of theoretical perspectives that range from the dependency school to Immanuel Wallerstein's world-system approach. The neo-Gramscian approach, originally theorized by Robert Cox, is a perspective in IPE that focuses on change in historical processes, social structures, and social dynamics to understand world order and IPE. Fundamentally nondeterminist, this approach concentrates on the historical conditions for the emergence of a particular social order within a country and on its effects on world order. Contrary to the problem-solving theories that Cox identifies with orthodox theorists, the neo-Gramscian approach has an explicit normative aim. The neo-Gramscians' greatest contribution to the debates in IPE is their concept of hegemony, which they see as a form of structural power based not just on military strength and possession of the means of production, but also on ideas and civil society. Hegemony becomes an intersubjective process.

The neo-Gramscian school and the British school (see Chapter 7) mainly developed outside of and in opposition to the dominant paradigms in orthodox IPE presented in the previous chapters. The works of the neo-Gramscian and British schools share several points in common: they are very critical of the works produced by orthodox IPE and of the American obsession with quantitative methods and formal modelling. The two schools are post-positivist. Both of these schools have a compatible conception of globalization, both believe that production structures are essential to building the international political economy, and the authors in both perspectives have shaped structural or holistic conceptions of power. Moreover, these schools are not in opposition to one another, as is the case of the realist and liberal perspectives in orthodox IPE. The two schools even nourish each other, with citations from either perspective frequently being used by both schools.

Where the neo-Gramscian school and the British school differ is in the greater affiliation between the neo-Gramscian works of Robert Cox and his successors and the Marxist and neo-Marxist approaches. The neo-Gramscian school is in fact very often associated with Marxian approaches, which is only marginally the case for Susan Strange and the British school, even though the Marxist influence in the British school is an accepted and undeniable truth. As Marxism had a huge influence in IPE debates of the 1970s and 1980s and its influence is quite clear in the works of the neo-Gramscian school, this chapter will first provide a brief sketch of Marxist theory in IPE and then look more closely at the neo-Gramscian school. Marxism in IPE comprises a large assortment of theoretical perspectives that range from the dependency school to Immanuel Wallerstein's world-system approach.

Marxist Approaches in IPE

Long before the end of the 1980s and the collapse of the communist bloc, Marxism had suffered a significant loss of influence in IPE. As explained earlier, this paradigm had declined sharply in the United States. Since the 1990s, less than 10 per cent of the articles published in the 12 leading scientific journals fit the Marxist paradigm. In 2008, the TRIP project revealed that American researchers in international relations believed that Marxism was less important than the feminist perspective or the British school.

The decline of Marxism in IPE occurred before the fall of the USSR. Part of the explanation lies in the transformations on the international scene. Soviet diplomacy, for example, drew more from the realist paradigm than from the Marxist, and the end of import substitution strategies in Latin American countries hastened the decline of Marxism as an economic doctrine such that today, almost no country adheres to this once powerful ideology.

Another part of the explanation for the decline of Marxism is found within the epistemic community. David Lake suggests, for example, that Marxist analyses never succeeded in developing a robust and unified theory, contrary to the neoclassical economic theories on growth and underdevelopment. He also points out that Marxist theories were largely contradicted by the facts, whether in regards to international trade flows, development aid, foreign direct investment, or the causes of underdevelopment in the South and other issues that Marxists tried to explain (Lake, 2008: 760). It is very clearly a *degenerative* research program. Recently, however, notably following the financial crisis of 2008, the rise of the 1 per cent and the Occupy Wall Street movement, we are seeing a return of Marxist-inspired criticisms of capitalism and globalization.

In this discussion of Marxism, our focus will be less on the foreign policy of countries that endorse this ideology than about Marxist theory of world politics. These theorists concentrate their reflection on North–South economic relations rather than on relations between the major powers.

The very basic assumptions of Marxism are the following: the capitalist economy is based on two antagonistic social classes—the bourgeoisie and the proletariat. Marxists conceive of the economy as a place of exploitation and inequalities between the different social classes. They maintain that economic and political issues are interrelated, and that the economy structures or biases political relations in favour of the bourgeoisie. The bourgeoisie own the means of production while the proletariat have the labour power that they must sell to the bourgeoisie. As proletarians do more work than they are paid for in wages, the bourgeoisie appropriate this added value for themselves. In short, the profit of capitalism is derived from the exploitation of the proletariat by the bourgeoisie. Hence, contrary to liberal authors, Marxist authors are pessimistic about social progress. The economy is a negative-sum game, a game of exploitation of the poor by the rich.

Even though capitalism is based on the exploitation of the proletariat by the bourgeoisie, Marx did not see the growth of capitalism as exclusively negative or regressive. He even believed capitalism was synonymous with a certain advancement in society. In its first phase, capitalism destroyed the previous production relationship—feudalism—that had exploited peasants even more by keeping them in conditions comparable to slavery. In that case, capitalism was an improvement, because proletarians were now free to sell their labour power to the highest bidder. Marx also believed that Western expansionism was a necessary phenomenon because it allowed pre-capitalist societies to achieve a form of modernity. This spread of modernity was the essential condition for the worldwide diffusion of capitalism and subsequently of the socialist revolution.

For Marx, the evolution of capitalism paves the way for the socialist revolution in which the means of production are socialized and placed under the control of the proletariat, who make up the majority of the population. That is Marxism's revolutionary goal. The purpose of the Marxist project is the overthrow of the bourgeoisie by the proletariat. Most more contemporary authors have distanced themselves from this historical determinism found in Marx's writings. The Marxist conception of the world is materialist, which means that it is based on the idea that the central activity of any society is economic production. Economic production is the basis of all other human activities including politics. As the bourgeoisie dominate by their control of the means of production, they also control the political sphere, since the economy structures the politics.

In IPE, Marxian authors carry over these basic Marxist assumptions into their analyses of international political economy. For these authors, states are not independent and rational actors in international relations. Rather, the fundamental actors in international relations are social classes and it is the dominant class that controls the political sphere and, therefore, states. States produce policies that reflect the interests of the local bourgeoisie. Political relations between states, including wars, must therefore be understood in the larger context of a competition between the economic interests of the bourgeoisie of different countries.

Furthermore, the fundamental nature of capitalism is expansive. The history of capitalism is that of an expansion towards more markets and profits. With the expansion of capitalism, antagonism between the classes likewise spreads around the world. Imperialism and colonization are also the products of this expansion of capitalism and of this exploitation of the proletariat by the bourgeoisie. Even after colonies gain their independence, economic exploitation continues by other means.

It was Lenin who best theorized imperialism from the Marxist perspective. In his book *Imperialism, the Highest Stage of Capitalism*, published in 1917, he argued that in developed countries, capitalism destroys free competition. In capitalist societies, industrial and then banking monopolies are created. After that, the financial oligarchy exports its capital abroad to underdeveloped countries where high profits are still possible. Simultaneously, imperialist states wage war to annex colonies where they dominate national oligarchs. For Lenin, imperialism is the oligopolistic stage of capitalism. In his "law of uneven development," Lenin asserted that the expansion of capitalism is necessarily uneven between countries, as well as between industries and enterprises. Great Britain outpaced Germany throughout the nineteenth century. In consequence, Great Britain had a vast colonial empire while Germany had only a very small one. With the decline of Great Britain in the early twentieth century, Germany hoped for a redistribution of the spheres of influence that would reflect its status as a rising power. This new German ambition would lead to growing rivalries with the British Empire. The highest stage of capitalism is therefore monopolistic imperialism that gives rise to aggressive foreign policies and war. The history of Marxist-inspired IPE hence consists in the study of the expansion of capitalism around the world and the new means of exploitation.

> ⠐ **Box 6.1** ⠂   **The Expansive Logic of Capitalism According to Marx and Engels in the Manifesto of the Communist Party of 1848**
>
> The need of a constantly expanding market for its products chases the bourgeoisie over the entire surface of the globe. It must nestle everywhere, settle everywhere, establish connections everywhere.
>
> The bourgeoisie has through its exploitation of the world market given a cosmopolitan character to production and consumption in every country. To the great chagrin of Reactionists, it has drawn from under the feet of industry the national ground on which it stood. All old-established national industries have been destroyed or are daily being destroyed. They are dislodged by new industries, whose introduction becomes a life and death question for all civilized nations, by industries that no longer work up indigenous raw material, but raw material drawn from the remotest zones; industries whose products are consumed, not only at home, but in every quarter of the globe. In place of the old wants, satisfied by the production of the country, we find new wants, requiring for their satisfaction the products of distant lands and climes. In place of the old local and national seclusion and self-sufficiency, we have intercourse in every direction, universal interdependence of nations. And as in material, so also in intellectual production. The intellectual creations of individual nations become common property. National one-sidedness and narrow-mindedness become more and more impossible, and from the numerous national and local literatures, there arises a world literature.

Dependency Theory

Among the neo-Marxian works that have had the most impact on the research community, dependency theory has made a noteworthy contribution, and it has had a considerable influence in the development of IPE.

Dependency theory, which was so influential in the 1960s and 1970s, was developed by Latin American authors and specialists. Dependency theorists reject the optimism of liberals and of theorists of modernization or political development, asserting that industrialized countries prevent third world countries from developing by keeping them in a relationship of dependency.

Drawing on Marxism and Latin American economic structuralism, dependency specialists focus exclusively on North–South relations. There is a great variety of works and theses related to dependency theory. The works of André Gunder Frank and, a little before him, Raúl Prebisch quickly gained

The bourgeoisie, by the rapid improvement of all instruments of produc-tion, by the immensely facilitated means of communication, draws all, even the most barbarian, nations into civilisation. The cheap prices of commodities are the heavy artillery with which it batters down all Chinese walls, with which it forces the barbarians' intensely obstinate hatred of foreigners to capitulate. It compels all nations, on pain of extinction, to adopt the bourgeois mode of production; it compels them to introduce what it calls civilisation into their midst, i.e., to become bourgeois themselves. In one word, it creates a world after its own image.

The bourgeoisie has subjected the country to the rule of the towns. It has created enormous cities, has greatly increased the urban population as compared with the rural, and has thus rescued a considerable part of the population from the idiocy of rural life. Just as it has made the country dependent on the towns, so it has made barbarian and semi-barbarian countries dependent on the civilised ones, nations of peasants on nations of bourgeois, the East on the West.

The bourgeoisie keeps more and more doing away with the scattered state of the population, of the means of production, and of property. It has agglomerated population, centralised the means of production, and has con-centrated property in a few hands. The necessary consequence of this was political centralisation. Independent, or but loosely connected provinces, with separate interests, laws, governments, and systems of taxation, became lumped together into one nation, with one government, one code of laws, one national class-interest, one frontier, and one customs-tariff. (Marx and Engels, 1848: 16)

influence in Marxist groups, particularly in the United States and Europe. Later, the work of Fernando Henrique Cardoso and Enzo Faletto (1979) established itself as the essential reference. The approach of these latter authors is less doctrinarian and radical.

Dependency theorists dispute the liberal theorists' claim that the economic problems of developing countries are the result of ineffective do-mestic policies, and that greater North–South interdependence would foster the development of these less advanced countries. Instead, dependency the-orists assert that external factors are responsible for this dependency. The key concepts of dependency theory are: core, periphery, and dependency. The dependency of developing countries extends from the area of trade to the financial, technological, and social areas. That said, there are some dif-ferences among the authors who espouse dependency theory. André Gunder Frank believed that countries are not only "dependent," they were inten-tionally "underdeveloped" (1966). Fernando Henrique Cardoso and Enzo

Faletto focused their attention on international and local variables like class struggle (1979). In general, most dependency theorists agree that the elite of developing countries align themselves with the preferences of the elite of developed countries and contribute to maintaining the world capitalist order so as to preserve their own social status. Local elites thus act in support of the interests of the bourgeoisie of developed countries and strengthen the dependency of undeveloped countries.

The political prescription for ending this dependency is to break with the global capitalist economy, as the dependency relationship is part of the structure of the system that seeks to reproduce itself. The dependency school eventually freed itself from proletarian internationalism, adopting a more affirmed nationalism and supporting import substitution policies. These approaches are largely obsolete nowadays.

The World-System Approach

Another author who has had a lot of influence through his redefinition of Marxism is Immanuel Wallerstein. Wallerstein's original approach was to combine elements of Marxist analysis with the *longue durée* (long-term) approach of historian Fernand Braudel to build on Braudel's world-system concept. A world-system does not mean it encompasses the whole world; more precisely, it is a particular form of political and economic structure. A world-system is defined as a unit with a single division of labour and multiple cultural systems (Wallerstein, 1976: 5). World-systems unite the economic and the political in a certain dependency relationship. Over the course of history, two varieties of world-systems have coexisted. The first system consists of world empires, such as the Roman Empire, in which the political and the economic are controlled from a unified centre. The second system is represented by world economies that are linked economically by a single international division of labour, but where the political authority remains decentralized at the national level of each state. Wallerstein's analysis is based on the modern world-economy characterized by capitalism (Wallerstein, 1976, 2004).

For Wallerstein, the world-economy developed throughout the "long" sixteenth century (1450 to 1640) and was based on an international division of labour that covered Europe in a first phase, then spread throughout the Western world and finally to certain other parts of the world (Wallerstein, 2000). From this division of labour came a capitalist world-economy built on a hierarchy of cores, semi-peripheries, and peripheries. Core countries specialize in complex and advanced activities such as mass industry and sophisticated agriculture. These activities are controlled by the local bourgeoisie. Periphery countries create simple products such as grains, wood, sugar, and so on. The labour force is often made up of slaves or exploited workers. When a periphery has a manufacturing base, it is generally under the control of the capitalist bourgeoisie of the core country. Semi-periphery countries are a hybrid of the two.

In this system, exchanges are necessarily unequal: the surpluses of the peripheries are transferred towards the core. This transfer of wealth is accentuated by the fact that the developed states of the core possess institutional structures capable of imposing such a system of exploitation while developing states do not have this possibility.

Wallerstein argues therefore that the capitalist economy is the main unit of analysis of the international political economy, and that states are not independent actors but are determined largely by their positioning in the world-economy. Even before the collapse of the Soviet Union, Wallerstein did not believe that socialism could exist in a capitalist world-economy. According to the author, there is currently no socialist system in the world-economy, nor are there any feudal systems because there is *one* world-system. It is a world-economy that is by definition capitalist (Wallerstein, 1976: 35).

This unequal exchange system naturally creates tensions in the system. These tensions are eased thanks to the presence at the core of a powerful hegemony that, supported by its military and economic superiority, imposes norms and institutions that regulate international relationships for the benefit of the core. The Netherlands was the hegemonic power of the seventeenth century, Great Britain held that power in the nineteenth century, and the United States was the twentieth century's hegemonic power.

The semi-peripheries are also important because they provide the system with relative stability; core countries do not exploit a unified front. The semi-peripheries serve as a buffer zone. Furthermore, the system envisaged by Wallerstein is not static: peripheries may transform into semi-peripheries and semi-peripheries into the core and vice versa. The goods and services that are exchanged in the world-economy can also change. At one point in history, it was textiles, then industrial machinery, and nowadays it is new information of technologies, biotechnologies, and financial services. But for Wallerstein, the nature of the system remains fundamentally intact, with a hierarchy of cores, semi-peripheries, and peripheries that interact in an unequal exchange system.

Other authors, such as Christopher Chase-Dunn, are followers of the world-system approach. Samir Amin and André Gunder Frank include certain elements of Wallerstein's approach in their works on dependency. However, this research paradigm is losing popularity.

The Neo-Gramscian School

The neo-Gramscian approach, originally theorized by Robert Cox, is a perspective in IPE that focuses on change in historical processes, social structures, and social dynamics to understand world order and IPE. Fundamentally nondeterminist, contrary to the approaches presented above, this approach concentrates on the historical conditions for the emergence of a particular social order within a country and on its effects on world order. The basic unit of international relations is the "state/society complex" (Cox, 1981: 127). There are numerous levels of analysis designed to understand changes in the world order. The neo-Gramscian approach stresses the importance of contextualization and historical perspective. It examines material conditions but also institutions and ideas. Well before the emergence of constructivism in international relations, the neo-Gramscian approach was focusing on the importance of intersubjectivity and the social construction of ideas, because any changes in shared collective ideas lead to changes in the civil society.

Contrary to the problem-solving theories that Cox identifies with orthodox theorists, the neo-Gramscian approach has an explicit normative aim. Neo-Gramscians are critical theorists because they do not accept the world as it is. They believe that theory and practice are not separated from thought and action. Neo-Gramscian authors maintain that the realist and liberal perspectives in orthodox IPE are fundamentally conservative approaches because they ensure the reproduction of the international system. Hence, these problem-solving theories serve the interests of the powerful because they seek to preserve the status quo, including its unequal relationships.

Neo-Gramscians believe that it is essential to develop critical thinking about the historical conditions that have produced injustices and the modes of social stratifications and domination. The theory set out to understand the fundamental operating modes of the world as it is, in order to transform it into a more just and equitable world. Representatives of the neo-Gramscian school basically focus on the structural sources of the social inequalities in the international system, and they clearly express the desire to find a way to modify this system. It is precisely this emancipating and very normative orientation that discredits this approach for the orthodox in IPE, who qualify it as "unscientific."

The neo-Gramscians' greatest contribution to the debates in IPE is their concept of hegemony, which they see as a form of structural power based not just on military strength and possession of the means of production but also on ideas and civil society. Hegemony becomes an intersubjective process. The power of the dominant class is also based on its ability to gain acceptance for a social order that is favourable to the dominant class itself. In their analyses of global and local politics, neo-Gramscians place considerable importance on historical structures. This section presents the works of three authors who are closely identified with the neo-Gramscian approach, beginning with its founder, Robert Cox, and following with two of his successors: Stephen Gill and Mark Rupert.

Robert Cox

Robert Cox, a Canadian (and an English Quebecer), is considered the founding father of the neo-Gramscian school. He has had a huge influence on this perspective. In Susan Strange's review of his book *Production, Power, and World Order: Social Forces in the Making of History*, published in 1987, Strange wrote that Cox was "a loner, a fugitive from the intellectual camps of victory, both Marxist and liberal" (1988b: 269–70). Cox himself acknowledges this: in the preface of a book he co-wrote with Timothy Sinclair, Cox says that their book could have been subtitled *Apart from the Mainstream*. He writes, "The approach I have called historical dialectic has for long been outside the mainstream of social sciences, especially in America" (Cox and Sinclair, 1996: ix).

Cox was much read and cited in the 1980s and 1990s. He still figures today among the most influential authors in IPE. This is explained notably by his many works on globalization. He was the intellectual leader of a new generation of post-Marxist critical researchers. Cox's 1981 article "Social Forces, States and World Order: Beyond International Relations Theory" offered, for many, a credible alternative to the neorealist positivism that, at the time, was perceived as being at its height in the United States.

Cox was born in Montreal in 1926, the son of an English-speaking, conservative family. He developed an interest in the history of the French Canadians, who were clearly under the domination of the English in the 1940s and 1950s. He became a militant in the centre-left French Canadian nationalist political movement led by André Laurendeau. He made frequent references to Quebec and the sovereignist movement in his works. While he had some sympathy in the 1970s for the Parti Québécois, a party that promoted Quebec independence, he had difficulty accepting that party's enthusiastic support of the free trade agreement between Canada and the United States in the 1980s.

Cox earned a master's degree in history from McGill University in Montreal. He was never trained or socialized in the profession of professor or in the conventions of the international relations discipline or IPE. He became a university professor quite late in life, which probably accounts for his unconventional approach to international politics. His interest in international politics surfaced after the Second World War, in the International Labour Organization (ILO) where he worked for nearly 25 years.

Cox was deeply marked by his experience in the ILO. He believed that to survive as an institution, the ILO needed to ensure the support of the United States, especially of those in the United States who accused the structure of being infiltrated by communist agents. The ILO also had to maintain its role as an organization with a universal vocation, which, in practical terms, meant making Western bloc countries accept the presence of Eastern bloc countries as members of the institution. Lastly, it must try to maintain a reasonable degree of coherence in a bureaucratic system divided into feudal-type baronies (Cox and Sinclair, 1996). In the 1970s, Cox felt increasingly restricted in the ILO and he resigned to begin his university career at Columbia University in New York, then at York University in Toronto.

Cox, and subsequently the neo-Gramscians, share a strong, but not exclusive, inspiration in the Marxist tradition. Their works are full of Marxist-inspired language and concepts. Cox, for example, shares with the Marxist tradition the idea that production and labour are fundamental activities that condition a large spectrum of other human activities and the organization of society (Cox, 1987). Production also affects forms of state and, ultimately, world order. Production generates the material capabilities on which the state's power is built. Control of production and the power relations that it generates between social forces directly influence the state and the form it will take. Production provides the material basis for all forms of social existence, and the ways in which human efforts are combined in the productive process affect all other aspects of social life, including politics.

For Cox, production is a broad concept that includes, besides the production of material goods, the production of ideas and of intersubjective meanings, norms, institutions, and social practices. Putting production at the centre of the analysis is simply a way to think about collective life. Social structures of production represent the context in which production takes place, what kinds of things are produced, and how they are produced. Social structures of production symbolize the priorities of a society and in turn reflect the hierarchies in the social relations of that society. How things are produced exemplifies the manner in which the dominant social power organizes production (Cox, 1987: 10–11). Cox's emphasis on production is so great that several people have criticized his works, deeming them too reductionist.

Cox is therefore a historical materialist, which quite clearly links him to the Marxist tradition. He himself asks, "How is Marxism linked to this world-order method or approach?" From the outset, he admits that Marxism cuts across several currents of thought. According to Cox, there are two main currents: Marxism that reasons in historical terms and tries to explain and promote change in social relations; and Marxism as an analytic framework to study the capitalist state and society. The first approach is that of historical materialism, which Cox associates with Eric Hobsbawm and Antonio Gramsci. This approach has also influenced researchers who do not identify with Marxism, such as members of the French *Annales* school and in particular Fernand Braudel. The second is the structural Marxism approach that Cox associates with the works of Louis Althusser and Nicos Poulantzas. He maintains that this second approach has several points in common with the neorealist approach: they are both ahistorical and have an essentialist epistemology. Cox identifies with historical materialism and the historical dialectic approach, an approach that focuses on contradictions and conflicts as a guide for explanation of world politics (Cox, 1996b: 58).

Contrary to neorealists, who believe that the state is the main actor in international relations, neo-Gramscians focus not on the reified and universal state of neorealists but on the forms of state that are changing, if only slowly over time, due to pressures from below (i.e., from civil society) and from above (i.e., from the world order). Neo-Gramscians make change and social transformations a central aspect of international relations. They clearly distinguish themselves from the problem-solving approaches favourable to the status quo.

Cox analyzes world politics and political economy by introducing the concept of historical structure that is defined as "a particular configuration of forces" (Cox, 1981: 126). For Cox, a historical structure is comprised of three interacting forces: material capabilities, ideas, and institutions. In his research, he explores the interface between these three forces, and their effects on forms of state. He seeks to understand how this particular configuration of forces defines and maintains world order. He departs from traditional Marxist historical materialism by adding the forces of ideas and institutions to the force of material capabilities. When we find a relatively stable order, says Cox, we can speak of a "historical bloc." Here, he differs from structuralists, because, for him, there is no one-way determinism among these three forces (Cox, 1981). He argues that structures are the result of collective human actions and that, whilst human actions are influenced by structures, structures are also influenced by human action.

Neo-Gramscians think that revealing the historical transformations of an object is essential to understanding the world and how it works. Political institutions, for example, do not arise from the natural order of things or from the natural selection process, but rather are the consequence of human actions over time. Hence, we cannot assume, as orthodox theorists do, that states represent relatively homogeneous entities and that they behave like rational actors.

For neo-Gramscians, the researcher's job is to try to reconstruct the processes involved in producing historical structures. Researchers must also didactically determine the main contradictions of this order, as well as the moments when a qualitative break in history occurs and during which the configuration of forces is transformed. Neo-Gramscians are therefore interested in the succession of hegemonic cycles since the Industrial Revolution and have a special interest in the American hegemonic period after 1945.

The Rediscovery of Gramsci

Robert Cox has had a number of intellectual influences that are not among the usual references in the political sciences and in IPE. He acknowledges owing a special debt to several authors. From Edward Hallett Carr, who is associated with realism, Cox learned that there are important links between industrialization and changes in forms of state, in ideas, and in world order (Cox, 1996a: 127). From Georges Sorel, Cox learned that we can be influenced by Marxist analyses without swallowing the whole package. According to Cox, Sorel's view was that historical materialism had to be understood as the relationship between mentalities and material conditions of existence. Sorel rejected the determinism of various Marxist currents of thought and knew that social struggles arise from political passions that become overwhelmingly important. The concept of historical structures, which is central in Cox's work, derives from the writings of Fernand Braudel. From Giambattista Vico, Cox learned that the historicist method is the most appropriate approach to human knowledge (Cox, 1996b: 53). Finally, Cox drew even greater inspiration from the works of Antonio Gramsci and he helped introduce Gramsci's work to IPE theorists.

Cox's most important contribution to IPE theories comes from his works on American hegemony that were inspired by the analyses of Antonio Gramsci. Drawing on this Italian thinker, Cox built his theory on the idea of hegemonic control in capitalist societies to explain how the dominant ideas about the social order help to maintain that order. It is important to point out that Gramsci wrote almost nothing on international relations, but he believed that international relations grew out of social relations and not the other way around (Cox, 1996a: 133). In his works, Cox transposes Gramsci's ideas and concepts regarding domestic politics (hegemony, historic bloc, organic intellectuals, etc.) to construct and explain his own conception of world order. The neo-Gramscian approach in international relations projects Gramsci's ideas onto the international scene. It is of secondary importance here to know whether Cox does justice to Gramsci in his interpretation of Gramsci's writings (Germain and Kenny, 1998). Instead, we can judge him on the goal he set for himself. According to Cox, his works are not a critical study of Gramsci, but rather a derivation of certain useful ideas with which to revisit current theories in international relations (Cox, 1996a: 124).

Gramsci, a theoretician and a communist activist, was deeply involved in the fight against fascism in Italy. He was imprisoned for nearly 10 years under Mussolini (1922–1943). During these years in prison he wrote *The Prison Notebooks* (1926–1937). The neo-Gramscian school's interest in this work is explained by the original conception of hegemony that Gramsci proposed. For him, hegemony is the ability of a dominant class to hold power (or authority) over dominated classes with the latter's consent. He exposed the logic behind this ability to exercise intellectual and moral leadership in order to convince the dominated that their interest converges with the interests of the dominant class. The power of the dominant class relies not simply on open coercion or explicit threat, but also on its ability to expand its ideological power through a set of institutions. For Gramsci, these institutions are the state and civil society. The state can, if necessary, use coercion to defend the interests of the dominant class; civil society includes the economy, religion, political parties, clubs, and other non-state institutions. Contrary to liberal thinking, civil society is not only composed of actors or groups that seek first and foremost to defend their interest, it is also an important actor in the constitution of a historic bloc—that is to say, a particular alignment of forces that use hegemony.

The dominant class thus acquires a hegemonic power over civil society when institutions (public and private) do not call into question its power and when, in addition, they defend the interests of the dominant class by seeking to legitimize the hegemonic order. In Gramsci's mind, to overthrow this order, instigating a *coup d'état* is not enough; it is also necessary to change the hegemonic discourse anchored in civil society. For example, Gramsci explained the failure of Italian Marxists by their inability to introduce a counterhegemonic bloc within Italian society.

For specialists of the neo-Gramscian approach, the analyses of power neglect a fundamental dimension: power is not only relational, it is also structural; it is anchored in civil society. As well, power does not depend exclusively on material capabilities; it relies on a combination of material aspects, ideas, and institutions. The legitimacy of a social order, which favours the status quo, is integrated in the dominant ideology. For Cox, hegemony is the way a social group exercises power. Consensus in a society is achieved by making sure that certain benefits are distributed to subordinate groups; these actions can plausibly be presented as representing the common interest.

According to Cox, Gramsci's originality lay in his use of the concept of hegemony, as he applied it to the bourgeoisie and to the hegemonic apparatus or mechanisms of the dominant class. This allowed him to distinguish the bourgeoisie who had achieved a hegemonic position over other classes from those that had not achieved this objective. In northern Europe, for example, in the countries where capitalism first took hold, the bourgeois hegemony was the most complete. To achieve this, concessions had to be made, as they were in Sweden, for example, where capitalism was preserved while at the same time it was made more acceptable for the working class.

Because hegemony was deeply rooted in civil society, the bourgeoisie were not even obliged to run the state directly. Other classes could do that for them, provided that these rulers recognized and accepted the hegemonic structures of civil society and the limits of their political action.

In this perspective, the state is not limited to just the government and its institutions. It underpins the political structure of civil society. In Gramsci's era, the institutions making up civil society were the church, the education system, the press—in short, all the institutions that helped to create in people certain behaviours and certain expectations that support the hegemonic social order. The hegemony of the dominant class thus forms a bridge between the conventional categories of state and civil society.

Gramsci's concept of hegemony is a combination of consent and coercion. When the consensual aspects of power are in the forefront, hegemony prevails. Coercion is always latent, but it is only applied in marginal and deviant cases. As Cox writes, "Hegemony is enough to ensure conformity of behavior in most people most of the time" (Cox, 1996a: 127).

Gramsci illustrates his concept of hegemony by using the experience of the 1917 Bolshevik revolution to show how to make a revolution in Europe. He used a military analogy, comparing wars of movement and wars of position. According to Gramsci, the basic difference between Western Europe and Russia lay in the strength of the state and the civil society. In Russia, the administration and the coercive apparatus of the state were imposing, but they were also vulnerable because civil society was underdeveloped. A small, well-led working class was able to plunge the state into a war of movement. This working class met with no resistance from civil society. The revolutionary movement was able to take control of the power and found a new state, and to ensure its domination by using the state's coercive means and by trying to create a new legitimacy for the new power.

In contrast, in Western Europe, civil society under bourgeois hegemony was much more structured and took different forms. A war of movement was not impossible in this context, even though, in the long term, the experience would probably be doomed to failure. A war of movement cannot be effective against a hegemonic relationship between state and civil society. The alternative strategy is the war of position that patiently builds the foundations of a new state. In Western Europe, argued Gramsci, the battle must be won within civil society before an assault on the state could be successful. A premature attack on the state would just underscore the weakness of the opposition movement and would facilitate the re-imposition of bourgeois domination. The only way to change a hegemonic order is thus to build a counterhegemony within the existing hegemony.

A historic bloc cannot exist without a hegemonic social class. When such a social class does exist, it maintains the cohesion, the identity within the bloc as it propagates a common culture. Intellectuals play an essential role in the creation of a historic bloc. They are not a separate class. For Gramsci, they are organically linked to the dominant social class. Their social function is to develop and preserve the mental images, technologies, and organizations that unite the members of a class and a historic bloc in a common identity. Organic intellectuals act in this way for the whole society in which the bourgeoisie dominate. They play an essential role in expressing the interests of the bourgeoisie in universal terms (Cox, 1996a: 133).

For Gramsci, the state is the basic entity in international relations and the place where social conflicts occur. It is the changes in the domestic social structures of states that transform international relations. States are also the places where class hegemonies are built. However, the Gramscian vision of the state is broader than the classic definition of the state in international relations, where a state is often viewed merely in terms of the size of its army and its foreign affairs bureaucracy. With regard to foreign policy itself, great powers have a certain liberty to determine their foreign policies, which is not the case for smaller countries.

Cox set out to transpose the Gramscian concept of hegemony to the world scale. States that succeed in establishing a hegemonic order are powerful states that have undergone major social and economic revolutions. These revolutions do not simply modify the state's economic and political structures, they also unleash energies that spread beyond state borders. As Cox writes,

> Hegemony at the international level is thus not merely an order among states. It is an order within a world economy with a dominant mode of production which penetrates into all countries and links into other subordinate modes of production. It is also a complex of international social relationships which connect the social classes of the different countries. World hegemony can be described as a social structure, an economic structure, and a political structure; and it cannot be simply one of these things but must be all three. World hegemony, furthermore, is expressed in universal norms, institutions and mechanisms which lay down general rules of behavior for states and for those forces of civil society that act across national boundaries, rules which support the dominant mode of production. (1996a: 137)

Cox stresses the importance of the periodization of hegemonic orders. In his works, he proposes two different periodizations. In the periodization he outlined in 1983, Cox distinguished four periods. The first extended from 1845 to 1875, the second from 1875 to 1945, the third from 1945 to 1965, and the fourth began in 1965. In the periodization he outlined in 1987, he reduced the number of periods to three: the first period, which extended from 1789 to 1873, saw the emergence of the international liberal economy; the second, from 1873 to 1945, was the period of rival imperialisms; and the third, that of the neoliberal world order, started in 1945 (Cox, 1981, 1987).

The difference between the periodizations is that the first was longer, covering the hegemonic period of the British Empire based on comparative advantage theory, free trade, and the gold standard; and that, in this first periodization, Cox viewed the American hegemony period as being in decline since 1965. In his 1987 periodization, he changed his mind. Since

1945, a hegemonic order has been built in response to the capacity of the United States—the dominant power—to define the norms of the desired order in universal terms that are compatible with the interests of other states. American hegemony is not a simple imperial relationship, but rather "leadership by consent." This form of political domination is not experienced as such by those who are under it. The dominant power instead manages to have others adhere to this order, sometimes at the cost of certain sacrifices. Once implemented, neo-Gramscian hegemony moves from a relational to a structural power relationship.

International organizations such as the UN, the World Bank, the IMF, GATT, and nowadays the WTO are mechanisms through which the universal norms of the world hegemony are expressed and diffused. For Cox, international institutions mirror the contemporary hegemonic consensus in regards to a particular international issue.

International institutions are the product of hegemony. The characteristics of international institutions that strengthen the hegemon's power are: "(1) the institutions embody the rules which facilitate the expansion of hegemonic world orders; (2) they are themselves the product of the hegemonic world order; (3) they ideologically legitimate the norms of the world order; (4) they co-opt the elites from peripheral countries; and (5) they absorb counterhegemonic ideas" (Cox, 1996a: 138).

Cox claims that the hyperliberal model, supported by American power, became rooted in international institutions and thus managed to overshadow other models of thought. The key words of the hyperliberal ideology are competitiveness, deregulation, privatization, and restructuring. Hyperliberalism is still the dominant ideology in the United States. For Cox, international organizations have contributed to the particular structure of the international order by strengthening the dominant forms of state. International organizations become organs for spreading the interests of the dominant power. The ideological dimension is very strong, transcending states to form a true international social order. Individuals, NGOs, and international organizations identify with this order and defend its foundations.

This world order is not just state-centric, because it is the product of the external expansion of the interests of the dominant social class. The dominant social class therefore operates at the world scale and presents its social, economic, cultural, and technological institutions as models to imitate. For Cox, social forces are therefore very important, being composed of groups of people who occupy a particular place in the world-economy due to their role in the organization of production. Certain social forces, such as individuals who own or work in competitive industries, will become defenders of free trade, while other social forces will oppose free trade because it is a threat to their interests. Analyzing these forces helps to understand the state of development of the capitalist economy in the world. Cox argues that it is within social forces that we can trace the indicators of a future change in the existing order through the creation of a counterhegemonic historic bloc comprised of the poor in wealthy countries and of the new working class created by the globalization of capitalist modes of production (Cox, 1996a: 140). Backed by the United Nations Conference on Trade and Development, the demands of developing states for the creation of a new world economic order are an example of counterhegemonic contestation.

In summary, Cox theorizes the complex dynamic between the political and the economic that takes the specific form of an interaction between social forces, forms of states, and world order. The goal for the analyst is to try to understand how these interactions impact the current phase of human history. Cox's argument is difficult to follow, but the essence can be summarized as follows: since 1945, capitalist social forces have been in an intense movement of economic globalization that is urging internationalization of production combined with migrations from underdeveloped to developed countries. The dominant class produces, regulates, and organizes the neoliberal world order. In this context, international organizations such as the WTO are institutions in which power relations are crystallized, and these organizations relay the interests of the dominant social classes to the subordinate. The WTO and the IMF look after the commercial interests of developed countries before those of underdeveloped countries (Cox and Schechter, 2002).

With regard to forms of states, transformations on the international scene have variable effects, because states are embedded in the global political economy in different ways. However, states have generally transformed their role as protectors of the domestic economy against sudden fluctuations in the international economy and have become transmission belts carrying the dominant hegemon's ideology from the global economy to the national economy (Cox, 1990). This means that states compete with one another to obtain competitive advantages, because they believe that integration in the international economy is inevitable.

The Structural Power of Capital

After Robert Cox, the neo-Gramscian approach has been developed notably through the works of Stephen Gill. Two of Gill's fundamental contributions have to do with the structural power of capital and American hegemony.

Gill is a professor of political sciences at York University in Toronto, Canada. He was born in Britain and presents himself as a refugee from Thatcherism. He is generally considered to be Cox's successor within the neo-Gramscian school. As with Cox, the scope of his work makes it difficult to classify him simply as a researcher in IPE. Gill holds a doctorate in sociology and considers his principal works to be a continuation of those of Cox, with whom he shares the normative ambition.

With David Law, Gill co-authored a textbook on the global political economy (Gill and Law, 1988). In this reference manual, the two authors seek to integrate the various approaches, orthodox and heterodox, in IPE theories, from the realist-mercantilist perspective, the liberal and public choice perspective, the Marxist and world-system approaches, to the neo-Gramscian approach. They attempt to demonstrate that, although IPE as a self-aware field of study emerged in the 1970s, its roots can be traced to the first authors who took an interest in political economy (mercantilists, liberals, and Marxists). Gill and Law reject the American tendency to separate the disciplines by specialization. They do not accept the growing separation between the economic and the political, or the separation proposed by international relations specialists between domestic politics and international politics. They also reject the distinction between high politics, linked to security issues, and low politics, linked notably to free trade issues, currency, and foreign investment issues. In the second part of their book, they discuss a variety of basic research themes, including the power of capital, the military-industrial rivalry, the postwar international system, monetary and financial issues, multinational companies and global processes of production, free trade and protectionism, energy and oil, North–South relations, communist states and East–West relations, and American hegemony. They conclude that the globalization of national economies is a fundamental trend, that the supremacy of the military-industrial complex over security issues is huge, and that the effect of globalization on global ecological challenges is deepening (Gill and Law, 1988).

An interesting contribution of this book, which the authors also developed in a separate article, is that it tackles the issue of the structural power of capital from a neo-Gramscian perspective (Gill and Law, 1989). For these authors, power has several dimensions: material, normative, behavioural, and structural. They refer explicitly to Cox's concept of neo-Gramscian hegemony. According to Gill and Law, the power of capital is structural. It is not necessary for the holders of capital to weigh a direct threat because their power is structural. The flexibility and mobility of multinational companies that hold capital to invest abroad enable these companies to easily obtain concessions from countries that want to host them. The domination logic is reversed: it does not come from the threat to invest on a territory, but rather from the lack of interest by investors. Capital has a structural power because countries anticipate the desires of investors and modify their behaviour in order to be perceived as "attractive." Investors do not even have to intervene directly because capital is so internationally mobile, that companies will compare the investment climates in different countries before choosing where to locate. The consequence is that governments are increasingly forced to imitate the economic policies of other countries, which paves the way to a race to the bottom. Even France, which under Charles de Gaulle had adopted a very nationalistic attitude against US investments, had to modify its policies in the 1970s when it became apparent that the result of those policy choices was that multinational companies were directing their investments to other countries in the European Community (Gill and Law, 1989: 485).

Another important book by Gill deals with American hegemony and the Trilateral Commission (1990a). This work proposes a theory of transnational American hegemony and contests the idea that this hegemony has been in decline since the 1970s. Instead, says Gill, it is in transformation due to globalization, the growing mobility of capital, and the neoliberal ideology supported by strong states and dominant classes, notably in the United States, that favour opening up the international trade system.

Gill draws on the works of Cox and the Gramscian concepts of hegemony, historic bloc, and organic intellectuals, while at the same time comparing his viewpoints with neorealist and liberal neo-institutionalist authors. Essentially, Gill's thesis is based on the idea that the ideological and cultural aspects of hegemony, which are not discussed by the orthodox school, show that the United States is not experiencing a decline in its hegemony, but rather an increase.

Gill's empirical field is the Trilateral Commission. His purpose is not to expose conspiracy theories on the secret power of this institution, but rather to analyze it as a meeting place for the world's elites who come together to forge consensuses on the world's major economic and political issues. The commission was created in 1973 with financial backing from David Rockefeller. Its original aim was to foster cooperation between North America, Europe, and Japan, with the collaboration of actors from the private sector that is concerned with international affairs. These associations are comprised of members of the different countries' elites, who frequently travel between the various places of power in the countries: businesses, governments, universities, media enterprises, and law firms.

For Gill, the commission's members are organic intellectuals. Gramsci made a distinction between traditional intellectuals, who perceive their role as being separate and autonomous from the political and social conflicts of their era, and organic intellectuals, who see themselves as public intellectuals and who have an essential role in articulating and justifying the ideologies of the dominant class. The fundamental difference between the two types is that organic intellectuals are fully aware of their role in theorizing, popularizing, and transmitting the ideologies of the dominant class, using a universalist language that presents these ideologies as being to everyone's benefit. On the whole, organic intellectuals are favourable to a form of transnational liberalism, and they play a crucial part in reconciling, at the domestic level, some of the conflicts emerging between the transnational capitalist class and the domestic classes. These elites represent the status quo and play a critical role in spreading the ideas of the dominant class. In the case of the Trilateral Commission, the transnational dominant class, whose nerve centre is in the United States, seeks the constitution of a transnational liberal order.

Towards the end of the 1990s, Gill shifted his focus to the dynamic of the power of globalization and neoliberalism, coining the term *disciplinary neoliberalism* to designate "a concrete form of structural and behavioural power" combining "the structural power of capital with 'capillary power' and 'panopticism'" (Gill, 2003: 130). Gill drew on the notions of "disciplinary power" and "panopticism" in the works of French philosopher Michel Foucault (1975). A panopticon is a type of prison envisioned by the utilitarian philosopher Jeremy Bentham. The architecture of this type of prison is designed to enable a prison guard to observe all the prisoners without them knowing whether or not they are being watched. In this type of incarceration unit, prisoners are under the impression they are always being observed and, having interiorized this feeling, they tend to discipline themselves. Foucault used this abstract concept in *Discipline and Punish* and made it the model for a disciplinary society (Foucault, 1975).

Gill argues that neoliberalism has a disciplinary power comparable to the panopticon. The disciplinary society concept must be understood as a combination of two levels of power: macro and micro. For Gill, disciplinary neoliberalism draws upon his ideas regarding the structural power of capital, as shown by the example of the "new constitutionalism" and its strong contention that the neoliberal values of individuals, the market, privatizations, competition, and so on are becoming pervasive and are making their way into the micropractices of everyday life for the majority of people around the world.

The new constitutionalism refers to all the new legal instruments, such as laws, treaties, and institutions, that are gradually ensuring that an ever greater part of people's lives conform to the disciplinary neoliberalism logic, thereby limiting democratic control (Gill, 2002). Disciplinary neoliberalism is institutionalized at the macro level of power. According to Gill, the discourse on global economic governance is reflected in the policies of the Bretton Woods organizations (that is to say, the conditionality imposed by the IMF and the World Bank, demanding changes to forms of state and economic policies) and in quasi-constitutional regional arrangements such as NAFTA, the Maastricht Treaty, and the multilateral regulatory framework of the new World Trade Organization. It is also reflected in the global trend towards independent central banks, with their macroeconomic policies that prioritize "the fight against inflation" (Gill, 2003: 131).

Like many others, Gill accuses the IMF of practising market fundamentalism and of seeking to penalize states that have deliberately chosen not to implement orthodox neoliberal policies. One might argue with Gill that these countries, through their poor management of public finances, in fact dug their own graves and that they can always refuse IMF intervention, as no country is forced to accept its assistance. Gill's answer to this objection is his concept of the "structural power of capital." Conditionality, he says, is actually desired by the international private investors upon which less developed countries depend. The IMF is merely the transmission belt for the interests of the dominant transnational class.

Gill defines "market civilization" as a historical structure or a set of transformative practices involving the myth or ideology of capitalist progress. Market civilization also involves processes of disintegration, notably practices that create exclusionary and hierarchical social relations. At the micro level, it means the implementation of the neoliberal ideology in everyday life, either by the value placed on the individual, private property, the market, and privatization, or by the hierarchization of social relations. Examples of this transformation include the growing commodification of health care, health insurance, religion, the human genome. Gill is worried about the panopticon effect of the massive accumulation of digital data on individuals as consumers, from their credit history, consumer habits, and demographic information to data on their insurability. He is also concerned by the rising trend to monitor public spaces and workplaces using the new technologies.

The Politics of Mass Production

While not as well known as Cox and Gill, Mark Rupert, of Syracuse University in the state of New York, is also identified with the neo-Gramscian school. In 1995, he published *Producing Hegemony: The Politics of Mass Production and American Global Power*. Contrary to Gill, who speaks of a coalition amongst the economic elites of various countries to explain American hegemony in the world, Rupert claims that American power was shaped by the way in which mass production (and its underlying ideology) was institutionalized in the United States and then exported throughout the world.

The author explains how the "historic bloc" comprised of American statespersons, capitalists, and centrist union leaders, as secondary partners, produced a political consensus in the United States. This liberal order was then globalized. The author examines the "productivist" ideology and the reasons for its spread around the globe, particularly in France, Italy, Germany, and Japan.

According to Rupert, the production of an unprecedented volume of mass goods after the Second World War fostered the reconstruction of a world order under American leadership. More specifically, he examines the case of the Ford Motor Company, centring his analysis on labour relations and moderate unionists as junior partners in the constitution of this hegemonic bloc. The author shows how this "Fordist" model of work organization functioned as a hegemony in the Gramscian sense of the term. Yet, according to Rupert, since the 1970s, this model has been in crisis. He concludes that its erosion and the pressures of transnational competition, as well as the neoliberal reaction of the 1970s and 1980s, are opening the way to new possibilities and transformations.

In another work, on the "ideologies of globalization," Rupert proposes a critical analysis of the interpretation of political and ideological struggles pertaining to the meaning and the future of globalization, drawing in particular on Gramsci's concept of "common sense" to better understand how particular ideologies are profoundly influenced by changing economic conditions (Rupert, 2000). For Gramsci, the notion of "common sense" must be differentiated from the concept of "good sense." Common sense is a fragmentary and often contradictory amalgam of popular, cultural, and religious beliefs.

According to Rupert, protests in the United States, especially against the WTO meeting in Seattle in November 1999, and elsewhere in the world have shown profound disagreement over the meaning of globalization and over the new world order. In *Ideologies of Globalization*, the author examines the link between the United States and the global political economy. He divides his work into several chapters that tackle subjects such as the historical context of the development of globalization and its relation to the structures of US political economy, the emergence of opposition movements, especially against NAFTA and the WTO, and the reaction of nationalist movements and extreme right populist groups.

Conclusion

Although neo-Gramscians have not acquired a central place in the debates in IPE, several authors are pursuing the works of this school from various perspectives. Worthy of mention are the works of Jeffrey Harrod (2002, 1987) on the theories and strategies of unionism in the global political economy and unprotected workers; the works of Christina Gabriel and Hélène Pellerin (2008) on labour migrations; those of Kees van der Pijl (1998) on transnational classes and international relations; and those of Craig Murphy and Douglas Nelson on global institutions, development, and marginalization (2005). Neo-Gramscianism is therefore, in the words of Imre Lakatos, a progressive research program, even though it is on the fringes of the dominant theories.

Among the critics of the neo-Gramscian school, there are those who reproach Robert Cox for being too detached from the works of Marx, and those who think that he has misinterpreted Gramsci (Germain and Kenny, 1998). Some critics link Cox with Marxist, Gramscian, or Weberian perspectives, or with the Frankfurt school, and then reproach him for having deviated from these thinkers or these schools (Schechter, 2002). Several others reproach him for being overly pessimistic.

The most frequent criticism, particularly from scholars in the United States, is that even though the works of Cox or Gill have a strong empirical dimension, these authors do not attempt to falsify their hypotheses. Some critics, for example, argue that Gill's work on the Trilateral Commission is merely hypothetical, as it has not been demonstrated with the scientific rigour accepted in leading US universities.

Like Susan Strange, Cox is largely ignored by the orthodox school and is not studied in US universities. The explanation may be found in the fact that Coxian ontology puts "modes of production" rather than states at the centre of the analysis. It is difficult to merge Cox's emphasis on the "state–society complex" with the state-centric tradition of the dominant orthodox approach in the United States. Cox's approach is so far removed from the orthodox in IPE that it is pushed to the semi-periphery. It cannot easily be simplified into a logical theorem, it is just the opposite of a parsimonious approach, and its methodology does not always easily identify falsifiable propositions.

Questions

1. What are the basic assumptions of Marxism?
2. What does being "dependent" mean for dependency theorists?
3. What is the main unit of analysis of IPE for Immanuel Wallerstein?
4. Why do we say that the neo-Gramscian school has an explicit normative aim?
5. Why is production, according to Cox and the Marxists, conditioning the organization of society?
6. What is the influence of Marxism on the neo-Gramscian school?
7. How does neo-Gramscian hegemony differ from hegemonic stability theory?
8. What does the structural power of capital mean for Stephen Gill and David Law?
9. What is an organic intellectual according to Gramsci?

Further Reading

On the foundations of the neo-Gramscian approach in IPE:

Cox, Robert W., with Timothy J. Sinclair. *Approaches to World Order*. Cambridge: Cambridge University Press, 1996.

Gill, Stephen, and David Law. *The Global Political Economy: Perspectives, Problems and Policies*. Baltimore, MD: Johns Hopkins University Press, 1988.

Gill, Stephen. *Power and Resistance in the New World Order.* New York: Palgrave Macmillan, 2002.

The author most associated with the neo-Gramscian approach is Robert Cox. Here are his most important publications:

Cox, Robert W. "Social Forces, States and World Order: Beyond International Relations Theory." *Millennium: Journal of International Studies* 10.2 (1981): 126–55.

Cox, Robert W. "Gramsci, Hegemony and International Relations: An Essay in Method," *Millennium: Journal of International Studies* 12.2 (1983): 162–75.

Cox, Robert W. *Production, Power, and World Order: Social Forces in the Making of History.* New York: Columbia University Press, 1987.

Cox, Robert W. "Production, the State and Change in World Order." In *Global Changes and Theoretical Challenges: Approaches to World Politics for the 1990s*, edited by Ernst-Otto Czempiel and James N. Rosenau, 37–55. Toronto: Lexington Books, 1989.

Cox, Robert W. "Toward a Post-Hegemonic Conceptualization of World Order: Reflections on the Relevancy of Ibn Khaldun." In *Governance without Government: Order and Change in World Politics*, edited by Ernst-Otto Czempiel and James N. Rosenau, 132–59. Cambridge: Cambridge University Press, 1992.

Cox, Robert W., and Michael G. Schechter. *The Political Economy of a Plural World: Critical Reflections on Power, Morals and Civilization.* London: Routledge, 2002.

On the work of Robert Cox:

Leysens, Anthony. *The Critical Theory of Robert W. Cox: Fugitive or Guru?* Basingstoke, UK: Palgrave Macmillan, 2008.

The British School

Chapter Contents

- The Heterodox British School in IPE
- Globalization
- Structural Power
- Markets
- Finance.
- Conclusion

Reader's Guide

There is broad consensus dating the birth of IPE in Great Britain to a 1970 article by Susan Strange that proposed building bridges between international economics and international politics. The institutionalization of IPE in Great Britain owes a great deal to Strange, and her desire to build IPE on multidisciplinary foundations became a distinctive trademark of the British school. The British school's lack of a coherent research paradigm has led to a very great diversity of works. Causal theories are often absent and formal modelling non-existent. The main strength of these works is that they target problems, underscore injustices, and show up areas of absence of governance, order, or authority. While the orthodox approach aspires to scientific "objectivity," the heterodox approach is more openly normative in the tradition of pragmatism and moral philosophy. The heterodox school adopts a less formal methodology that is closer to interpretive historical sociology. This method Is more compatible with the larger ambitions of heterodox researchers. The orthodox school is more intensive while the heterodox school is more extensive. From this large variety of works, this chapter focuses on those that most directly participated in the founding debates of IPE—namely, the conception of globalization, American hegemony, structural power, the relationship between states and markets, and, lastly, an important element that is distinctive of the British school, international finance.

In the British school, the lack of a coherent research paradigm has led to a great diversity of works. The research is consequently less cumulative than in the case of the orthodox approach. From this large variety of works, this chapter focuses on those that most directly participated in the founding debates of IPE—namely, the conception of globalization, American hegemony, structural power, the relationship between states and markets, and, lastly, an important element that is distinctive of the British school, international finance. But before tackling these themes, the chapter provides an overview of the genesis of the heterodox British school.

The Heterodox British School in IPE

Although there is broad consensus dating the birth of IPE in Great Britain to a 1970 article by Susan Strange that proposed building bridges between international economics and international politics, several authors rightly point out that IPE's historical roots lie much deeper. For Matthew Watson, as well as for Ben Clift and Ben Rosamond, the British school in IPE has a long tradition of research that is compatible with the more contemporary works in political economy (Watson, 2005). It is for this reason that Clift and Rosamond contend that not all researchers consider international relations as the necessary, or even necessarily useful, starting point from which to analyze the global political economy (Clift and Rosamond, 2009: 95).

In Great Britain, John A. Hobson's Marxian works criticizing imperialism, and his critiques of the thinking of orthodox economists, had more than a little influence on the eventual development of IPE. The works of Norman Angell on economic and financial interdependence and on the obsolescence of war also played a role. Keynes's work was an undeniable stimulus, as was the equally noteworthy work of Karl Polanyi. Indeed, the influence of authors with Marxian leanings was much greater in Great Britain than in the United States (Clift and Rosamond, 2009: 99).

That said, the institutionalization of IPE in Great Britain owes a great deal to Susan Strange. Even Clift and Rosamond describe her as a "colossus of British IPE" (2009: 95). According to Barry Gills, one of the founders of the *Review of International Political Economy*, "She founded IPE as we know it here in Britain and she left a great hole in it when she left" (quoted in Cohen, 2007: 208). In fact, Strange's legacy is so important that it is still influencing researchers in the heterodox school, despite her death in 1998.

Strange held only an undergraduate degree in economics (albeit with first-class honours) from the London School of Economics and Political Science (LSE). At the age of 23, she began working as a correspondent for *The Economist* and *The Observer*. Three years later, in 1949, she obtained her first position at University College in London, where she taught international relations. In 1964, she joined the Royal Institute of International Affairs, better known as Chatham House. From 1978 to 1988, she pursued her career in the department of international relations at LSE and finally ended her career at the European University Institute in Florence and at Warwick University.

At Chatham House, Strange had been hired to produce works on the pound sterling and British monetary policy. It was there that she became interested in the political aspects of international financial issues. The relations between power, influence, the role of reserve currencies, and the domestic economy were fundamental topics, but few research studies were being done on the political aspects of monetary issues. The politics of international monetary and financial affairs became the hallmark of Strange's works and, subsequently, of British IPE.

Following the publication in 1970 of her pioneering manifesto, Strange founded the International Political Economy Group in 1971 (Murphy and Nelson, 2001: 393). This research group, which is still active, aimed to bring together not only scholars and students but also journalists, politicians, and civil servants to discuss issues related to international political economy.

While her manifesto article of 1970 called for a form of synthesis of works in international relations and in international economics, in the mid-1980s, she proposed expanding the multidisciplinary approach, notably to establish a contrast with orthodox IPE. In 1984, Strange published *Paths to International Political Economy*, a collective work representative of this desire to broaden the range of IPE. In this book, Roger Tooze defined IPE as a subdiscipline of international relations, while other authors from various disciplines explained what their field of specialization could bring to IPE. David Wightman, for example, provided a chapter on the contribution of economic history; Dennis Pirages introduced the ecological approach; and Sol Picciotto focused on international law (Wightman, 1984; Pirages, 1984; Picciotto, 1984).

Strange's desire to build IPE on multidisciplinary foundations became a distinctive trademark of the British school. During the 1990s, Robert Denemark and Robert O'Brien did a comparative analysis of IPE course plans in the United States and in Great Britain (1997). Their conclusion confirmed the tendency: IPE courses in Great Britain were more inclusive, they integrated several disciplines and approaches, and they transcended disciplinary boundaries more freely than those offered in the United States. Given this context, Stephen Gill and David Law, and then Ronan Palan, proposed using the term *global political economy* to distinguish orthodox IPE from heterodox IPE (Gill and Law, 1988). Others, such as Nicola Phillips, kept the term *international political economy*, but called for a true globalization of the research field and for extending research beyond the triad of industrialized countries (Phillips, 2005). Phillips criticized orthodox IPE for its ethnocentrism, its habit of seeing the world through the lens of capitalist society, with its history, its concept of development, and its dominant ideology. Her work seeks to demonstrate the poverty of the dominant orthodox IPE, expose its ideological biases and its methodological problems, and propose solutions to correct them, such as developing a truly multidisciplinary approach.

In 1994, with the publication of the first issue of the *Review of International Political Economy* (*RIPE*), the bias for a multidisciplinary approach became the norm. The inaugural editorial stated,

> *RIPE*'s raison d'être is to bring together these exciting new attempts to understand contemporary social change by facilitating dialogue and debate across existing academic divides. This will be our contribution to nurturing a new IPE. The implications of this are that, in traditional terms, the journal will inevitably be "multidisciplinary" in scope and "interdisciplinary" in spirit. (*RIPE*, 1994: 2)

The journal's international editorial board reflected this great diversity of approaches and viewpoints. As these boards are often symbolic, the selection of members is significant. The original board members included, for example, geographer John Agnew, anthropologist Jonathan Friedman, professor of management Uma Kothari, and political scientist Jeffry Frieden. Two years later, in 1996, the *New Political Economy* (*NPE*) journal made its debut. Today, it is the chief rival of the *RIPE* on the heterodox side. Like the *RIPE*, the *NPE* encourages conversation between disciplines.

In 2000, Ronen Palan edited the book *Global Political Economy*. He proposed a critical reading of "contemporary theories" in IPE and gave only marginal notice to the theories developed by the orthodox school. Apart from one chapter on game theory and a second on institutionalism (the liberal perspective), the 14 other chapters demonstrated this commitment to develop the British school on multidisciplinary and eclectic foundations. The articles discussed a variety of issues, such as development theory (Pieterse, 2000), race, gender, and culture in the postcolonial order (Ling, 2000), the contribution of historical sociology and global transformations (Shaw, 2000), as well as labour and IPE (O'Brien, 2000). All these themes are largely ignored by orthodox IPE. Since then, multidisciplinarity and eclecticism have been the trademarks of the heterodox works in IPE, which deal with a vast set of subjects.

The hallmark approach of British IPE as developed by Strange is also highly critical, being nourished by a strong skepticism regarding orthodoxy. Strange's antipathy for the "establishment" and "the barons and the top brass" of academia is especially evident (Strange, 1995: 295). Her aversion to the works of orthodox researchers and more particularly to realists, perceived at the time as dominant, is undeniable. Even though she admired certain aspects of American culture—Robert Keohane said of Strange that she liked the openness and the irreverence of American society and that, by instinct and by temperament, she was a woman of the American West (Keohane, 2000: 14)—Strange denounced the egotism of the power and arrogance of American researchers whom she attacked ruthlessly.

Roger Tooze noted that Strange's work was marked by a series of contributions that were "outside of the mainstream and in practice as constituting a 'critical' approach, and that it was received and considered as such by most of us in IR/IPE" (2000: 280). Strange's disdain for the production in American IPE stemmed from the fact that she believed these works had the normative objective to produce knowledge in the service of American power. Strange set out to denounce the misuse of American power and to call attention to that country's privileged place in the world.

She therefore drew a quite unflattering portrait of orthodox IPE: according to her, it was not true international political economy, but rather an inadequate and misguided political approach to international economic relations based on a narrow conception of the economic relations between states. In a now famous text on international regimes, she compared American political scientists to medieval scholars who, in their ignorance and superstitions, imagined dragons beyond the European horizon (Strange, 1982). In another controversial article, "Wake up, Krasner! The World Has Changed," written in the form of a rebuttal, she targeted Stephen Krasner, a leader in IPE in the United States, demanding that he open his eyes to the reality of globalization (Strange, 1994). In her opinion, Krasner's theories made no sense when compared with the real world.

If Strange openly criticized the orthodox approach in IPE, she was even harder on orthodox economists. She opposed their imperialism in the social sciences. In the book *Paths to International Political Economy*, which she edited, no economists were included among the collaborators. For her, economists produced "phony science, not social sciences" (Strange, 1994: 217). "Always attack the economists!" she often said (cited in Halliday, 2008).

This oppositional thinking developed by Strange is another characteristic of the British school in IPE. The inaugural editorial of the *RIPE* defined the journal in opposition to the orthodox school in IPE. In that text, the editors asserted that globalization had provoked a crisis in the social sciences because the "institutionalized orthodoxies" within the various disciplines were mute in the face of the massive changes produced by globalization. The social sciences were, in the 1990s, poorly equipped to explain the processes underway. The editorial criticized three key research fields: international relations theories, neoclassical economics, and orthodox development theories.

The *RIPE* editorial's authors readily stated that international relations was the most important area for the development of IPE. They wrote, "In fact this is the only discipline where an IPE has developed as a recognized subdiscipline" (*RIPE*, 1994: 2). According to the authors, the dominant theory in international relations, realist theory, was inadequate to understand contemporary transformations. Critics of the realist school claimed the approach was much too state-centric, that it ignored not only ideologies and culture, but also key economic issues, and that it was obsessed by security issues. The works of the realists underestimated the importance of globalization; they were static and ahistoric, which made them inadequate to understand the rapid transformations on the international scene. As for the liberals, although they did stress the transformations associated with globalization and complex interdependence, they made the mistake of thinking that the world was becoming interdependent, suggesting by that fact that states had been "independent" in the past. In short, the lack of historical perspective was a major problem in both these cases.

The complex changes linked to globalization required another approach. The authors of the *RIPE* editorial wrote that these transformations had created a growing interest in Marxism and the need to develop "a more holistic and total world-view, one which accepted the force of structured relationships, pervading hegemonic practices and group interests, but one which could also deal with the uncertainties of history and social struggle" (*RIPE*, 1994: 6). Put simply, an approach focused on structures rather than on actors. Neo-Gramscianism was presented as a useful approach for understanding contemporary globalization (see Chapter 6). From the heterodox perspective, research must make room for broader theoretical debates. It also must accept more ambitious social and historical explanations and transcend the old Marxist and liberal categories so popular in the 1970s and 1980s. In other words: "IPE is seen in its own historical specificity: contemporary globalization" (*RIPE*, 1994: 7).

The editorial's authors also called into question the works of orthodox economists. In their view, since 1945, economics had been dominated by the neoclassical synthesis. This synthesis and the resulting economic theories were developed for national economies, or for closed economies, and therefore did not take globalization into account. Questions related to globalization or international trade were secondary. The change of paradigm from Keynesianism to neoliberalism and monetarism starting in the 1970s did not fundamentally change the situation. National economies were still the focus of the analysis of economists: "Quite simply the emerging global economy escaped from the orthodox conceptualization of the international economy" (*RIPE*, 1994: 7).

The authors also invited contributors to revisit the works of several renowned heterodox economists, such as Marx, Myrdal, Hirschman, Kaldor, Kapp, Veblen, and Polanyi, in order to produce a more socialized and institutionalized conception of economics. They reaffirmed the relevance of the neo-Gramscian approach and its holistic or structural explanation of the world. They encouraged researchers to reject the separation between economic and non-economic processes. They invited researchers to consider that the economic life of firms is embedded in social and cultural relations and is dependent on processes of cognition and therefore on different forms of rationality.

They also called for the rejection of the methodological individualism of neoclassical economists, proposing instead that economics, like all other social actions, be based on institutions and processes of institutionalization (*RIPE*, 1994: 9). According to the editors, IPE research needed to focus on the habits and routines that persist over time. Finally, in a complete break from orthodox economists, the editors believed it important to integrate irrational behaviours, uncertainty, and imperfect knowledge as pillars of economic activity. They wrote, "The great challenge of our time in economics is to develop analytical frameworks which are capable of simultaneously recognizing the durable driving forces of global capitalism as well as its many nuances, twists and turns, and unexpected outcomes" (*RIPE*, 1994: 9).

Globalization also triggered a questioning of orthodox development theories that had been built upon an overly universalist logic. The editorial's authors considered the transformations in developing and developed countries to be part of the same world-system, as shown by the theories of Immanuel Wallerstein and André Gunder Frank. Wallerstein believed that there was a need to rethink the social sciences to better understand the transformations taking place. He also considered it essential that development theories integrate cultural and identity issues, notably the issue of the relationship between global cultural influences and the heterogeneity of local cultures. Simply put, the heterodox regard globalization as an important phenomenon that, due to its new intensity, is permanently altering political practices.

Globalization

Susan Strange was very critical of the use of the term *globalization* because it might refer "to anything from the Internet to a hamburger. All too often it is a polite euphemism for the continuing Americanisation of consumer tastes and cultural practices" (Strange, 1996: xiii). However, the perspective that she and the British school in IPE adopted is quite clearly hyperglobalist. According to Strange, in the 1990s, IPE specialists were divided into two groups: those who believed that the world had not changed and that therefore it was not necessary to revise the analytical perspectives to study international relations; and those who believed that the world had changed a lot as a result of globalization and that a complete revision of the main approaches was necessary.

In "Wake up, Krasner! The World Has Changed," Strange expressed her profound disagreement with Krasner's statement that globalization was not a new phenomenon. Although it is true that everything is not new,

Strange admitted, it is false to claim that nothing is new, that nothing has changed. Krasner did not see the change or even the significance of the changes for states and world politics (Strange, 1994: 208). For Strange, the problem with academic journals such as *International Organization* was that they were not open enough to the diversity of viewpoints, including those of non-American authors, and that they did not adequately present the major changes in world politics caused by globalization (Strange, 1994: 209).

In 1994, the members of the *RIPE* editorial committee were clearly at variance with the realist theorists of international relations on the issue of globalization. In that first editorial, they asserted that the key point justifying in their eyes the creation of a new journal and a new heterodox approach was related to the fact that

> we recognize that we are living in an age of extraordinary social change in all realms of human activity. One crucial common denominator of this social turmoil has been the process of "globalization." Second, there has been a crisis of the social science disciplines in their treatment of this massive social change. In field after field, orthodox frameworks have been exposed as unsuitable vehicles through which to understand globalization. (*RIPE*, 1994: 2)

The authors linked the very foundation of the heterodox school to the globalization phenomenon that required revising ways of doing research and that called for developing new approaches to make the world understandable.

For the *RIPE* editorial committee, the orthodox were unable to properly account for the qualitative changes linked to globalization, which justified the creation of a new journal and the adoption of a new multidisciplinary approach. Six aspects of globalization were deemed to be of particular importance (*RIPE*, 1994: 3–4).

The first aspect was the emergence of a global financial market created by the increase in Eurocurrencies and the deregulation of the 1980s. In consequence, national authorities lost their ability to regulate their domestic financial markets. At a deeper level, this phenomenon also showed the importance of the financialization of economies and the financial world's capability to exercise its structural power.

The second fundamental aspect of contemporary globalization was the transnationalization of technology, with all that implies in terms of speed of change and the accelerated obsolescence of old technologies. This aspect of globalization has made Strange's "knowledge structure" an increasingly central concern. Knowledge and the new technologies are a new force in the economy, but these factors are unequally distributed and accentuate ipso facto the divisions between the rich and the poor.

The third aspect was linked to the fact that many firms have no other choice but to internationalize very early on in their existence. Thus, it is difficult to determine a firm's nationality. The effects of this are considerable for both the development of national economies and the functioning of the world-economy. The most powerful multinationals hold more and more power in the world-economy.

The fourth aspect was the rise of a transnational economic diplomacy and the globalization of the power of states, which signified entry into a new era in which governments and firms negotiate in order to determine new rules of the game worldwide. The effect of this is to challenge the idea that the state is the sole key actor in economic life and international relations.

The intensification of communication networks and of international immigration formed the core of the fifth aspect. These two factors led to the emergence of a form of global culture and to the de-territorialization of symbols, meanings, and identities. It is not an Americanization of the world culture, but rather a complex recomposition of cultures that involves mergers, imitation, and adaptation processes, but also rejections.

Finally, the last aspect was related to what can be called the development of the global geography. The changes produced by globalization involve the advent of a world in which the traditional borders are breached. For some, this means that the world-economy is a place in which flows of capital, goods, and services circulate. For others, the world is seen as a space where there is a concentration of power in the hands of a small number of large globalized cities. Regardless of the conception of the new geography, the identity of cities, regions, and countries is increasingly shaped in global networks rather than in the internal networks of the countries (*RIPE*, 1994: 3–4).

For Angus Cameron and Ronen Palan, globalization is also, in part, the fruit of the imagination of actors. For these authors, globalization is not simply a "real" phenomenon. It is also a story (Cameron and Palan, 2004: 3). In a work published in 2004, the authors question the link between the "facts" and the "fictions" of globalization. What relations exist between the concrete processes of globalization and the various myths, stories, and ideologies that define globalization in the public discourse? How do the theories, discussions, and debates about globalization construct how we imagine it to be? How are conceptions of the state, society, and politics transformed under globalization? The authors show how our conceptions or narratives of globalization have served to construct the political responses to it, both from states and from firms. Rather than accepting a disintegration of the state as the necessary starting point, Cameron and Palan introduce the concept of *imagined economies of globalization* and explain how this invention of the market and of globalization becomes an integral part of the politics of globalization. For the authors, the concept of "imagined economies" has to be understood in the same sense as the definition of the concept of nation for Benedict Anderson, that is, as "imagined communities" (1991). Economies are thus largely imagined by the people, and it is that perception that influences politics.

Structural Power

Power and structural power are fundamental concepts for specialists of British IPE. The research agenda established by Strange has had a considerable influence that persists to this day (Langley, 2009). Strange described herself as a *new realist*. She wrote, "This new realism . . . is quite different from the neo-realism developed by writers in international relations" (Strange, 1996: xv). The central question of her work was "*Cui bono?*" Who benefits from the situation? Power was therefore a core issue in her questioning. Just like realists in IPE, Strange was interested in power relationships and in the expression of power in the international political economy with the fundamental difference that, for her, power is not the prerogative of the state. Many other actors demonstrate power or authority, including multinationals, the market, and the financial world. The relations between these actors and states are not limited to issues of war, peace, and conflict. Power is at the core of international political economy issues and may be exercised in different ways. Strange emphasized structures rather than relations between actors. Power is structural and it establishes the importance, in IPE, of authority in specific historical circumstances. For Strange, power cannot be understood through universal generalizations.

Strange endorsed the neo-Gramscian criticism of international organizations and their rules that are largely determined by the great powers. She wrote,

> The international organisation is above all a tool of national government, an instrument for the pursuit of national interest by other means. The elementary perception of old fashioned realists is obscured—probably unconsciously—by most of the rather extensive literature on the international regimes. Too often, a regime is represented as merely the consequence of a harmonising process, through which governments have coordinated their common interests. The power element is underplayed. (Strange, 1996: xiv)

For Strange, most international regimes are not, in reality, the result of an assembly of equals, but the consequence of a strategy employed by a dominant state or a group of dominant states. The creation of a regime is sometimes the product of a negotiation with less powerful countries. It is, in fact, as the neo-Gramscian approach maintains, "a subtle exercise in political hegemony" (Strange, 1996: xiv). According to Strange, the liberal perspective of the study of international regimes, institutions, and organizations tends to excessively reify them; it neglects power relationships, it is too American-centred, it does not anticipate change because it is biased in favour of order, and it is too state-centric, thus forgetting non-governmental actors (Strange, 1982).

In the second half of the 1980s, Strange joined the debate on the decline of American hegemony with a thesis that was a direct response to the American declinist school, whether represented by Robert Gilpin, Stephen Krasner, or Robert Keohane. For Strange, hegemonic stability theory is vague and ambiguous, as the existence of a hegemonic power only partially explains why one order prevails at certain times, but not at others.

She also disagreed with the observation that the United States had lost power and that this decline of American power explained the disorder within the international system. For Strange, this idea that had dominated the debates in the United States since the 1970s was largely a myth. The theory of the decline of hegemonic stability served simply to excuse the refusal of the United States to assume its role as the leading world power, a position that it still held in the 1980s, according to Strange. In contradiction to declinist theories, she proposed a new theory of power in international relations, that of "structural power" (Strange, 1987, 1988a).

Strange's theory of structural power, which she began to build in the mid-1980s, has a certain similarity with that of her LSE colleague, Michael Mann. Strange's theory aimed to demonstrate that the American Empire was not in decline, but, on the contrary, that it held the power necessary to exercise leadership at the world scale, not only for its own interest but also for the international system as a whole. To prove her argument, Strange explained how American power was deployed without overt coercion and why, despite an increasingly persistent impression of the erosion of American power, the United States was still the dominant power in the world-economy. The result is a theory of structural power, not just of relational power as amongst realists and liberals.

In Strange's view, in the realist definition of power, security issues inevitably take precedence over all other matters, including wealth creation, freedom, or justice. So it is not surprising that, for realists, the main focus of attention and study is the relation between states since, historically, it was chiefly states that had the capacity to upset or maintain world order. However, if power is defined as the capacity to create or destroy wealth and to influence issues such as justice and freedom, it is then essential to take into consideration, and even prioritize, the study of actors other than states and to expand the conception of security.

Another error made by declinists, observed Strange, is that they equate a state's economic base with the industrial resources based on the national territory. In other words, they overestimate the importance of the manufacturing sector as a power factor. This postulate was valid in the time of Adam Smith and Friedrich List, but it was no longer the same in the 1990s. In our modern economies, the services sector supersedes industry, something that declinists seem to fail to understand. What is essential is not the location of the firm, but who makes the important decisions in that firm (Strange, 1994). According to Strange, in the 1980s, the share of the world gross product in the control of American firms still far exceeded the shares belonging to their competitors taken individually. In short, declinists underestimated the importance of the American economy.

Strange found absurd the notion that US power was in decline, because in the world as we know it, structural power is shaped more by the economy, finance, knowledge, and communication than by the size of an army. The United States forms a "non-territorial empire" organized around large transnational firms. The US trade balance deficit should not be understood as a sign of the decline of the empire, as the subsidiaries of American firms abroad repatriate their profits through financial circuits, which allows them to pay their shareholders and to minimize, or even cancel, the effects of the trade deficit on the US economy.

According to Strange, in the competition between the USSR and the United States, the Soviet empire developed according to a classical political, territorial, and military logic, while that of the United States is fundamentally a de-territorialized power that goes beyond the military framework to have an economic, financial, and social dimension. Contrary to the USSR, which reached the level of superpower based essentially on its military strength and its relational power, the United States attained superpower status by building a structural power and, contrary to the USSR, the United States did not fail miserably on the economic, financial, and social levels. The USSR lost the battle due to its territorial millstone and it could no longer keep up with the de-territorialized power and the penetrating power of American influence. Strange's thesis is not incompatible with the one Joseph Nye would develop on soft power in 1990.

Strange also refuted the idea that the decline of the British Empire and that of the American Empire were the result of the same logic. The British Empire was supported by a territorial empire managed by a small insular power and the establishment of indirect rule, while the *Pax Americana* was (and still is) supported by a non-territorial empire, managed by a large continental power. American hegemony is more comparable to Roman hegemony, whose secret of resiliency resided in its ability to have local elites participate in managing the empire. For Strange, the US government succeeded at that because its imperial bureaucracy stretched, beyond Washington, DC, to all the international organizations created after the Second World War, including the IMF, the World Bank, and the WTO. Here, Strange echoed the neo-Gramscian analysis (see Chapter 6).

Declinist theorists also err in their belief that the tensions within the international system in the 1960s and 1970s were a symptom of the decline of the American Empire. In an article written with David Calleo, Strange contested the widely accepted idea in orthodox IPE that the abandonment of the monetary system introduced by the Bretton Woods Agreement was an indicator of the decline of American power. On the contrary, this abandonment was a sign of American power and not of its fall. The United States simply saw their monetary interest change after 1945 and deliberately chose to end the fixed exchange rate system that was not working as the US had hoped. In this way, the United States imposed their new desire on the others by transforming the rules of the game to US advantage. It was a deliberated decision, an act of power, and not a symptom of American impotence.

Finally, Strange argued, declinists' fundamental error is that they adopt an exclusively relational conception of power. They establish a relationship between resources and outcomes that is too direct. Outcomes cannot be predicted based only on knowing that the United States holds such and such resources compared to another state. Furthermore, according to Strange, two types of power can be exercised in IPE: structural power and relational power. In the competitive game between states and firms, it is increasingly structural power that prevails. Relational power is a Weberian concept and manifests as the ability of an actor to have his will prevail, even against resistance. Strange gave the example of the German army in 1940 that obtained Sweden's consent to cross their "neutral" country (Strange, 1988c: 24–5). Instead, declared Strange,

> Structural power, on the other hand, is the power to shape and determine the structures of the global political economy within which other states, their political institutions, their economic enterprises and (not least) their scientists and other professional people have to operate. This structural power, as I shall explain it, means rather more than the power to set the agenda of discussion or to design (in American academic language) the international regimes of rules and customs that are supposed to govern international economic relations. . . .
>
> Structural power, in short, confers the power to decide how things shall be done, the power to shape frameworks within which states relate to each other, relate to people, or relate to corporate enterprises. The relative power of each party in a relationship is more, or less, if one party is also determining the surrounding structure of the relationship. (Strange, 1988c: 24–5)

The concept of hegemonic power among neo-Gramscians has obvious affinities with Strange's notion of structural power. Yet, contrary to Robert Cox, for whom hegemonic power comes chiefly from the production

---

Box 7.1   American Structural Power According to Susan Strange's Model

When we examine American structural power from the perspective of Strange's four structures, we see that the United States is still in the lead. Militarily, with a defence budget totalling, according to the Stockholm International Peace Research Institute, more than US$640 billion in 2013—an amount that represents 37 per cent of all military spending on the planet—the United States is far ahead of the pack. In comparison, China's spending is estimated at $188 billion, Russia's at $88 billion, Saudi Arabia at $67 billion, France at $61 billion, and Great Britain at $58 billion (Paquin, 2008).

In terms of production, of the 500 largest multinationals based on income, in 2012, 128 had their head office in the United States, 95 in China, 57 in Japan, 31 in France, 28 in Germany, 28 in the UK, (including Royal Dutch Shell that is incorporated in the UK and headquartered in the Netherlands), and 10 in Canada. If we exclude the financial sector, of the 100 largest multinationals, 55 come from four industries: automotive, electrical, oil and gas, and chemical. American multinationals are dominant in most of these sectors.

In 2014, US firms held close to half of the 100 top market capitalization valuations. Apple alone has a capitalization of close to US$470 billion, or more than the GDP of many countries. The top 5 per cent of the 100 largest

---

structure, Strange viewed this power as having four dimensions that are not hierarchical but in interaction. The four dimensions are: security, knowledge, production, and finance. The security structure is not restricted to conventional military aspects but includes all the agreements that determine the conditions to ensure the protection of citizens against threats. These agreements include, for example, protections against natural disasters. The knowledge structure has to do with the world of ideas, notably those produced by universities and research, a sector in which the United States dominates. It also concerns the agreements that enable the creation, dissemination, and accumulation of information. The production structure represents all the agreements that determine what is produced, who produces it, for whom, where, how, and under what conditions. Finally, the finance structure corresponds to the agreements that determine access to credit and its availability, as well as the cost, place, and relative value of currencies. For Strange, the four structures have the same ontological status. No structure has precedence over the others.

One of the difficulties with Strange's concept of structural power is that the four structures are not coordinated. It is therefore difficult to

firms listed on the world's stock markets are American with Apple, Exxon Mobile, followed by Google, Microsoft, and Berkshire Hathaway. In Europe, 18 European firms are ranked in the top 100 while in developing countries the number is just 11.

The portion of American currency in world reserves was 62.2 per cent in 2013 compared to 23.7 per cent for the Euro. Certain US banks and financial institutions are among the largest players in their industries, including Citigroup, Bank of America, Merrill Lynch, Morgan Stanley, and Goldman Sachs. US pension funds hold enormous power through their colossal investments.

In regards to the knowledge structure, the United States is again in the lead. American universities are always ranked among the best in the world in terms of research. They attract the world's best researchers—more than 400,000 European researchers work in the US—and they spread American ideas worldwide. The capability for technological innovation is very high, and the United States has the greatest number of Nobel Prize recipients. It also holds a very high number of patents compared to other countries. In 2005, international applications for patents published by the World Intellectual Property Organization reveal that Americans submitted 45,111 patent applications versus 25,145 by Japan, 15,870 by Germany, 5,522 by France, and 5,115 by Great Britain. In communications, the United States is also clearly dominant in the film, television and music industries.

Source: Adapted from Paquin, 2008: 93–4.

operationalize on the empirical field this conception of power, as structural power is practised without concerted effort, without minimal rationality and even without clear intent. The worlds of finance, business, knowledge, and the governmental elite do not have a common vision and are sometimes in open conflict. It is difficult to exercise power in these conditions. In such a complex environment, collective power loses its meaning, and unless it relates to a specific actor, power is just a difficult metaphor to operationalize on the empirical field. Despite all this, these four structures do not evolve independently and their interactions to a large extent determine the secondary structures such as transportation systems, international trade, energy, and the welfare state. For Strange, the United States incontestably held the highest structural power. It was at the summit of this power structure.

Markets

Markets are important actors for heterodox authors. In their view, and particularly for Susan Strange, markets have gained in importance since 1945.

The reversal of state–market balance of power represents a key feature of IPE. Strange wrote,

> The impersonal forces of the world markets, integrated over the postwar period more by private enterprise in finance, industry and trade than by the cooperative decisions of governments, are now more powerful than the states to whom ultimate political authority over society and economy is supposed to belong.
>
> Where states were once the masters of markets, now it is the markets which, on many crucial issues, are the masters over the governments of states. And the declining authority of states is reflected in a growing diffusion of authority to other institutions and associations, and to local and regional bodies, and in a growing asymmetry between the larger states with structural power and weaker ones without it. (Strange 1996: 4)

According to Strange, power had passed from states to markets under the effect of the internationalization of multinationals, the globalization of production, and the internationalization of world financial markets. World financial markets had short-circuited the authority of governments and become what Strange described as the Frankenstein of the world market. Neither the United States nor the G8 succeeded in enclosing the de-territorialized financial actors. For Strange, after three centuries during which the state's authority over society was more and more centralized, the world had evolved towards a new medievalism that was characterized by the dispersal of powers and direct competition between the various actors who held the authority (Strange, 1996: 44–65).

Strange contended that intrafirm trade was so intense that, to a large extent, it was transnational firms that decided, based on their trade strategies, what goods transited from one country to another. The penetration of the Japanese market by American firms in the 1980s and 1990s was related more to those firms' own contacts than to the efforts of the American government to open the Japanese market. Nowadays, governments have very little influence on the decisions of firms. Traditional ways of doing things have only a marginal influence.

For Strange, the fight for the acquisition of market shares had replaced the fight for the conquest of territory and possession of natural resources. In this new international game, the search for alliances between states continues, not to strengthen military capability, but to increase bargaining power, like the European Union with the WTO. As well, international negotiations are not restricted to states and intergovernmental organizations. States also negotiate with foreign firms. These firms can be convinced, in exchange for stable access to a good or growing market, to find financing, to use new technologies and to procure management techniques. The traditional notion of interstate diplomacy must be enlarged to include the interactions between states, between states and multinational firms, and between firms themselves (Stopford and Strange, 1991: 1–5).

In an indirect reply to democratic peace theory, Strange claimed that people are now favourable to free trade, not because it fosters peace and co-operation between societies but because it is the condition for their prosperity. At the foreign policy level, the consequence of these changing mindsets is that states no longer compete to obtain new territories but to obtain new market shares: economic prosperity in domestic politics is the most effective means to consolidate social peace. If the economic machine breaks down, social troubles begin. Thus, in this context, industrialized states prioritize efforts to offer an attractive environment for the foreign investments of multinational firms. Strange wrote,

> As washing machines, vacuum cleaners, dishwashers, central heating and refrigerators and freezers spread down the income levels, more people had more to lose from inter-state conflict. Comfort bred conservatism in politics. Moreover, the new wealth was being acquired by the Germans and the Japanese who had actually been defeated in World War II. Acquiring territory was no longer seen as a means to increase wealth. Losing territory did not mean the state became poorer or weaker. Gaining market shares in the world outside the territorial borders of the state, however, did enable formerly poor countries like Japan, Taiwan or Hong Kong to earn the foreign exchange with which to buy capital goods, foreign technology and the necessary resources of energy and raw materials. As John Stopford and I have argued, competition for world market shares has replaced competition for territory, or for control over the natural resources of territory as the "name of the game." (Strange, 1996: 9)

The great paradox of Strange's work is that she acknowledged, with the publication of her book *The Retreat of the State*, that markets had supplanted the authority of states and that even the American government was grappling with the same type of problem as the other countries in the world, even though its structural power was huge compared to that of others. According to her, the world had changed very rapidly and the effect of this change was that markets had come to hold more power than governments.

In addition to multinationals, and to the world of finance and bankers, several other "authorities" have sufficient power to influence very significantly the course of IPE. In *The Retreat of the State*, Strange looked at non-state and unconventional authorities. She analyzed six: the telecommunications world, the Mafia, the insurance world, large auditing firms, cartels, and international organizations. Her conclusion was that states were no longer the primary actors on the international scene; they had been pushed aside by other actors who benefitted from sizeable resources (Strange, 1996).

In the same year that Strange published *The Retreat of the State*, Ronen Palan and Jason Abbott published their book, *State Strategies in the Global Political Economy* (Palan and Abbott, 1996), in which they qualified Strange's thesis on the retreat of the state, maintaining that states are not in decline or withering away, but that they are changing and evolving in order to face the challenges linked to globalization. States are transforming into "competitive states," to use Philip G. Cerny's term (2000). These transformations include a number of profound changes for public policies. Now, instead of relying on a specific industrial sector, states tend to try to guarantee a competitive economic environment.

Palan and Abbott examined the multiple possible strategies that states can use, from the hegemonic strategies of the most powerful states, to the parasitical strategies of mini-states that serve as tax havens, to the creation of continental economies such as the European Union and NAFTA in North America. In short, there are many possible strategies that do not follow the same path or promote the same policies. The authors bluntly attacked the idea that states are interchangeable units and that globalization forces them to follow the same direction. States do not adopt standardized responses to globalization, but instead, in accordance with their historical context, seek to base their reforms on their competitive advantages.

Finance

For Ronen Palan, what most clearly distinguishes heterodox IPE from orthodox IPE is the study of international finance. For the heterodox, the relationship between politics and international finance is fundamental in IPE. What currency should be used for international transactions? Who should manage this international currency? How should credit be allocated and created on the international scene? What is the place of the state in international financial governance? What is the power of private actors in these areas?

These are critical questions and they have been the source of political conflicts and power struggles not only between states, but also with private actors that hold more and more power over these aspects. Hence, questions about money and credit in IPE are central in determining "who gets what, when and how," as Strange put it (1998, 1986). The contrast with orthodox IPE could not be greater, as financial issues have always been on the periphery of the central debates in orthodox IPE, despite certain important contributions such as those of Jeffry Frieden, Benjamin Cohen, Barry Eichengreen, or Jonathan Kirshner.

For Ronen Palan, this situation can be explained by the methodological choices of the two schools. He writes, "American IPE resolutely adopts methodological individualism, and is increasingly doing so. British IPE is less interested by the 'actors' and their preferences and behaviours. It is more concerned with structural and historical changes" (2009: 391). The insistence on methodological individualism makes it difficult to conduct research, in accordance with the recognized standards of orthodox IPE, on international financial issues.

According to Benjamin Cohen, one of the differences between the orthodox and heterodox schools is that the former systematically confronts theories with facts. The orthodox therefore produce more empirical research than researchers in the heterodox school. Stung by this analysis, Palan wrote, "Privately, 'American' perception of the British school is of a group of fuzzy thinkers and navel gazers—big on statements, weak on empirics" (2009: 391). For Palan, the American orthodox school is not perceived as being more "empirical" than the heterodox school or in sync with developments in the real world.

This viewpoint is shared by the Canadian Eric Helleiner. For him, the latest generation of orthodox researchers in IPE have much less historical knowledge of the global economy and the works in political economy than the previous generation. This difference is quite a recent phenomenon and, these researchers, who in Helleiner's opinion are neither humble nor open-minded, should exhibit a little modesty in their assertions (Helleiner, 2009).

As theory is only valid, according to the orthodox approach, if it holds up when confronted with facts, Palan proposed this test of reality in regards to the 2008 financial crisis. If the heterodox approach is as theoretically and methodologically weak as claimed, the analyses proposed by heterodox scholars should be invalidated by the crisis. Yet, according to Palan, the theses presented by the specialists identified with the British school did quite well compared with those of authors from the orthodox school. He wrote,

During the 1980s—a period that saw great debates in American IPE on the merits of regime theory, hegemonic stability theory and two-level game theory—Strange wrote her seminal contribution, *Casino Capitalism* (1986). *Casino Capitalism* was a trenchant critique of the post–Bretton Woods American dominated global economy, cantering on what Strange considered the most serious flaw in the fledgling global economic system, namely, unregulated finance prone to bouts of speculation. In retrospect, it appears she had a point. If anyone thinks this was a fluke, then let us remember that when she learned of her terminal illness, she decided to write her last testament, *Mad Money* (1998). Nearly everything she wrote about in these two prophetic works is applicable to the crisis that we are experiencing today. (2009: 387)

Strange was not the only member of the British heterodox school to have this "obsession" (according to certain orthodox researchers) with international financial issues. In 1996, Helleiner published a book called *States and the Reemergence of Global Finance*. In it, he explains how, with Bretton Woods, the world moved from an open trade system but with capital controls to a system embracing open trade and freely circulating capital. He shows that the international order was created on Keynesian compromises that took into account not only international interests but also the need to protect the welfare state. This Keynesian order was gradually abandoned. At odds with the conventional wisdom, the author shows that it was not the advent of technologies and market forces that were responsible for these choices. For Helleiner, they were the conscious and deliberate choices of states, notably the most powerful ones.

In *Who Elected the Bankers?*, Louis Pauly, who has worked for the IMF, explains why the citizens of various countries, such as France, Canada, Mexico, and Russia, are concerned about the development of the financial world (1998). He describes how financial actors have more and more power over government policy. Pauly also demonstrates that the economic and financial system in which we live is the result of policy decisions made by the democracies of industrialized countries. His book describes the various historical attempts, mainly unsuccessful, to create instruments of multilateral economic surveillance, including the League of Nations, the IMF, the G8, and the European Union.

Palan has published several studies on tax havens. In a 2012 book, co-authored with Richard Murphy and Christian Chavagneux, he presents the history of tax havens, how they operate, their role, and their impact on international finance. According to the authors, tax havens serve as the legal home of two million corporate entities and half of all international lending banks, and they hold up to $13 trillion of personal wealth—the equivalent of the annual US gross national product (Palan, Murphy, and Chavagneux, 2010). They contend that, rather than being peripheral to the global economy, tax havens are an integral part of it. If tax havens are not the cause of the 2008 crisis, they played a fundamental role in it.

In 2007, Anastasia Nesvetailova published a book on the fragility of finance and the issues of debt, speculation, and crisis, in which she predicted that the subprime crisis would trigger an international financial crisis. The fragility of international finance derives from an explosive combination of financial innovations, excessive borrowing, and the lack of progressive liquidity in the system. In *Fragile Finance*, Nesvetailova develops a historical analysis by examining the evolution of these factors since the 1980s (2007). In 2010, she published a second work, *Financial Alchemy in Crisis*, in which she focuses on the absence of liquidity in the system and the credit pyramid. She is harshly critical of financiers and bankers who think they can create wealth and money (2010).

To these authors we can add several others who have worked on related financial issues, authors such as Timothy Sinclair, who published *The New Masters of Capital: American Bond Rating Agencies and the Politics of Creditworthiness* in 2008. The credit agencies that Sinclair writes about play an important role in the global economy and their opinions affect several billions of dollars in borrowing, notably by governments. The difference between the AA and BB rating costs governments millions, even billions, of dollars. It is these agencies that set the standards to compare governments and that assign good and bad points. In a more recent book, co-written with Lena Rethel, Sinclair examines the transformations of banks and, more particularly, their increasing tolerance of risk (Sinclair and Rethel, 2012). In 1997, Randall Germain published a work on the international organization of credit. In this book, he describes the historical transformations of international finance through an examination of investment banks. He argues that the organization of credit is relatively unstable and that the role and the capability of states are increasingly precarious.

Conclusion

As we have observed, the construction of the works and research in British IPE involves a very different logic from those of orthodox IPE. The research studies of the British school do not take the form of paradigmatic debates. Instead, they set out to explain why things are as they are. Causal theories are often absent and formal modelling non-existent. The main strength of these works is that they target problems, underscore injustices, and reveal areas of absence of governance, order, or authority. While the orthodox approach aspires to scientific "objectivity," the heterodox approach is more openly normative in the tradition of pragmatism and moral philosophy (Cohen, 2007: 200). The heterodox school adopts a less formal methodology that is closer to interpretive historical sociology. This method is more compatible with the larger ambitions of heterodox researchers. The orthodox school is more intensive while the heterodox school is more extensive.

This lesser attention to methodology has historically affected the reception in the United States of works from the British school. Even though Susan Strange had been elected president of the International Studies Association in the 1990s, Katzenstein, Keohane, and Krasner's 1999 article about the history of the *International Organization* journal since 1970 made just two small mentions of Strange's work. As Cohen writes,

> Strange did have ideas of her own, of course—lots in fact—but she rarely took the time to develop them in a systematic fashion. In the United States, Strange's lack of formal rigor was considered a distinct liability. She was

admired for her daring—her willingness, even, eagerness, to defy conventional wisdom. As one U.S. scholar wrote to me, she "was never swayed by fashion [and was] always ahead of the curve." But for most Americans in the field, the erstwhile journalist was more pundit than profound, more agent provocateur than savant. Her book, in general, was not thought to be particularly compelling. Yet in Britain her writing took on the aura of gospel, inspiring devotion and emulation. (Cohen, 2008: 51)

In conclusion, Palan recognizes that the works of the British school, notably on international finance, tend to be very critical and that the tone is relatively apocalyptic, even conspiracy-seeking. There is a feeling that a crisis of global proportion is on our doorstep and that it is important to act to avoid the worst. And the worst happened in 2008. The orthodox approach, for its part, saw nothing. In this regard, the great strength of the British school is to have built theories and concepts that allow us to better understand what occurred at that time (Cohen, 2009a: 436–44). Ultimately, Palan writes, "The proof of the pudding is in the eating" (2009a).

Questions

1. Why do we say that the institutionalization of IPE in Great Britain owes a great deal to Susan Strange and her desire to build IPE on multidisciplinary foundations?
2. What were the "institutionalized orthodoxies" within the various disciplines in social sciences that needed to be contested according to the *Review of International Political Economy* inaugural editorial?
3. Why are Susan Strange and the British school "hyperglobalist"?
4. Why did Strange find absurd the notion that US power was in decline in the 1980s?
5. What are the key dimensions of structural power according to Susan Strange?
6. Why have the impersonal forces of the world markets become so important since the end of the Second World War?
7. Susan Strange wrote in the 1990s that states are no longer the primary actors on the international scene. Do you agree?
8. For Ronen Palan, what most clearly distinguishes heterodox IPE from orthodox IPE is the study of international finance. Do you agree?
9. According to Benjamin Cohen, one of the differences between the orthodox and heterodox schools is that the former systematically confronts theories with facts. Do you agree?
10. What is the key difference between the neo-Gramscian school and the British school?

Further Reading

On the foundation of the British school:

Palan, Ronen, ed. *Global Political Economy: Contemporary Theories*. London: Routledge, 2000.

Phillips, Nicola, ed. *Globalizing International Political Economy*. Basingstoke, UK: Palgrave Macmillan, 2005.

Strange, Susan, ed. *Paths to International Political Economy*. London: George Allen & Unwin, 1984.

Stubbs, Richard, and Geoffrey R.D. Underhill, eds. *Political Economy and the Changing Global Order*. 2nd ed. New York: Oxford University Press, 2006.

The author most associated with the British school is Susan Strange. Here are her most important publications:

Strange, Susan. "International Economics and International Relations: A Case of Mutual Neglect." *International Affairs* 46.2 (1970): 304–15.

Strange, Susan. "*Cave! hic Dragones*: A Critique of Regime Analysis." *International Organization* 36.2 (1982): 479–96.

Strange, Susan. *Casino Capitalism*. Oxford: Blackwell, 1986.

Strange, Susan. "The Persistent Myth of Lost Hegemony." *International Organization* 41.4 (1987): 551–74.

Strange, Susan. "The Future of the American Empire." *Journal of International Affairs* 42.1 (1988): 1–17.

Strange, Susan. *States and Markets: An Introduction to International Political Economy*. London: Pinter Publishers, 1988.

Strange, Susan. "States, Firms and Diplomacy." *International Affairs* 68.1 (1992): 1–15.

Strange, Susan. "Wake up, Krasner! The World Has Changed." *Review of International Political Economy* 1.2 (1994): 209–19.

Strange, Susan. "ISA As a Microcosm." *International Studies Quarterly* 39.3 (1995): 289–95.

Strange, Susan. *The Retreat of the State: The Diffusion of Power in the World Economy*. Cambridge: Cambridge University Press, 1996.

Strange, Susan. "Territory, State, Authority and Economy: A New Realist Ontology of Global Political Economy." In *The New Realism: Perspectives on Multilateralism and World Order*, edited by Robert W. Cox, 3–19. Basingstoke, UK: Palgrave Macmillan, 1997.

Strange, Susan. *Mad Money: When Markets Outgrow Governments*. Ann Arbor: Michigan University Press, 1998.

Stopford, John, and Susan Strange, with John S. Henley. *Rival States, Rival Firms: Competition for World Market Shares*. Cambridge: Cambridge University Press, 1991.

On Susan Strange's work:

Lawton, Thomas C., James N. Rosenau, Amy C. Verdun, eds. *Strange Power: Shaping the Parameters of International Relations and International Political Economy*. Aldershot, UK: Ashgate, 2000.

Tooze, Roger. "Susan Strange: Academic International Relations and International Political Economy." *New Political Economy* 5.2 (1999): 280–9.

Tooze, Roger, and Christopher May. *Authority and Markets: Susan Strange's Writings on International Political Economy*. Basingstoke, UK: Palgrave Macmillan, 2002.

8 Green and Feminist IPE

Chapter Contents

- Green IPE
- The Orthodox Approach in Green IPE
- Critical Green IPE
- Feminist IPE
- Feminist Ontology in IPE
- Feminist Epistemology in IPE
- Conclusion

Reader's Guide

The chapter is about two peripheral theoretical approaches in IPE: green and feminist IPE. Though they are very important, they remain on the periphery, as the majority of IPE specialists address them only rarely. A great many green IPE theories are compatible with the debates of the orthodox school. For the orthodox, environmental issues have become new topics that can be analyzed using analytic tools and existing theoretical frameworks. A heterodox and critical school also exists in green IPE theory and green IPE shares many points with heterodox approaches. Feminist approaches, for their part, are definitely positioned on the fringes of IPE. Their affinity with heterodox approaches and their rejection of positivism fosters this marginalization. In IPE, none of the paradigms of the orthodox approach has been significantly influenced by feminist works, and despite signs of sympathy, the neo-Gramscian and the British school do not use gender as a category of analysis.

This chapter examines two peripheral theoretical approaches in IPE: green and feminist IPE. These are not emerging theories—some articles date from the 1980s—and though they are very important, they nevertheless remain peripheral, as the majority of IPE specialists address them only rarely, or never. These perspectives are generally absent from introductory textbooks, syllabi, and reading lists for general examinations.

While feminist IPE theories are losing ground, green IPE theories are burgeoning. As we will see in this chapter, a large share of green IPE theories are compatible with the debates of the orthodox school, which makes them more acceptable to that school. For the orthodox, environmental issues become new topics that can be analyzed using analytic tools and existing theoretical frameworks. That said, a heterodox and critical school also exists in green IPE theory and green theory shares many points with heterodox approaches.

Feminist approaches are definitely on the fringes of IPE. Their affinity with heterodox approaches and their rejection of positivism fosters this marginalization. In IPE, none of the paradigms of the orthodox approach has been significantly influenced by feminist works, and despite signs of sympathy, the main approaches presented previously in this book, from the neo-Gramscian to the British school, do not use gender as a category of analysis. These approaches are mentioned only rarely in textbooks and even more rarely in syllabi. This chapter first examines green IPE theories and then turns to feminist IPE theories.

Green IPE

Environmental issues are increasingly influencing IPE theories. The acceleration of globalization is having a considerable effect on the environment. The importance of environmental issues, in particular biodiversity, climate change, and decarbonization of economies, is resulting in the integration of environmental issues in IPE debates. The nature and the origin of the change are the subject of passionate debates.

Orthodox and heterodox approaches already address environmental issues, but without making them the focus of analysis. While orthodox theories tend to present environmental issues as new issues that can be analyzed using existing theories, other more heterodox and critical approaches have also been developed. These approaches do not share the positivist epistemology of the dominant theories, they do not use a state-centric analytical framework, and they have a very pessimistic discourse on environmental issues. Heterodox and critical works are also more obviously normative: we must save the planet. Questions of environmental justice are omnipresent.

This section on green IPE theories is divided into two parts. The first part presents the orthodox green IPE theories, and the second, the heterodox green theories.

The Orthodox Approach in Green IPE

Within the orthodox school, realists and liberals tend to treat environmental issues as new issues that can be analyzed in their pre-existing theoretical framework. Realists have largely neglected the analysis of environmental issues as this topic belongs to the realm of "low politics." Nevertheless, certain themes are of interest for realists, themes such as conflicts over the appropriation of scarce natural resources, the internationalization of the national environmental standards of the most powerful countries, and climate refugees.

It is the liberals who have tackled environmental issues most in their works. Liberals have a fundamentally optimistic vision of globalization and environmental issues. For them, when tallying the plus and minus columns, the plus side wins out. Liberals argue that the accelerated growth of the world-economy has fostered a rapid decline in poverty, and it has also contributed to the growth of per capita income, while at the same time promoting global awareness of environmental problems.

Thomas Malthus (1798) had predicted that with the "geometrical" or exponential growth of the population, the Earth would one day run short of resources. For liberals, this prediction is only half true. Even though the world population has grown exponentially over the last 200 years, the planet is not in a shortage situation. The green revolution of the 1960s and 1970s fostered the emergence of more resilient agriculture and rapid growth that helped to considerably reduce the world's malnutrition problems. Food prices have dropped by two-thirds since the 1960s. As well, life expectancy at birth, according to the World Health Organization, rose from 36 years in 1900 to close to 70 years in 2013 (Dauvergne, 2014: 374).

Economists Gene Grossman and Alan Krueger (1994), in their influential article, introduced the Kuznets curve into the environmental field. Kuznets curve (1955) claims that after a certain development threshold level, measured by the increase in per capita income, economic inequality in a country is reduced. Grossman and Krueger contend that, after a certain development threshold level is reached, a country's pollution level decreases. When per capita income reaches between US$5,000 and $8,000 per year, say the authors, pollution begins to fall. The explanation is simple: at this threshold, the population lobbies for better living conditions. In addition, at this threshold, governments and businesses own more resources that allow them to reduce pollution. If these predictions are accurate, pollution levels should begin to fall in countries such as China, as they did in postwar Japan, which experienced a comparable process.

For liberals, the debate chiefly has to do with finding the balance between economic growth, poverty reduction, and environmental protection. The essence of the theoretical problem, according to liberals, lies in "common pool resources," meaning the transnational management of an international common good. Essentially, the aim of liberal theories is to explain and predict the behaviour of states and to propose solutions to create stronger and more effective international environmental regimes. These theories draw inspiration from a paper written by ecologist Garrett Hardin titled

"The Tragedy of the Commons." In this astonishing paper published in the journal *Science* in 1968, Hardin drew an analogy between the destruction of British common lands and the modern "commons," which include the atmosphere, the high seas, and unregulated forest. Nowadays, a number of authors illustrate the climate change problem with this metaphor.

The tragedy of the commons goes like this: imagine a pasture open to everyone. Under these conditions, we can assume that livestock producers, who want to maximize their interest, will put as many animals as possible in this pasture because it is in their self-interest to do so. Eventually, if all producers adopt the same behaviour, it will lead to overuse of the resource, which will create innumerable problems for the collective. The solution to this problem is (1) to create private property where the land is divided into parcels, (2) to institute an auction system or a lottery, or (3) to institute a quota regime to regulate the system. To do nothing is not a good solution in the long term. In all cases, state intervention is desirable, as a series of rational individual behaviours leads to an irrational collective outcome.

In Hardin's opinion, this problem possesses a logic similar to pollution. For polluters, it is more rational economically to release their pollution into a common resource, such as the air or the ocean, than to assume the cost of reducing this pollution. Since air or oceans cannot be sold in the form of private property, and since they are common resources that belong to no one, state intervention either through taxation, regulation, or even criminalization of environmentally damaging acts becomes inevitable. When pollution has transnational repercussions, as in the case of climate change, the coordinated action of several states at the global level is the only solution. Collective action theory and the management of international common goods thus require the creation of international institutions, regimes, and treaties to manage the resource or to regulate pollution.

For liberals, the solutions to environmental problems require international cooperation, for several reasons. Although the biosphere is indivisible, the Earth is fragmented into a multitude of states. As well, environmental issues affect a great many public and private interests. States have no other choice than to cooperate, if only to ensure the proper management of a watershed, knowing that pollution does not respect a country's borders. Moreover, some sources of pollution have significant effects on the planet as a whole. CO_2 emissions in New York or Beijing accentuate the global problem of climate change. Worsening environmental problems may turn into an international crisis, as with drought-plagued climate refugees, for example. Finally, some environments, such as international seabeds or the Antarctic, belong to the global commons and their management requires interstate collaboration.

As presented in Chapter 4, liberal theorists are therefore interested in the creation of international institutions or regimes on environmental issues. The number of regional and international negotiations pertaining

---

Box 8.1   International Environmental Agreements, Regimes, or Institutions

Convention on Wetlands of International Importance (1971)

London Convention on the Prevention of Marine Pollution (1972)

United Nations Environment Programme (UNEP) (1973)

Convention on International Trade in Endangered Species of Wild Flora and Fauna (1973)

Convention on the Conservation of Antarctic Marine Living Resources (1980)

United Nations Convention on the Law of the Sea (1982)

Montreal Protocol on Substances that Deplete the Ozone Layer (1987)

World Commission on Environment and Development Report (Brundtland Commission) and Sustainable Development (1987)

Basil Convention on the Control of Transboundary Movements of Hazardous Wastes and Their Disposal (1989)

Earth or Rio Summit (1992)

Convention on Biological Diversity (1992)

United Nations Convention to Combat Desertification (1994)

Stockholm Convention on Persistent Organic Pollutants (2001)

Kyoto Protocol to the United Nations Framework Convention on Climate Change (1998)

---

to environmental issues has increased significantly. According to Ronald Mitchell, since the 1970s, there have been more than 1,100 multilateral environmental agreements, including protocols and amendments.

The effectiveness of these kinds of international regimes to enforce and regulate environmental agreements and policies is also a concern in the field. Several international regimes are weak and non-binding. They have not had sufficient influence on the behaviour of states or of multinational corporations. One of the problems stems from the fact that it is difficult to clearly establish the causes, consequences, and solutions to ecological or environmental problems.

Furthermore, in the matter of climate change, the whole question of historical responsibility makes it difficult to reach an agreement between developed and developing countries. This explains the notion of "common but differentiated responsibility" in international climate negotiations, or even why, in the development aid policies of developed countries, subsidies are granted to developing countries so that they adopt policies, such as reforestation, to mitigate greenhouse gas production (Roberts and Parks, 2006).

When powerful interests, such as those of the oil or gas industry, are affected, it is easy to predict that the industry will mobilize against restrictive measures. The oil industry's influence on the Conservative Party of Canada and on the US presidency and Congress have succeeded in limiting the involvement of these countries in the fight against climate change.

Despite all this, liberals will maintain that the creation of a large number of international standards, institutions, and legal instruments to protect the planet is a positive accomplishment. Even if climate change negotiations are at an impasse, several international initiatives have proven to be successful. One example is the Montreal Protocol of 1987, which has led to developed countries substantially reducing their production and consumption of substances (such as CFCs) that have depleted the ozone layer.

Critical Green IPE

While "orthodox" green approaches are dominant in the debates, green heterodox critical theories are also present. These approaches may be qualified as critical as they are "problem-posing" rather than "problem-solving," to use Robert Cox's terms. They are essentially multidisciplinary, and, above all, very obviously normative in their orientation. Critical green IPE theorists, in their aim to promote environmental justice, seek to theorize the ecological injustices of the industrialization and globalization eras.

These theories are naturally very critical of orthodox green approaches, and the criticism takes several forms. Heterodox green theorists are critical of the hidden normative biases of orthodox theorists and of the ethical problems posed by these biases. The orthodox, with their propensity for problem solving, accept the world as it is, while the heterodox believe a radical questioning is necessary.

To begin, green theorists criticize realists for having only marginally integrated environmental issues in their reflection. Their silence or their relegation of environmental issues to the realm of "low politics" is seen by the green movement as a form of implicit support for the unbridled exploitation of the planet. Green theorists strongly criticize those who claim that it is futile to cooperate on environmental matters if a state does not make absolute gains. They also criticize the realist theorists' narrow version of the concept of "security" when environmental degradation causes numerous security problems beyond the obvious one of climate refugees. As well, realist theoretical models are unable to explain why we are seeing such a significant increase in the number of international treaties and regimes in the environmental field.

Then again, critical green theorists are also skeptical of rationalist analyses based on liberal regime theory. According to green theorists, to understand the creation of international regimes to protect wilderness areas like the Antarctic, or threatened species such as whales or elephants, or the atmosphere, requires a social and historical analysis rather than one based on rational choice theory. Critical green theorists argue that the "interest-based bargaining" of liberal theorists is too limited to explain the growing number of agreements, protocols, and regimes. It is important to consider the entrepreneurs of environmental standards, their discourse, and their action plans. Critical green theorists take a positive view of the rise in the influence of non-state actors, transnational social movements, and democratization of the international scene. These deficiencies of regime theories fostered the emergence of a constructivist and critical conception of environmental regimes.

What is more, analyzing environmental problems in terms of international regimes draws our attention away from the real driver of environmental degradation, the capitalism and industrialization dynamic. Green theorists criticize the "rational" overexploitation of the Earth. Critical green theorists in IPE are skeptical of the economic planning so dear to mercantilists, and they are opposed to trade liberalization projects as proposed by liberals (Bernstein, 2001).

Critical green IPE authors are more clearly in the category of pessimists. For them, environmental degradation caused by human activity has a long history. It was not until after the Second World War, however, that the extent and the persistence of environmental problems became a global problem. Rapid demographic growth, the development of new modes of transportation and new technologies, as well as the increased consumption of energy and natural resources, are certainly contributing factors. The ramp-up of consumption in society produced enormous pollution and waste that resulted in the rapid erosion of the planet's biodiversity. Even though it is undeniable that in several countries, hygiene measures have improved and pollution has decreased, the overall environmental balance sheet remains very negative. Ecosystem degradation is a fact and natural resources are being overexploited.

The problem has reached such a level that some authors question not only the secondary effect of economic growth, but also economic development itself. A key influence in this debate has been the Club of Rome report published in the 1970s, titled *The Limits to Growth*. Nowadays, population growth, with close to 200,000 births every day, is a ticking time bomb, notably due to the improved standard of living of the populations in emerging countries. If the Chinese adopt American lifestyle habits, the environmental outlook is devastating. How can the Earth in 2050 support nearly 10 billion people? Humans will have to produce more food in the next 40 years than they did in the previous 10,000 years. How can we do this without destroy-ing the planet?

Eric Helleiner brought the ideas of Leopold Kohr to the discussion in critical green theory (2013). Austrian Leopold Kohr, who received the Alternative Nobel Prize in 1983, promoted the "small is beautiful" notion, that life in small communities is preferable to large groups. As a correspon-dent for *The New York Times* in Europe during the Spanish Civil War, he became a fierce opponent of fascism and communism. After fleeing Austria, he spent much of the remainder of his life as a professor of various subjects at Rutgers and other universities. His landmark book *The Breakdown of Nations* was published in the 1950s.

According to Kohr, the "bigness" of political and economic life in the industrial era reduces the capacity of humans in society to live a full and bal-anced life within their community, a community that would be more demo-cratic and respectful of the individual. Kohr promoted the idea that the large nation-states that emerged with the industrial age fostered the rise of authoritarianism. In such large communities, citizens are not able to moni-tor the actions of the state (Helleiner, 2013).

Adapted to environmentalists' concerns, Kohr's theses imply that glo-balization of the economy and finance erodes diversity and local autonomy. In this globalized environment, local economies are pressured by global competition, which is harmful to the environment. The concentration of power of the large multinationals drives them in a race for profit at the expense of the environment and biodiversity. Increased toxic waste and pollution on the planet are symptoms of this unbalanced life.

A source of concern is that in this globalized environment, human be-ings lose touch with nature. Kohr claimed that the problems caused by the "bigness" of nation-states would be eliminated if the world were made up of "self-reliant 'small states'" as it was in medieval times (Helleiner, 2013: 331).

In adapting Kohr's theses, we realize that the units of analysis of criti-cal green theorists are not nation-states, individuals, social classes, but local communities. The overall structure is not the interstate system of real-ists, the globalized environment of liberals, or the capitalism of Marxists, but rather the industrialization era. This industrialization era produces an imbalance between nature and the environment and economic develop-ment. The normative aim of green theorists is "act locally, think globally" (Helleiner, 2013: 335).

Critical green theorists have made this slogan, coined by René Dubois during the Stockholm Earth Summit in 1972, the catchphrase of their move-ment. Act locally means that individuals' foremost concern must be to deal with problems within their community. The slogan represents support for the decentralization and valorization of local political and economic life. Underlying this slogan is a criticism of industrial society. The accelerated period of industrialization and then the ramp-up in society of consumption created an imbalance in the relationship between development and the environment.

While liberals contend that environmental problems are the consequence of political market failure that can be solved by enforcing a carbon tax or by establishing international regulatory institutions for example, greens tend to see environmental problems in apocalyptic terms. The industrial era lifestyle is the problem. Green theorists favour local purchasing and local production, small markets, and local economic initiatives. Some have called this "neo-medievalism." This approach has led to a new reflection on the nature of sustainable development, on environmental justice, and on ecological security.

Critical approaches in green IPE also criticize liberal approaches for neglecting several important phenomena, including economic domination structures and ecological risk distribution between states, regions, and social classes. The importance of the emphasis placed on environmental justice is crucial in critical green IPE.

According to green theorists, environmental injustice occurs when actors "externalize" the environmental costs of their practices and their decisions onto other actors. Alf Hornborg developed an ecological theory of imperialism (2013). In this approach, capitalism can only be understood at the global economy scale and through the exploitation of the periphery by the centre. This imperial-like relationship constitutes an "unequal exchange in an ecological direction" (Hornborg, 2013: 340). It is an unequal exchange of energy and matter between the centres and the resource peripheries.

Environmental injustice also occurs when a privileged class appropriates more than its share of the environment, leaving a disproportionate ecological footprint (Wackernagel and Rees, 1998) or when countries "delocalize their pollution," thereby increasing their "ecological shadow." The concept of ecological footprint was coined by William Rees and Mathis Wackernagel and represents, in the case of a person, the total area in global hectares required to sustain his or her lifestyle. This concept allows researchers to measure and compare the average ecological impact of people in different countries. The concept of an ecological shadow arises "as economies, through both intentional and unintentional patterns of consumption, trade, investments, and financing transfer the environmental harm of its citizen outside its territory" (Dauvergne, 2014: 376). In a globalized environment, pollution may decrease in a country such as Sweden, but if Swedish firms are subcontracting out to China, the problem is merely being relocated. Hence, although Sweden's ecological footprint decreases, its ecological shadow increases. In the end, the Earth is not any better off.

More radical approaches promote zero growth, a position that goes further than the proposal to make development sustainable, which was advocated by the Brundtland Report. Many green theorists criticize the sustainable development approach because, in its focus on intergenerational equity, it ignores the issue of biodiversity. Even more problematic, the report assumes that sustainable development can be achieved through the acceleration of economic growth. Critical green economists reject the position of neoclassical economists who believe that by putting a price on pollution, we will change the behaviour of actors and thereby reduce pollution (Schlosberg, 2007).

For critical green theorists, this is precisely the paradox of sustainable development: environmental protection is more likely to occur in a context of economic growth but growth creates big environmental problems. Ulrich Beck argued that ecological problems persist because they are produced by the economic, scientific, and political elites that we ask to solve those problems. Better environmental standards cannot be arrived at by achieving greener growth, but by changing the system.

Feminist IPE

What are feminist approaches in IPE? Feminism entered the debates in international relations and international political economy theories almost simultaneously towards the late 1980s and the early 1990s (Tickner, 1997, 2011, 2013a, 2013b). The main goal of feminist theories is to make gender visible in the real world (Paul and Amawi, 2013: 294). Feminist theorists analyze IPE through the lens of gender, but IPE feminists want not simply "an IPE with women in it, but the creation of a fully gendered IPE" (Paul and Amawi, 2013: 294). V. Spike Peterson further asserts that gender "is constitutive of contemporary international political economy itself" (Peterson, 2013: 309). To promote research on women in world politics, a specialized journal was created (*Feminist Journal of International Studies*), and a databank on the marginality and the subordination of women in world politics was established. The Woman Stats Project (www.womanstats.org) is the most important and comprehensive compilation of information on the status of women in the world. The website includes information on over 360 indicators in 175 countries. In IPE, the contribution of feminist approaches can be seen at two levels: the first is ontological—feminists want women to have their rightful place in the analysis in IPE. The second is epistemological and theoretical.

Feminist Ontology in IPE

In the first category of works that aim to include women in IPE, we see a variety of research themes that are at odds with traditional subjects dealt with in IPE. Feminists want to understand why women are marginalized and speculate about how this situation affects the structure of world politics. They wish to expose the fact that orthodox approaches make women invisible. Through their research, feminists in IPE want to show the importance of nothing less than half of humanity. Since the majority of women are on the fringes of IPE, on the fringes of power, they offer a totally new perspective, very different from the "state-centric focus" of orthodox theories. Feminist studies have thus extended the ontological base of IPE towards new issues. The use of gendered lenses by a researcher reveals a very different reality from that observed through orthodox lenses.

Feminists in IPE are concerned with the subordination of women in world politics. Feminist works deal notably with the gendered division of labour. This division arose in seventeenth-century Europe with the new division of labour produced by the creation of remunerative work, essentially male, in the public sphere versus unremunerated work, essentially female, in the private sphere. Men became "breadwinners" while women became "housewives." With the acceleration of industrialization, women who entered the labour market found themselves disproportionately in underpaid jobs in the textile, services, or subsistence farming sectors. The history of capitalism is also the history of the marginalization and subordination of women (Tickner, 2011).

Starting from this idea of marginalization, IPE feminists have focused on a variety of topics rarely studied by their male colleagues, such as unequal access to jobs; economic and social inequalities in developing countries; the implications of trade liberalization on the condition of poor women; development issues where women are more present than men; global maternal mortality; unequal access to education; genital mutilation; inequities in family law; life expectancy and poverty rates among women; the condition of women refugees; human rights violations that afflict women such as rape in wartime and sex trafficking (Peterson and Runyan, 2010; Enloe, 2004).

These works have shed light on the fact that, globally, women earn lower wages than men and occupy a disproportionate place among the poor and vulnerable people in all societies. Even when women do get better jobs, they tend to earn lower wages than men. Women are also clearly marginalized at the executive, legislative, and judicial power levels in all countries, even in Scandinavian countries that have the best record of reducing the gender gap.

The invisibility of women in IPE theories led J. Ann Tickner, in 1991 (see Tickner 2013b), to recommend a rereading of the three analytical categories in IPE proposed by Robert Gilpin: liberalism (Chapter 4 of this book), economic nationalism (or IPE realism from Chapter 3), and Marxism (Chapter 6). She observed that none of these approaches addressed the issue of gender, not even Marxism. Even worse, several researchers present these analytical categories as being gender-neutral, which means that the interactions between states and markets (how Gilpin defines IPE) can be understood without taking gender differences into consideration. Tickner tells us that feminists cannot accept this assertion.

Feminists believe instead that we cannot understand IPE without including gender differences, in the same way Marxists maintain that we cannot understand IPE without referring to social classes. At the theoretical level, feminists criticize the idea that IR and IPE are gender-neutral disciplines and that researchers can distinguish "facts" from "values" based on a notion promoted by the orthodox school. Tickner writes, "Ignoring gender distinctions hides a set of social and economic relations characterized by inequality between men and women" (2013b: 297).

When we analyze the claim of gender neutrality in the three perspectives put forward by Gilpin, we realize, says Tickner, the significance of the bias in these perspectives at two levels: their explanation of IPE, and their normative prescription, which is biased in favour of male interests. According to Tickner, the feminist perspective in IPE would begin its analysis with very different "assumptions" about categories of analysis in IPE in regards to individuals, states, and social classes. For feminists, gender is a

> set of socially constructed characteristics describing what men and woman ought to be. Characteristics such as strength, rationality, independence, protector, and public are associated with masculinity while characteristics such as weakness, emotionality, relational, protected, and private are associated with femininity. It is important to note that individual men and women may not embody all these characteristics—it is possible for women to display masculine ones and vice versa. Rather, they are ideal types; the ideal masculine type (in the West—white and heterosexual) is sometimes referred to as "hegemonic masculinity." (Tickner and Sjoberg, 2013: 206)

These gendered characteristics, according to Tickner, are relational, meaning that they depend on one another to find their meaning, that they are defined in opposition to one another. They are also unequal or biased in favour of men, because masculine characteristics are more valued than feminine ones (Peterson, 2013: 309 10). As Tickner puts it, "There is evidence to suggest that both women and men assign a more positive value to masculine characteristics" (1997: 614).

Liberalism, which is the dominant orthodox approach, takes as its starting point the analysis of the individual. For liberals, individuals are by nature "economic animals driven by rational self-interest. Rational economic man is assumed to be motivated by the laws of profit maximization. He is highly individualistic, pursuing his own economic goals in the market without any social obligation to the community of which he is part" (Tickner, 2013b: 299). The feminist critique of these assumptions questions this idea of rational man that is extrapolated from Western male behaviour and that is supposed to represent all of humanity at all times. At the very least, says Tickner, this calculating behaviour cannot be used as a reference for the behavioural norms of women. In most countries, women are already concentrated in reproductive rather than productive activities. Their role does not conform to the behaviour prescribed by the theories mentioned above. Moreover, women who are in the labour market, when they are not completely marginalized, tend to choose caring professions such as teaching, nursing, and social work, professions that are poorly adapted to the idea of profit maximization. Rational choice theory is therefore revelatory of the male domination of the IPE discipline.

The idea of individual economic rationality, an idea drawn from liberal political theory, does not concord with a feminist reading that would put more emphasis on interdependence, community, and cooperation. The market, which is the sphere of action of *homo economicus*, is a male construct. Liberal development theories that view the market as a driver of change generate a bias favourable to men and against women who favour collaborative approaches. Tickner, for example, rejects the idea that rationality is a fundamental, natural characteristic of self-interested individuals. She believes instead that rationality is socially constructed. An alternative form of feminist rationality would be present not in the market and competition, but in "caring roles." Power must also be defined in such a way as to move the concept away "from autonomy and domination" and toward "mutual enablement." Feminist theory also focuses on what is taking place in the reproductive sphere.

Liberals and realists in IPE use game theory to explain the behaviour of states on the international scene. When cooperation exists, it is explained not in terms of community, but in terms of rational actors that want to maximize their interests. However, Tickner cites the works of Birgit Brock-Utne, who maintains that men and women behave differently when they play a simulation of game theory. Hence, at a very fundamental level, the explanation using game theory excludes female values from the equation.

Gilpin's economic nationalism (the realist approach in IPE in this book) is a critique of liberalism. The key actor is no longer the individual but the state, which is presumed to be rational, seeking to maximize its power, wealth, and autonomy. State action is guided by the concept of national interest. A feminist critique of these assumptions puts the social construction of the state in its historical context to demonstrate the marginality of women, particularly in foreign affairs and the military. As well, the prescription of Gilpin's nationalist approach was largely a male construct. The idea of maximizing the power of the state and promoting the development of its army favours men more than women. In societies where military spending is maximized, Tickner (2013b) tells us, women are often the first to suffer the economic effects when social programs are sacrificed for military priorities.

For nationalists, the military-industrial complex is an important part of the national economy that must have state protection. Women would prefer economic and social security.

Given that Marxists focus on the less fortunate in the world-economy, it would seem that this perspective is more readily compatible with feminism. It is true that feminist theory owes a debt to Marxist theories. Like Marxists, a large number of feminist theorists accept the idea that knowledge is embedded in human activity. Feminist theories widely accept the relationship between knowledge and power. They contend that most of human knowledge was developed by men and based on male interests. And like Marxists, feminists reject the idea of a universal and abstract rationality.

Marxist theories are nevertheless biased in favour of men because they place production spheres, where men are dominant, at the centre of the analysis, while they tend to completely ignore the reproduction spheres where women are in the majority. For Tickner, the problem of capitalist societies lies not only in the exploitation of the proletariat by the bourgeoisie, but also in the structure of male domination or patriarchy of society. The very visible production sphere overshadows the reproduction sphere. The construction of the private sphere as being associated with women is the cause of the devaluation and neglect by mainstream approaches.

For V. Spike Peterson, the exclusion of women from theoretical frameworks is no accident. As the core of the research deals with fundamentally male research topics, the exclusion of women is not "accidental or coincidental but *required* for the analytical consistency of reigning paradigms" (Peterson, 2013: 310). In plain language, women cannot be added to the existing paradigms without fundamentally changing the underlying assumptions of these paradigms.

Feminist works can be divided into various categories. Liberal feminism is interested in institutions and practices and asks what a world in which women had a more important role would be like. In general, liberal feminism asserts that a world with more women in the spheres of power fosters cooperation, negotiation, and a more peaceful world. Liberal feminism promotes women's equality and wants the obstacles that block women's path towards equality to be removed in the name of liberal tradition so that women have the same opportunities as men.

A number of feminists disagree with this approach. Post-liberal feminists argue, for example, that inequalities continue to be present even when men and women have obtained equality in law. The fight must go further. Postmodern feminism faults liberal feminism for producing knowledge that legitimizes a new repressive discourse on the pretext of wanting to free women. Gender hierarchies are still very present. Critical feminist theorists for their part maintain that power relations are hidden in the ideas and material structures that were chiefly built by men. The feminist standpoint even

contends that women reason and think differently from men while constructivist feminists concentrate on gender representations and the influence of
these representations on world politics. Feminists in the Marxist tradition
focus on the question of gender and social classes, while postcolonial feminists
believe that feminists must adjust their analyses by race, class, and place (non-
Western societies versus Western societies, for example) (Tickner, 2013b).

Feminist Epistemology in IPE

The late 1980s saw an ongoing debate in the United States between positivists and post-positivists in international relations and IPE theories. It was
in this context that several researchers began to question the ontological as
well as the epistemological foundations of IR and IPE theories. Post-positivist
research, which includes critical theories, certain forms of constructivism,
poststructuralism, and postmodernism, began to question the dominant approaches that were positivist, rationalist, and materialist—in other words,
the fundamental principles of the orthodox school in IPE.

Feminism emerged in the 1980s as a new perspective in IR and IPE research, as awareness grew of the marginalization of women, as a subject of
research, in these fields. Feminist theorists criticized these disciplines as
they kept women on the fringes. The first works, briefly outlined above,
were ontological critiques of the mainstream works that neglect to give a
larger place to women. The second generation of works were epistemological
critiques of IPE theories. Feminist theorists criticized the positivist epistemology of the orthodox theories of the late 1980s and the early 1990s.

From the theoretical point of view, the majority of feminist theories in
IPE are post-positivist. The aim of these theories is not simply to highlight
the unequal distribution of gains or the marginality of women in world
politics but also to explain how gender structures IPE.

A great many feminist approaches are more in tune with critical theories as defined by Robert Cox. Feminism is more explicitly normative than
orthodox approaches; it seeks the emancipation of women, equality, and the
elimination of "unequal gender relations." Even though feminist approaches
do not necessarily have to be post-positivist, they tend to be because of their
acceptance of a wide variety of methodological and disciplinary approaches.
Feminist analyses are based on a variety of philosophical, sociological, and
anthropological traditions outside mainstream approaches in IPE or in political science.

Feminist approaches tend to be very skeptical of positivist approaches
that insist there is a separation between facts and values and that "facts" are
neutral. While a number of feminists detect structural realities that persist
over time, such as patriarchy, they tend to think that these realities are socially constructed and variable over time rather than universal and natural.

A theory that defines itself by production, rationality, accumulation of capital is not objective about real facts in the world but expresses a clear masculine bias. The normative objective of feminist theories is thus to promote the emancipation of women.

Problem-solving approaches essentially accept the world as a basis or framework for action. Since feminists are united in their perceptions that gender hierarchies are detrimental to women, they find it difficult to accept this epistemological positioning.

Orthodox authors, who adopted the scientific methods of the natural sciences, tend to consider feminist approaches atheoretical. The most frequent criticism made by orthodox authors is that women can simply be included in the existing paradigms. But for Tickner, "feminists and IR scholars are drawing on very different realities and using different epistemologies when they engage in theorizing about international relations" (1997: 613). It is therefore difficult for feminist theorists to dialogue with orthodox researchers as, for the latter, feminist ways of doing things do not constitute "legitimate scientific inquiry." Feminist epistemology seeks concretely to redefine the analytical and conceptual core of IPE.

The fundamental problem probably lies in the fact that feminist research topics are often peripheral to the IPE field. Furthermore, due to orthodox theorists' adherence to the precepts of "rational economic man," to the idea that unitary states operate in an anarchic and asocial environment, or to the fixation of Marxist theorists on the production sphere, there is little space or point of entry to include feminist theories (Tickner, 2013a). Also, post-positivist approaches reject rationalist methods and causal theories and develop more interpretative approaches centred on ideas, values, and tools derived from sociology in order to understand world politics. This makes them irrelevant, according to orthodox theorists.

Conclusion

It is still too early to say whether green theories will become more important or if a new discipline (Green Political Economy) will be institutionalized alongside IPE and security studies due to the importance of environmental issues and climate change. The publication of several synthesizing works tends to confirm the latter hypothesis (Clapp and Dauvergne 2005; LaFerrière and Stoett, 2006). But for now, environmental debates, when they find their way into IPE textbooks, are generally on the periphery of the fundamental debates of the discipline. That said, the links between international politics, states, markets, and the environment are so important that the other scenario is that these debates will be reflected even more at the core of the theoretical approaches, to take a more central place in IPE alongside financial issues and free trade.

The feminist perspective, on the other hand, seems to be losing ground in IPE. J. Ann Tickner, who started her career as a specialist in IPE and North–South relations before becoming the author of reference on feminist theories in international politics, stated in a 2013 interview that the influence of feminist approaches on mainstream works continues to be marginal. Even though Robert Keohane called for dialogue between mainstream approaches and the feminist perspective, these dialogues have been very limited (Keohane, 2008). In 1997, Tickner wrote, "the lack of attention paid to feminist perspectives by other critical approaches has also been disappointing" (611). Feminist researchers have essentially dialogued with themselves (Tickner, 2013a).

Questions

1. Why are green and feminist theoretical approaches considered to be peripheral?
2. What are the major differences between the "orthodox" green IPE theories and the critical green IPE theories?
3. What is the "Tragedy of the Commons" according to Garrett Hardin?
4. Why are capitalism and industrialization the real drivers of environmental degradation?
5. What is an environmental injustice?
6. What is the main goal of the feminist theories in IPE?
7. Why is the gendered division of labour key to understanding the marginalization of women in IPE?
8. Feminists criticize the idea that IPE is a gender-neutral discipline and that, according to the thinking of the orthodox school, researchers can distinguish "facts" from "values." Do you agree?
9. Why are feminist theories ignored by the orthodox school, according to Tickner?
10. Do you agree that the heterodox school does not pay enough attention to feminist perspectives?

Further Reading

Bibliography for green international political economy approaches:

Bernstein, Steven. *The Compromise of Liberal Environmentalism*. New York: Columbia University Press, 2001.

Clapp, Jennifer, and Peter Dauvergne. *Paths to a Green World: The Political Economy of the Global Environment*. Cambridge, MA: MIT Press, 2005.

Dauvergne, Peter. "Globalization and the Environment." In *Global Political Economy*, 4th ed., edited by John Ravenhill, 372–98. Oxford: Oxford University Press, 2014.

Haas, Peter M., and James Gustave Speth. *Global Environmental Governance*. Washington: Island Press, 2006.

Hardin, Garrett. "The Tragedy of the Commons." *Science* 162 (1968): 1243–8.

Helleiner, Eric. "International Political Economy and the Greens." In *The Theoretical Evolution of International Political Economy: A Reader*, 3rd ed., edited by Darel E. Paul and Abla Amawi, 327–39. New York: Oxford University Press, 2013.

Hornborg, Alf. "The Thermodynamics of Imperialism: Toward an Ecological Theory of Unequal Exchange." In *The Theoretical Evolution of International Political Economy: A Reader*, 3rd ed., edited by Darel E. Paul and Abla Amawi, 340–8. New York: Oxford University Press, 2013.

LaFerrière, Eric, and Peter J. Stoett. *International Ecopolitical Theory: Critical Approaches*. Vancouver: University of British Columbia Press, 2006.

Paterson, Matthew. *Understanding Global Environmental Politics: Domination, Accumulation, Resistance*. London: Palgrave, 2000.

Rees, William. "Ecological Footprints and Appropriated Carrying Capacity: What Urban Economics Leaves Out." *Environment and Urbanization* 4.2 (1992): 121–30.

Roberts, J. Timmons, and Bradley Parks. *A Climate of Injustice: Global Inequality, North-South Politics, and Climate Policy*. Cambridge, MA: MIT Press, 2006.

Schlosberg, David. *Defining Environmental Justice: Theories, Movements, and Nature*. Oxford: Oxford University Press, 2007.

Wackernagel, Mathis, and William Rees. *Our Ecological Footprint: Reducing Human Impact on the Earth*. Gabriola Island, BC: New Society Publishers, 1998.

The feminist approach in IPE:

Enloe, Cynthia. *The Curious Feminist: Searching for Woman in a New Age of Empire*. Berkeley, CA: University of California Press, 2004.

Keohane, Robert. "Beyond Dichotomy: Conversations between International Relations and Feminist Theory." *International Studies Quarterly* 42.1 (2008): 193–7.

Paul, Darel E., and Abla Amawi. *The Theoretical Evolution of International Political Economy: A Reader*, 307–309. New York: Oxford University Press, 2013.

Peterson, V. Spike, and A.S. Runyan. *Gender Issues in the New Millennium*. 3rd ed. Boulder, CO: Westview Press, 2010.

Peterson, V. Spike. "How (the Meaning of) Gender Matters in Political Economy." In *The Theoretical Evolution of International Political Economy: A Reader*, edited by Darel E. Paul and Abla Amawi, 309–23. Oxford: Oxford University Press, 2013.

Shepherd, Laura J., ed. *Gender Matters in Global Politics*. New York: Routledge, 2010.

Tickner, J. Ann. "Gender in World Politics." In *The Globalization of World Politics*, 5th ed., edited by John Baylis, Steven Smith, and Patricia Owens, 262–78. Oxford: Oxford University Press, 2011.

Tickner, J. Ann. "Ann Tickner on Feminist Philosophy of Science: Engaging the Mainstream and (Still) Remaining Critical in/of IR: Theory Talk #54." *Theory Talks*, 22 April 2013. http://www.theory-talks.org/2013/04/theory-talk-54.html.

Tickner, J. Ann. "On the Fringes of the World Economy: A Feminist Perspective." In *The Theoretical Evolution of International Political Economy: A Reader*, edited by Darel E. Paul and Abla Amawi, 297–308. Oxford: Oxford University Press, 2013.

Conclusion

Our understanding of world politics would be totally inadequate without the principal theoretical contributions developed by IPE specialists since the 1970s. There is no doubt that this discipline is essential and that any internationalist worthy of the name cannot ignore the key debates in IPE, whether they are about globalization and interdependence, international finance, transformations of power, American hegemony and hegemonic stability theory, or regime theory and international cooperation. Nowadays, it is unthinkable to isolate major economic and financial issues from other key international issues.

As we have seen in this book, the debates in IPE are broadly determined by two very different and largely incompatible scientific cultures—on one side, the orthodox school and on the other, the heterodox school. The latest generation of orthodox researchers in IPE claim they are developing more rigorous theoretical frameworks that better satisfy the demanding principles of positivism and empiricism. This approach, they believe, facilitates the generalization and accumulation of knowledge. The orthodox consider heterodox approaches too eclectic, or even eccentric, to be valuable. They condemn them as unscientific and relegate them to the semi-periphery or periphery of the debates in IPE.

The positivist approach, mobilizing quantitative methods at will, finds its strengths chiefly in the construction of the research methodology. Overall, what makes this school attractive is the fact that the methodology is at the forefront, that it is clearly stated. This makes it much easier for a student to emulate an orthodox researcher in IPE than to emulate Robert Cox or Susan Strange. In heterodox IPE, there is no very precise guide about how to conduct research and about what constitutes acceptable research. The demarcation line between ideology and scientific research is not always very clear. Few heterodox researchers are concerned about the falsification criterion, advocated by Popper, which is crucial in orthodox IPE.

That said, the quantitative turn and the recent obsession with formal modelling have led orthodox IPE to become increasingly abstract and have reduced the complexity of the world to its simplest expression. The greatest problem with contemporary works in orthodox IPE is that the perverse quest for rationality and the overuse of statistical methods to explain how the world functions disconnect these works from the real world. The sophistication of theoretical models separates them from this reality rather than bringing it closer. In addition, positivists are fundamentally incapable of taking into account non-observable realities such as ideology, reason, identity, or the construction of social life.

For Benjamin Cohen, the major difficulty with the works of the mainstream approach in orthodox IPE lies in the deficit of imagination amongst researchers, and more particularly in their inability to envisage or even to consider radical systemic changes. Since the 1990s, the new generation of IPE researchers has completely forgotten or ignored key issues. They are no longer asking themselves the big questions about world politics. Consequently, according to Cohen, the latest IPE researchers are deadly dull and are failing to see the fundamental and important issues for the real world.

Regarding the performance of orthodox IPE works and the financial crisis of 2008, Cohen did a quick survey of the articles published over the 10-year period preceding the crisis in the most important US journals, including *International Organization*, *International Studies Quarterly*, *World Politics*, *American Political Science Review*, and *American Journal of Political Science*. He found very few analyses on financial issues. For Cohen, of the handful of studies dealing with the financial crisis, "Not a single one of these analyses gave even a clue that a major systemic change might be just around the corner" (2009a: 436). He concluded that the performance of orthodox IPE in foreseeing the financial crisis was quite simply embarrassing. A researcher who reads nothing but works produced by orthodox IPE theorists would conclude that we are living in a more stable world than the reality tells us. Orthodox IPE is incapable of explaining change, contrary to heterodox works. Even if heterodox works do not have the methodological rigour and the standards of the orthodox school, on the whole, they did anticipate the financial crisis.

The major theories of the orthodox IPE school have failed to imagine or read events on too many occasions to live up to their claims: they announced the end of American hegemony in the early 1970s, and then changed their mind . . . several times; they were not able to predict the breakup of the Soviet Union, the September 11 attacks or, as just mentioned, the 2008 financial crisis. Their failure is so flagrant that today few orthodox theorists still believe in the predictive capacity of their theoretical models. They recognize that the world is highly complex and largely unpredictable. In other words, the orthodox are living intellectually beyond their means.

Why was the orthodox school unable to anticipate the financial crisis and on a broader scale the great upheavals of the past? According to Cohen, the dogmas of orthodox IPE make it difficult to think outside the box. Orthodox IPE has epistemological criteria and methodological standards that are biased in favour of building mid-level theories that mainly examine causal relations. This approach greatly limits researchers' ability to understand multifactor or random systemic changes. Hence, it is the epistemology of the orthodox school that is to blame for its narrow-mindedness.

Robert Keohane now shares this point of view. On the subject of the recent evolution of IPE, he writes, "I view it with a gnawing sense of dissatisfaction" (2009: 38). For Keohane, what is most lacking in contemporary orthodox IPE is an interpretation and an understanding of change. He continues, "Substantively, what is missing for me in contemporary IPE is the synthetic interpretation of change" (2009: 40).

Rudra Sil and Peter Katzenstein propose that researchers must stop formulating research questions with the aim to advance the debates between competing paradigms. Instead, they suggest focusing on important problems and employing methodological eclecticism to analyze them (Sil and Katzenstein, 2010). In this way, historical or institutionalist analyses are rehabilitated. The key is to encourage analytic eclecticism that accepts borrowing concepts, theories, and methodologies from a wider variety of traditions in order to answer the significant questions of the real world. These key questions must be the focus of researchers' attention, not just the questions that can be answered using quantitative methods. Sil and Katzenstein argue for research based on important substantive questions rather than on paradigmatic controversies or debates.

In short, the problem with orthodox IPE is its obsession with the debates between paradigms, with epistemology and methodology, and its neglect of crucial matters such as financial crises. In IPE's founding years, IPE researchers asked significant and fundamental research questions and used any methodological tool available to answer these questions. We must get back to this way of thinking, but with greater rigour.

Heterodox approaches are multidisciplinary, normative, and very critical of orthodoxy. It is difficult to pass global judgment on the works of the heterodox school, as these works are so varied and unequal in quality. While some authors approach genius, others are literally mediocre. Some problems arise from the fact that, in many cases, the methodology is not explained or the works do not take into consideration the existing research in the field. Therefore, the research is only somewhat cumulative. Heterodox approaches do not provide a guide for students to conduct future research, for example.

In addition, the poor mastery of statistical and quantitative methods sometimes impairs the quality of the analysis. Some works of the heterodox school are so methodologically problematic that it is hard to imagine a government basing an important decision on such studies. The content of some heterodox school works is very remote from the preoccupations of decision makers and political science in general. The analyses of Robert Cox or of critical authors in green IPE are hermetic for students, not to mention for practitioners. These works are fashioned to be on the fringes of mainstream debates due to their very critical approach and their eclecticism.

Is there a place for compromise and perhaps even synthesis? In IPE, the two schools complement one another on the objects of study, and the multidisciplinary approach of the heterodox school would allow importing new ideas and new debates in the United States. Nevertheless, the heterodox could develop sounder methodological approaches.

But as we have seen in this book, since the 1970s, the orthodox and heterodox approaches have steadily grown apart. For many years now, there has been minimal dialogue between the two schools. Stanley Hoffmann wrote in 1977 that international relations was an American social science. Twenty years later, Ole Waever (1998) proposed a sociological analysis of the discipline and came to a similar conclusion. For Waever, not only are American researchers hegemonic regarding the discipline, they are also quite closed to what is happening beyond their borders. Susan Strange shared this opinion: in 1995, during her presidential address to the International Studies Association (ISA), she declared the ISA could serve as a hearing aid for American researchers because the latter "appear to be deaf and blind to anything that's not published in the U.S.A" (Strange, 1995: 290). Nicola Phillips, of the University of Manchester, is also of the opinion that the IPE practised in the United States and the IPE practised in Great Britain have evolved separately, identifying little with one another as parts of the same enterprise (Phillips, 2005: 12).

How do we explain the intellectual "clash of civilizations" between the orthodox school and the heterodox school? For some, this evolution is explained by the fact that a small number of individuals has taken control of professorships in the most prestigious universities in the United States and dominates the editorial committees of leading scientific journals such as *International Organization*. In short, the canons of what is acceptable as IPE research for this small group of people has had the effect of excluding authors with heterodox leanings (Germain, 2009). It is true that the major American scientific journals publish only a limited number of heterodox authors or works. But is that the cause of the problem or its consequence (Katzenstein, 2009)?

For others, the academic training offered by major American universities and the socialization of young professors are chiefly responsible. The curriculum in these universities imposes a weighty level of study that stresses learning the reference authors and the dominant perspectives in the form of seminars and comprehensive exams. Students have little choice but to fit their works within the dominant perspectives. According to the TRIP project team, in the late 1980s and early 1990s, it seemed impossible to publish an article or to defend a thesis in an American university if the researcher did not situate his or her work in the framework of the dominant paradigms. Between 1980 and 2006, in the specialized journals selected in the TRIP project, the proportion of published articles that did not propose an orthodox theoretical framework fell from 47 per cent to just 7 per cent (Maliniak et al., 2011: 441–5; Maliniak and Tierney, 2009).

In addition, the doctoral training in major American universities emphasizes the learning of quantitative methods while courses in qualitative methods are more rarely mandatory. After conducting a comparative analysis of the university IPE programs in the United States, Henry Farrell and

Martha Finnemore concluded that quantitative methods held a place of honour in American academic training (2009).

As a result, students from renowned American universities develop a relatively similar scientific culture. In the career path of a young professor in the United States, the pressures to publish and the search for grants in order to obtain a permanent position and career promotions mean that this young professor seeks above all to publish either articles in the top (American) peer-reviewed journals, or a book with a recognized university publisher. The situation is clear: journals for the most part publish works that respect the standards of the American orthodox school and have a favourable bias for quantitative methods. Young American researchers are well-enough informed of the situation to understand that it is in their interest to adhere to the majority standard in order to advance in their careers or even to have a career.

To this situation is added the fact that American academics specializing in international relations and IPE are not very open to the idea of hiring young graduates from non-American universities. To the question "What percentage of academic researchers in international relations have a degree from an American university?" the answer is 96 per cent in the United States, 31 per cent in Canada, 14 per cent in Australia, and just 9 per cent in Great Britain. This shows that the political science departments in the United States are reticent to hire researchers who have graduated from European or even Canadian universities. It also shows that in the Canadian and British cases, American universities are not as hegemonic as is sometimes claimed (Maliniak et al., 2009: 8).

In addition, IPE specialists in the US have been trained by a very small number of universities. Almost half of American IPE researchers hold doctorates from just a dozen academic institutions (Yale, Columbia, Cornell, Harvard, University of California–Berkeley, University of California–Los Angeles, University of Wisconsin, University of Michigan, MIT, Princeton University, Stanford University, and University of North Carolina–Chapel Hill) (Maliniak and Tierney, 2009: 15). Since the 1980s, researchers in these institutions have produced about 30 per cent of the articles published in the 12 most "important" journals of the discipline. Yet these universities represent only about 1 per cent of the academic programs in the United States. Between 1972 and 2006 (with the exception of a four-year interlude in the 1990s), the editorial committee of the discipline's most important journal, *International Organization*, always included professors from Harvard (Germain, 2009). There is a firmly established hierarchy among American universities, a very strong concentration of intellectual power.

An analysis of the textbooks, course outlines, and reading lists for comprehensive exams used in the major American universities confirms that the reference works are generally published in the United States and abide by the principles of the orthodox school. Cohen explains why this is so:

Most of the IPE readings [in my doctoral seminar] are indeed by American authors, contrary to my own preferences. I do offer a graduate seminar on alternative approaches to IPE from Britain, Asia, and elsewhere. But we don't make it part of the comprehensive exam, for a simple reason: to make our students as competitive as possible in the US academic job market. It won't help them get a job in a US university or college if they know something about the British or other non-US styles of IPE. To get a job in the US they need to know what is considered mainstream in the US. All very regrettable, but in my view necessary. (personal communication, quoted with permission, 2011)

Looking at who publishes in the 12 leading journals, we observe that an overwhelming majority of the researchers are American. From 1995 to 2006, Americans represented approximately 80 per cent of the authors published. Compared with the *Review of International Political Economy (RIPE)*, a reference in heterodox IPE, the contrast is remarkable, as no less than 60 per cent of the articles published in *RIPE* have always been by non-American authors. During the same period from 1995 to 2006, the percentage of American authors published in this journal even decreased, dropping from 40 per cent to 30 per cent (Maliniak and Tierney, 2009: 14).

These factors explain in large part why the works of American IPE specialists have evolved towards the orthodox model, towards this monoculture that today characterizes, for many, IPE in the United States. American students are socialized to integrate the codes and practices of the monoculture.

Doctoral training in Great Britain is more multidisciplinary. Course requirements, when they exist, are less weighty, and the learning of quantitative methods is the exception, not the rule. However, theses are often more consequential and the socialization of young professors is much less standardized. Canadian universities are increasingly aligning with the American standard, although the origin of professors' degrees is more varied and the practices are somewhat different from one university to another. As a sizeable proportion of Canadian professors were also trained in Europe, notably in Great Britain and in France for Quebec professors, they are more open to the diversity of approaches. As well, for self-identification reasons, the Canadians often seek to differentiate themselves from the Americans.

For all these reasons, a synthesis is unlikely. There is an American hegemony over the discipline and the majority of American researchers are convinced of the superiority of their approach. The progression of constructivism in international relations may permit an opening and some form of reconciliation between the schools in IPE. These rapprochements are, for the time being, rare. Yet they are desirable because, as Susan Strange suggested, in IPE, Catholic complexity is often preferable to Protestant parsimony.

Bibliography

Abbott, Frederick. "NAFTA and the Legalization of World Politics: A Case Study." *International Organization* 54.3 (2000): 519–47.

Abbott, Kenneth W., and Duncan Snidal. "Why States Act through Formal International Organizations." *Journal of Conflict Resolution* 42.1 (1998): 3–32.

Abdelal, Rawi, Mark Blyth, and Craig Parsons, eds. *Constructing the International Economy*. New York: Cornell University Press, 2010.

Acharya, Amitav, and Alastair Johnson, eds. *Crafting Cooperation: Regional International Institutions in Comparative Perspectives*. Cambridge: Cambridge University Press, 2007.

Adler, Emanuel. "Constructivism and International Relations." In *Handbook of International Relations*, edited by Walter Carlsnaes, Thomas Risse, and Beth Simmons. London: Sage, 2002.

Almond, Gabriel A., and Stephen Genco. "Clouds, Clocks and the Study of Politics." *World Politics* 29.4 (1977): 489–522.

Alt, James E., and Michael Gilligan. "The Political Economy of Trading States: Factor Specificity, Collective Action Problems and Domestic Political Institutions." *Journal of Political Philosophy* 2.2 (1994): 165–91.

Amable, Bruno. *The Diversity of Modern Capitalism*. Oxford: Oxford University Press, 2003.

Amin, Ash, and Ronen Palan. "Editorial: The Need to Historicize IPE." *Review of International Political Economy* 3.2 (1996): 209–15.

———. "Towards a Non-Rationalist International Political Economy," *Review of International Political Economy* 8.4 (2001): 559–77.

Amoore, Louise, Richard Dogson, Randall Germain, Barry Gills, Paul Langley, and Iain Watson. "Paths to a Historicised International Political Economy." *Review of International Political Economy* 7.1 (2000): 57–71.

Anderson, Benedict. *Imagined Communities*. London: Verso, 1991.

Andreff, Wladimir. *Les multinationales globales*. Paris: La Découverte, 2003.

Aron, Raymond. *Paix et guerre entre les nations*. 1962. 8th ed. Paris: Calman-Lévy, 1984.

Avey, Paul C., Michael C. Desch, James D. Long, Daniel Maliniak, Susan Peterson, and Michael J. Tierney. "The FP Survey: The Ivory Tower." *Foreign Policy* (January–February, 2012): 90–3.

Axelrod, Robert. *The Evolution of Cooperation*. New York: Basic Books, 1984.

Badie, Bertrand. *Culture et politique*. Paris: Economica, 1993.

Badie, Bertrand, and Marie-Claude Smouts. *Le retournement du monde: Sociologie de la scène internationale*. 3rd ed. Paris: PFNSP et Dalloz, 1999.

Bagwell, Kyle, and Robert W. Staiger. "An Economic Theory of GATT." *American Economic Review* 89.1 (1999): 215–48.

———. *The Economics of the World Trading System*. Cambridge, MA: MIT Press, 2002.

———. "Multilateral Tariff Cooperation During the Formation of Customs Unions." *Journal of International Economics* 42 (1997): 91–123.

Bailey, Michael, Judith L. Goldstein, and Barry Weingast. "The Institutional Roots of American Trade Policy." *World Politics* 49.3 (1997): 309–38.

Bakker, Isabella, and Stephen Gill, eds. *Power, Production and Social Reproduction: Human In/security in the Global Political Economy*. Basingstoke, UK: Palgrave Macmillan, 2003.

Baldwin, David A., ed. *Neorealism and Neoliberalism: The Contemporary Debate*. New York: Columbia University Press, 1993.

Barbieri, Katherine. *The Liberal Illusion: Does Trade Promote Peace?* Ann Arbor: University of Michigan Press, 2002.

Barbieri, Katherine, and Rafael Reuveny. "Economic Globalization and Civil War." *Journal of Politics* 67.4 (2005): 1228–47.

Barnett, Michael N., and Raymond Duvall. "Power in International Politics." *International Organization* 59.1 (2005): 39–75.

Barnett, Michael N., and Martha Finnemore. "The Politics, Power, and Pathologies of International Organizations." *International Organization* 53.4 (1999): 699–732.

Bates, R.H. *Open-Economy Politics: The Political Economy of the World Coffee Trade.* Princeton: Princeton University Press, 1997.

Bates, Robert H., Philip L. Brock, and Jill Tiefenthaler. "Risk and Trade Regimes: Another Exploration." *International Organization* 45 (1991): 1–18.

Bator, F. "The Anatomy of Market Failure." *Quarterly Journal of Economics* 72.3 (1958): 351–79.

Battistella, Dario. *Théories des relations internationales.* 4th ed. Paris: Presses de Sciences Po, 2012.

Baylis, John, Steve Smith, and Patricia Owen. Introduction to *The Globalization of World Politics: An Introduction to International Relations*, edited by John Baylis, Steve Smith, and Patricia Owens, 1–13. New York: Oxford University Press, 2011.

Bell, Daniel. "The World and the United States in 2013." *Daedalus* 166.3 (1987): 1–31.

Bernstein, Steven. *The Compromise of Liberal Environmentalism.* New York: Columbia University Press, 2001.

Blyth, Mark. *Austerity: The History of a Dangerous Idea.* New York: Oxford University Press, 2013.

———. *Great Transformation: Economic Ideas and Institutional Change in the Twentieth Century.* Cambridge: Cambridge University Press, 2003.

———, ed. *Routledge Handbook of International Political Economy (IPE): IPE As a Global Conversation.* London: Routledge, 2009.

Boudon, Raymond. "Review: What Middle-Range Theories Are." *Contemporary Sociology* 20.4 (1991): 519–22.

Brooks, Stephen G. "The Globalization of Production and the Changing Benefits of Conquest." *Journal of Conflict Resolution* 43.5 (1999): 646–70.

———. *Producing Security: Multinational Corporations, Globalization and the Changing Calculus of Conflict.* Princeton: Princeton University Press, 2007.

Brown, Chris. "'Our Side?' Critical Theory and International Relations." In *Critical Theory and World Politics*, edited by R. Wyn Jones, 191–204. Boulder, CO: Lynne Rienner, 2001.

Broz, Lawrence. "Political System Transparency and Monetary Commitment Regimes." In *The Political Economy of Monetary Institutions*, edited by William T. Bernhard, Lawrence Droz, and William Roberts Clark, 169–96. Cambridge, MA: MIT Press, 2003.

Buchanan, James M., and Gordon Tullock. *The Calculus of Consent: Logical Foundations of Constitutional Democracy.* Ann Arbor: University of Michigan Press, 1962.

Burchill, Scott. "Liberalism." In *Theories of International Relations*, 2nd ed., edited by Scott Burchill, Andrew Linklater, Richard Devetak, Jack Donnelly, Terry Nardin, Matthew Paterson, Christian Reus-Smit, and Jacqui True, 29–69. Basingstoke, UK: Palgrave Macmillan, 2001.

Buzan, Barry. "The Level-of-Analysis Problem in International Relations Reconsidered." In *International Relations Today*, edited by Ken Booth and Steve Smith, 198–216. Cambridge: Polity, 1995.

Cameron, Angus, and Ronen Palan. *The Imagined Economies of Globalization.* Thousand Oaks, CA: Sage Publications, 2004.

Cameron, David R. "The Expansion of the Public Economy: A Comparative Analysis." *American Political Science Review* 72.4 (1978): 1243–61.

Cardoso, Fernando Henrique, and Enzo Faletto. *Dependency and Development in Latin America.* Berkeley: University of California Press, 1979.

Carr, Edward H. *The Twenty Years Crisis, 1919–1939.* 2nd ed. London: Macmillan, 1946.

Carver, T., and P. Thomas, eds. *Rational Choice Marxism.* University Park: Pennsylvania State University Press, 1995.

Castles, Francis G. "A Race to the Bottom?" In *The Welfare State Reader*, edited by Christopher Pierson and Francis G. Castles, 226–44. Cambridge: Polity, 2006.

Cerny, Philip G. "The Competitive State." *Political Economy and the Changing Global Order*, 2nd ed., edited by R. Stubbs and G.R.D Underhill. Toronto: Oxford University Press, 2000.

Chalmers, Alan F. *What Is This Thing Called Science?* 4th ed. St Lucia: University of Queensland Press, 2013.

———. *Qu'est-ce que la science? Popper, Kuhn, Lakatos, Feyerabend.* Paris: La Découverte, 1996.

Chayes, Abram, and Antonia H. Chayes. "On Compliance." *International Organization* 47.2 (1993): 175–206.

Clapp, Jennifer, and Peter Dauvergne. *Paths to a Green World: The Political Economy of the Global Environment.* Cambridge, MA: MIT Press, 2005.

Clift, Ben, and Ben Rosamond. "Lineages of a British International Political Economy." In *Routledge Handbook of International Political Economy (IPE): IPE As a Global Conversation,* edited by Mark Blyth, 95–111. London: Routledge, 2009.

Cohen, Benjamin. *Advanced Introduction to International Political Economy.* Northampton, MA: Edward Elgar Publishing, 2014.

———. "Are IPE Journals Becoming Boring?" *International Studies Quarterly* 54.3 (2010): 887–91.

———. "A Grave Case of Myopia." *International Interactions* 35.4 (2009a): 436–44.

———. *International Political Economy: An Intellectual History.* Princeton: Princeton University Press, 2008.

———. "The Multiple Traditions of American IPE." In *Routledge Handbook of International Political Economy (IPE): IPE As a Global Conversation,* edited by Mark Blyth, 23–35. London: Routledge, 2009b.

———. Personal communication with the author (email). 11 March 2011.

———. "The Transatlantic Divide: Why Are American and British IPE So Different?" *Review of International Political Economy* 14.2 (2007): 197–219.

Cooley, Alexander. "Contested Contracts: Rationalist Theories of Institutions in America IPE." In *Routledge Handbook of International Political Economy (IPE): IPE As a Global Conversation,* edited by Mark Blyth, 48–61. London: Routledge, 2009.

Cooper, Richard. *The Economics of Interdependence: Economic Policy in the Atlantic Community.* New York: McGraw-Hill, 1968.

Cowhey, Peter F. "Domestic Institutions and the Credibility of International Commitment: Japan and the United States." *International Organization* 47.2 (1993): 299–326.

Cox, Robert W. "The 'British School' in the Global Context." *New Political Economy* 14.3 (2009): 315–28.

———. "Conversation with Randall D. Germain." *New Political Economy* 4.3 (1999): 389–98.

———. "Dialectique de l'économie-monde en fin de siècle." *Études internationales* 21.4 (1990): 693–703.

———. "Gramsci, Hegemony, and International Relations: An Essay in Method." In *Approaches to World Order,* by Robert W. Cox with Timothy J. Sinclair, 124–43. Cambridge: Cambridge University Press, 1996a.

———, ed. *The New Realism: Perspectives on Multilateralism and World Order.* Basingstoke, UK: Palgrave Macmillan, 1997.

———. "The Point Is Not Just to Explain the World But to Change It." In *The Oxford Handbook of International Relations,* edited by Christian Reus-Smit and Duncan Snidal, 84–93. New York: Oxford University Press, 2008.

———. Preface to *The Political Economy of a Plural World: Critical Reflections on Power, Morals and Civilization,* edited by Robert W. Cox and Michael G. Schechter, xii–xxiv. London: Routledge, 2002.

———. *Production, Power, and World Order: Social Forces in the Making of History.* New York: Columbia University Press, 1987.

———. "Production, the State and Change in World Order." In *Global Changes and Theoretical Challenges: Approaches to World Politics for the 1990s,* edited by Ernst-Otto Czempiel and James N. Rosenau, 37–55. Toronto: Lexington Books, 1989.

———. "Realism, Positivism and Historicism." In *Approaches to World Order,* by Robert W. Cox with Timothy J. Sinclair, 49–59. Cambridge: Cambridge University Press, 1996b.

———. "Social Forces, States and World Order: Beyond International Relations Theory." *Millennium: Journal of International Studies* 10.2 (1981): 126–55.

———. "Social Forces, States, and World Orders." In *Neorealism and Its Critics,* edited by Robert O. Keohane, 204–54. New York: Columbia University Press, 1986.

———. "Towards a Posthegemonic Conceptualization of World Order: Reflections on the Relevancy of Ibn Khaldun." In *Approaches to World Order* by Robert W. Cox with Timothy J. Sinclair, 144–73. Cambridge: Cambridge University Press, 1996c.

Cox, Robert W., and Michael G. Schechter, eds. *The Political Economy of a Plural World: Critical Reflections on Power, Morals and Civilization.* London: Routledge, 2002.

Cox, Robert, with Timothy J. Sinclair. *Approaches to World Order.* Cambridge: Cambridge University Press, 1996.

Dauvergne, Peter. "Globalization and the Environment." In *Global Political Economy*, 4th ed., edited by John Ravenhill, 372–98. Oxford: Oxford University Press, 2014.

Davis, Christina L. *Food Fights over Free Trade: How International Institutions Trade Liberalization.* Princeton: Princeton University Press, 2005.

———. "International Institutions and Issue Linkage: Building Support for Agricultural Trade Liberalization." *American Political Science Review* 98.1 (2004): 153–69.

Denemark, Robert A., and Robert O'Brien. "Contesting the Canon: International Political Economy at US and UK Universities." *Review of International Political Economy* 4.1 (1997): 214–38.

Deutsch, Karl W. *Political Community and the North Atlantic Area: International Organization in the Light of Historical Experience.* Princeton: Princeton University Press, 1957.

Dickins, Amanda. "The Evolution of International Political Economy." *International Affairs* 82.3 (2006): 479–92.

Doces, John, and B. Peter Rosendorff. "Intra-Democratic Variations and Trade Policy: Why Presidential Systems Have Less Open Trade." Unpublished paper, 2005.

Downs, George W., and David M. Rocke. *Optimal Imperfection? Domestic Uncertainty and Institutions in International Relations.* Princeton: Princeton University Press, 1995.

Downs, George W., David M. Rocke, and Peter N. Barsoom. "Is the Good News about Compliance Good News about Cooperation?" *International Organization* 50.2 (1996): 379–406.

Doyle, Michael W. "Liberal Internationalism: Peace, War and Democracy." *Nobelprize.org*, 22 June 2004. http://www.nobelprize.org/nobel_prizes/themes/peace/doyle/.

———. *Ways of War and Peace: Realism, Liberalism, and Socialism.* New York: W.W. Norton, 1997.

Drezner, Daniel W. *All Politics Is Global.* Princeton: Princeton University Press, 2007.

———. "Bottom Feeders." In *Debates in International Political Economy*, edited by Thomas Oatley, 148–76. New York: Pearson Education, 2010.

Dunn, Stephen P. *The Economics of John Kenneth Galbraith: Introduction, Persuasion, and Rehabilitation.* Cambridge: Cambridge University Press, 2011.

Eichengreen, Barry. "Dental Hygiene and Nuclear War: How International Relations Looks from Economics." *International Organization* 52.4 (1998): 993–1012.

Eichengreen, Barry, and David Leblanc. "Democracy and Globalization." BIS Working Papers, no. 219, 2006.

Enloe, Cynthia. *The Curious Feminist: Searching for Women in a New Age of Empire.* Berkeley: University of California Press, 2004.

Farrell, Henry, and Martha Finnemore. "Ontology, Methodology, and Causation in the American School of International Political Economy." *Review of International Political Economy* 16.1 (2009): 58–71.

Fearon, James D. "Bargaining, Enforcement, and International Cooperation." *International Organization* 52.2 (1998): 269–306.

Foucault, Michel. *Discipline and Punish: The Birth of the Prison.* New York: Random House, 1975.

Frank, André Gunder. "The Development of Underdevelopment." *Monthly Review Press*, September 1966.

Frieden, Jeffry A. *Global Capitalism: Its Fall and Rise in the Twentieth Century.* New York: W.W. Norton & Company, 2006.

———. "Invested Interests: The Politics of National Economic Policies in a World of Global Finance." *International Organization* 45.4 (1991): 425–51.

———. "Sectoral Conflict and U.S. Foreign Economic Policy, 1914–1940." *International Organization* 42 (1998): 59–90.

Frieden, Jeffry A., and David A. Lake, eds. *International Political Economy: Perspectives on Global Power and Wealth.* New York: Bedford/St Martin's Press, 2000.

Frieden, Jeffry A., and Lisa L. Martin. "International Political Economy: Global and Domestic Interactions." In *Political Science: State of the Discipline*, edited by Ira Katznelson and Helen V. Milner, 118–46. New York: W.W. Norton & Company, 2002.

Friedman, Milton. *Essays in Positive Economics*. Chicago: University of Chicago, 1953.

Friedman, Thomas L. *The World Is Flat: A Brief History of the Twenty-First Century*. New York: Farrar, Straus and Giroux, 2006.

Gabriel, Christina, and Hélène Pellerin, eds. *Governing International Labour Migration: Current Issues, Challenges and Dilemmas*. London: Routledge, 2008.

Galbraith, John K. "Power and the Useful Economist." *American Economic Review* 63.1 (1973): 1–11.

Garrett, Geoffrey. "Capital Mobility, Trade and the Domestic Politics of Economic Policy." *International Organization* 49.4 (1995): 657–87.

———. "Shrinking States? Globalization and National Autonomy in the OECD." *Oxford Development Studies* 26.1 (1998): 453–78.

Garrett, Geoffrey, and Deborah Mitchell. "Globalization, Government Spending and Taxation in the OECD." *European Journal of Political Research* 39.2 (2001): 145–78.

Gartzke, Eric, Quan Li, and Charles Boehmer. "Investing in Peace, Economic Interdependence and International Conflict." *International Organization* 55.2 (2001): 391–438.

Geertz, Clifford. *The Interpretation of Culture*. New York: Basic Books, 1973.

Germain, Randall. "The 'American' School of IPE? A Dissenting View." *Review of International Political Economy* 16.1 (2009): 95–105.

———. *Global Politics and Financial Governance*. Basingstoke, UK: Palgrave Macmillan, 2010.

———. *The International Organization of Credit: States and Global Finance in the World-Economy*. Cambridge: Cambridge University Press, 1997.

Germain, Randall, and Michael Kenny. "Engaging Gramsci: International Relations Theory and the New Gramscians." *Review of International Studies* 24.1 (1998): 3–21.

Gill, Stephen. *American Hegemony and the Trilateral Commission*. Cambridge: Cambridge University Press, 1990a.

———. "Constitutionalizing Inequality and the Clash of Globalizations." *International Studies Review* 4.2 (2002): 47–65.

———. "Epistemology, Ontology, and the 'Italian School.'" In *Gramsci, Historical Materialism, and International Relations*, edited by Stephen Gill, 21–48. Cambridge: Cambridge University Press, 1993.

———. "Finance, Production, and Panopticism: Inequality, Risk and Resistance in an Era of Disciplinary Neoliberalism." In *Globalization, Democratization, and Multilateralism*, edited by Stephen Gill, 51–76. Basingstoke, UK: Palgrave Macmillan, 1997.

———. *Power and Resistance in the New World Order*. Basingstoke, UK: Palgrave Macmillan, 2003.

———. "Two Concepts of International Political Economy." *Review of International Studies* 16.1 (1990b): 369–81.

Gill, Stephen, and David Law. "Global Hegemony and the Structural Power of Capital." *International Studies Quarterly* 33.4 (1989): 475–99.

———. *The Global Political Economy: Perspectives, Problems and Policies*. Baltimore, MD: Johns Hopkins University Press, 1988.

Gilpin, Robert. *Global Political Economy: Understanding the International Economic Order*. Princeton: Princeton University Press, 2001.

———. *The Political Economy of International Relations*. Princeton: Princeton University Press, 1987.

———. "Three Models of the Future." *International Organization* 29.1 (1975a): 37–60.

———. *U.S. Power and the Multinational Corporation: The Political Economy of Direct Foreign Investment*. New York: Basic Books, 1975b.

———. *War and Change in World Politics*. Cambridge: Cambridge University Press, 1981.

Goldstein, Judith L. *Ideas, Interest, and American Trade Policy*. Ithaca, NY: Cornell University Press, 1993.

———. "The Impact of Ideas on Trade Policy: The Origins of U.S. Agricultural and Manufacturing Policies." *International Organization* 43.1 (1989): 31–71.

Goldstein, Judith L., and Robert O. Keohane, eds. *Ideas and Foreign Policy: Beliefs, Institutions, and Political Change*. Ithaca, NY: Cornell University Press, 1993.

Goldstein, Judith L., and Lisa L. Martin. "Legalization, Trade Liberalization, and Domestic Politics: A Cautionary Note." *International Organization* 54.3 (2000): 603–32.

Goodman, John, and Louis Pauly. "The Obsolescence of Capital Controls? Economic Management in an Age of Global Markets." *World Politics* 46.1 (1993): 50–82.

Gourevitch, Peter. *Politics in Hard Times: Comparative Responses to International Economic Crises*. Ithaca, NY: Cornell University Press, 1986.

———. "The Second Image Reversed: The International Sources of Domestic Politics." *International Organization* 32.4 (1978): 881–912.

Gourevitch, Peter, Robert O. Keohane, Stephen D. Krasner, David Laitin, T. J. Pempel, Wolfgang Streeck, and Sidney Tarrow. "The Political Science of Peter J. Katzenstein." *PS: Political Science & Politics* 41.4 (2008): 893–9.

Gowa, Joanne. *Allies, Adversaries and International Trade*. Princeton: Princeton University Press, 1994.

———. "Anarchy, Egoism and the Third Images: The Evolution of Cooperation and International Relations." *International Organization* 40.1 (1986): 167–86.

Greenwald, Bruce C., and Joseph Stiglitz. "Externalities in Economies with Imperfect Information and Incomplete Markets." *Quarterly Journal of Economics* 101.2 (1986): 229–64.

Grieco, Joseph M. "Anarchy and the Limits of Cooperation: A Realist Critique of the Newest Liberal Institutionalism." *International Organization* 42.3 (1988): 484–508.

———. *Cooperation Among Nations: Europe, America, and Non-Tariff Barriers to Trade.* Ithaca, NY: Cornell University Press, 1990.

———. "The Relative-Gains Problem for International Cooperation: Comment." *American Political Science Review* 87.3 (1993): 301–38.

Grieco, Joseph M., and G. John Ikenberry. *State Power and World Markets: The International Political Economy*. New York: W.W. Norton & Company, 2003.

Grossman, Gene, and Alan Krueger. "Economic Growth and the Environment." NBER Working Paper, no. 4634, 1994.

Grossman, Gene M., and E. Helpman. *Interest Groups and Trade Policy*. Princeton: Princeton University Press, 2002.

———. "A Protectionist Bias in Majoritarian Politics." *Quarterly Journal of Economics* 120.4 (2005): 1239–82.

Haas, E.B. "The Obsolescence of Regional Integration Theory." Working Paper. Institute of International Studies, Berkeley, CA, 1975.

———. *The Uniting of Europe: Political, Social, and Economic Forces, 1950–57*. Stanford, CA: Stanford University Press, 1958.

Haas, Peter M. "Introduction: Epistemic Communities and International Policy Coordination." *International Organization* 46.1 (1992): 1–35.

Haas, Peter M., and James Gustave Speth. *Global Environmental Governance*. Washington: Island Press, 2006.

Haggard, Stephan. "The Institutional Foundations of Hegemony: Explaining the Reciprocal Trade Agreements Act of 1934." *International Organization* 42.1 (1988): 91–119.

Hall, Peter A. "The Movement from Keynesianism to Monetarism: Institutional Analysis and British Economic Policy in the 1970s." In *Structuring Politics: Historical Institutionalism in Comparative Analysis*, edited by Sven Steinmo, Kathleen Thelen, and Frank Longstreth, 90–113. New York: Cambridge University Press, 1992.

———. "Policy Paradigms, Social Learning, and the State: The Case of Economic Policymaking in Britain." *Comparative Politics* 25.3 (1993): 275–96.

Hall, Peter, and David Soskice, eds. *Varieties of Capitalism: The Institutional Foundations of Comparative Advantage*. New York: Oxford University Press, 2001.

Halliday, Fred. "The Revenge of Ideas: Karl Polanyi and Susan Strange." *Open Democracy*, 24 Sept. 2008.

Hamilton, Alexander. *Report on Manufactures*. N.p., 1791. http://www.constitution.org/ah/rpt_manufactures.pdf.

Hansen, Lene. "Poststructuralism." In *The Globalization of World Politics: An Introduction to International Relations*, edited by John Baylis, Steve Smith, and Patricia Owens, 166–81. New York: Oxford University Press, 2011.

Hardin, Garrett. "The Tragedy of the Commons." *Science* 162 (1968): 1243–8.

Harrod, Jeffrey. *Global Unions?: Theory and Strategy of Organized Labour in the Global Political Economy.* London: Routledge, 2002.

———. *Power, Production, and the Unprotected Worker.* New York: Columbia University Press, 1987.

Hay, Colin. "Globalization's Impact on States." In *Global Political Economy*, 2nd ed., edited by John Ravenhill, 314–45. Oxford: Oxford University Press, 2008.

Hay, Colin, and Daniel Wincott. *The Political Economy of European Welfare Capitalism.* New York: Palgrave Macmillan, 2012.

Hayek, Friedrich A. *The Constitution of Liberty.* Chicago: University of Chicago Press, 1960.

Heichel, Stephan, Jessica Pape, and Thomas Sommerer. "Is There Convergence in Convergence Research? An Overview of Empirical Studies on Policy Convergence." *Journal of European Public Policy* 12.5 (2005): 817–40.

Held, David, Anthony McGrew, David Goldblatt, and Jonathan Perraton. *Global Transformation, Politics, Economics and Culture.* Cambridge: Polity, 1999.

Helleiner, Eric. "Division and Dialogue in Anglo-American IPE: A Reluctant Canadian View." *New Political Economy* 14 (2009): 377–83.

———. "International Political Economy and the Greens." In *The Theoretical Evolution of International Political Economy: A Reader*, 3rd ed., edited by Darel E. Paul and Abla Amawi, 327–39. New York: Oxford University Press, 2013.

———. *States and the Reemergence of Global Finance: From Bretton Woods to the 1990s.* Ithaca, NY: Cornell University Press, 1996.

Henkin, Louis. *How Nations Behave: Law and Foreign Policy.* New York: Columbia University Press, 1979.

Hirschman, Albert O. *National Power and the Structure of Foreign Trade.* Berkeley: UCLA Press, 1945.

Hiscox, Michael J. *International Trade and Political Conflict.* Princeton: Princeton University Press, 2002.

Hoffman, Stanley. "An American Social Science: International Relations." *Daedalus* 106 (1977): 41–60.

Hollis, Martin, and Steve Smith. *Explaining and Understanding International Relations.* Oxford: Clarendon Press, 1991.

Hornborg, Alf. "The Thermodynamics of Imperialism: Toward an Ecological Theory of Unequal Exchange." In *The Theoretical Evolution of International Political Economy: A Reader*, 3rd ed., edited by Darel E. Paul and Abla Amawi, 340–8. New York: Oxford University Press, 2013.

Hülsemeyer, Axel, ed. *International Political Economy: A Reader.* Don Mills, ON: Oxford University Press, 2010.

Jabko, Nicolas. "Why IPE Is Underdeveloped in Continental Europe: A Case Study of France." In *Routledge Handbook of International Political Economy (IPE): IPE As a Global Conversation*, edited by Mark Blyth, 243–65. London: Routledge, 2009.

Jackson, Patrick Thaddeus. *The Conduct of Inquiry in International Relations. Philosophy of Science and Its Implications for the Study of World Politics.* London: Routledge, 2012.

Jensen, Nathan M. "Domestic Institutions and the Taxing of Multinational Corporations." *International Studies Quarterly* 57.3 (2013): 440–8.

———. *Nation-States and the Multinational Corporation: A Political Economy of Foreign Direct Investment.* Princeton: Princeton University Press, 2008.

Jervis, Robert. *Perception and Misperception in International Politics.* Princeton: Princeton University Press, 1976.

———. "Realism, Neoliberalism, and Cooperation: Understanding the Debate." In *Progress in International Relations Theory: Appraising the Field*, edited by Colin Elman and Miriam Fendius Elman, 277–310. Cambridge, MA: MIT Press, 2003.

Jessop, Bob. *The Future of the Capitalist State.* Cambridge: Polity, 2002.

Johnson, Chalmers. *MITI and the Japanese Miracle: The Growth of Industrial Policy, 1925–1975.* Stanford, CA: Stanford University Press, 1982.

Jones, R.J. Barry. *Globalization and Interdependence in the International Political Economy: Rhetoric and Reality.* London: Bloomsbury, 1995.

———. "International Political Economy (IPE)." In *The Routledge Encyclopedia of International Political Economy*, edited by R.J. Barry Jones, 813–14. London: Routledge, 2001.

Jordan, Richard, Daniel Maliniak, Amy Oakes, Susan Peterson, and Michael J. Tierney. *One Discipline of Many? TRIP Survey of International Relations Faculty in Ten Countries.* Williamsburg, VA: TRIP Project, Institute for the Theory and Practice of International Relations, College of William and Mary, 2009. https://www.wm.edu/offices/itpir/_documents/trip/final_trip_report_2009.pdf.

Kapstein, Ethan B. "Resolving the Regulator's Dilemma: International Coordination and Banking Regulations." *International Organization* 43.2 (1989): 323–47.

Katzenstein, Peter J., ed. *Between Power and Plenty: Foreign Economic Policies in Advanced Industrial States.* Madison: University of Wisconsin Press, 1978.

———, ed. *The Culture of National Security: Norms and Identity in World Politics.* New York: Columbia University Press, 1996.

———. "International Relations and Domestic Structures: Foreign Economic Policies of Advanced Industrial States." *International Organization* 30.1 (1976): 1–45.

———. "Sitting on the Knife's Sharp Edge." *Review of International Political Economy* 16.1 (2009): 122–35.

———. *Small States in World Markets: Industrial Policy in Europe.* Ithaca, NY: Cornell University Press, 1985.

Katzenstein, Peter, Robert O. Keohane, and Stephen D. Krasner. "International Organization and the Study of World Politics." *International Organization* 52.4 (1998): 645–85.

Keohane, Robert. *After Hegemony: Cooperation and Discord in World Political Economy.* Princeton: Princeton University Press, 1984.

———. Foreword to *Strange Power: Shaping the Parameters of International Relations and International Political Economy,* edited by Thomas C. Lawton, James N. Rosenau, and Amy C. Verdun, ix–xix. Aldershot, UK: Ashgate, 2000.

———. *International Institutions and State Power: Essays in International Relations Theory.* Boulder, CO: Westview Press, 1989.

———. "The Old IPE and the New." *Review of International Political Economy* 16.1 (2009): 34–46.

———. "Beyond Dichotomy: Conversations between International Relations and Feminist Theory." *International Studies Quarterly* 42.1 (2008): 193–7.

———. *Power and Governance in a Partially Globalized World.* New York: Routledge, 2002.

———. "Problematic Lucidity: Stephen Krasner's 'State Power and the Structure of International Trade.'" *World Politics* 50.1 (1997): 150–70.

———. "The Theory of Hegemonic Stability and Changes in International Economic Regime, 1967–1977." In *Change in the International System,* edited by Ole R. Holsti, Randolph Siverson, and Alexander L. George. Boulder, CO: Westview Press, 1980.

Keohane, Robert, and Lisa L. Martin. "Institutional Theory as a Research Program." In *Progress in International Relations Theory: Appraising the Field,* edited by Colin Elman and Miriam Fendius Elman, 71–108. Cambridge, MA: MIT Press, 2003.

———. "The Promise of Institutionalist Theory." *International Security* 20.1 (1995): 39–51.

Keohane, Robert, and Helen V. Milner, eds. *Internationalization and Domestic Politics.* Cambridge: Cambridge University Press, 1996.

Keohane, Robert, and Joseph S. Nye. *Power and Interdependence: World Politics in Transition.* 1977. New York: Longman, 2012.

Keynes, John Maynard. *The General Theory of Employment, Interest, and Money.* London: MacMillan, 1936.

Kindleberger, Charles P. *American Business Abroad: Six Lectures on Direct Investment.* New Haven, CT: Yale University Press, 1969.

———. *Power and Money.* New York: Basic Books, 1970.

———. *The World in Depression, 1929–1939.* Oakland: University of California Press, 1973.

King, Gary, Robert O. Keohane, and Sidney Verba. *Designing Social Inquiry: Scientific Inference in Qualitative Research.* Princeton: Princeton University Press, 1994.

Kirshner, Jonathan. *Appeasing Bankers: Financial Caution on the Road to War.* Princeton: Princeton University Press, 2007.

———. *Currency and Coercion: The Political Economy of International Monetary Power.*

Princeton: Princeton University Press, 1995.

———. "Realist Political Economy: Traditional Themes and Contemporary Challenges." In *Routledge Handbook of International Political Economy (IPE): IPE As a Global Conversation*, edited by Mark Blyth, 36–47. London: Routledge, 2009.

Koremenos, Barbara. "Contracting around International Uncertainty." *American Political Science Review* 99.4 (2005): 540–65.

Koremenos, Barbara, Charles Lipson, and Duncan Snidal. "The Rational Design of International Institutions." *International Organization* 55.4 (2001): 761–99.

Krasner, Stephen D. "The Accomplishments of International Political Economy." In *International Theory: Positivism and Beyond*, edited by Steve Smith, Ken Booth, and Marysia Zalewski, 108–27. Cambridge: Cambridge University Press, 2008.

———. *Defending the National Interest: Raw Materials Investments and U.S. Foreign Policy*. Princeton: Princeton University Press, 1978a.

———. "Global Communications and National Power: Life on the Pareto Frontier." *World Politics* 43.3 (1991): 336–66.

———. "International Political Economy: Abiding Discord." *Review of International Political Economy* 1.1 (1994): 3–19.

———, ed. *International Regimes*. Ithaca, NY: Cornell University Press, 1983.

———. *Sovereignty: Organized Hypocrisy*. Princeton: Princeton University Press, 1999.

———. "State Power and the Structure of International Trade." *World Politics* 28.3 (1976): 317–47.

———. "United States Commercial and Monetary Policy: Unraveling the Paradox of External Strength and Internal Weakness." In *Between Power and Plenty: Foreign Economic Policies in Advanced Industrial States*, edited by Peter J. Katzenstein, 51–87. Madison: University of Wisconsin Press, 1978b.

Krugman, Paul. *Pop Internationalism*. Cambridge, MA: MIT Press, 1996.

———. "What Economists Can Learn from Evolutionary Theorists." Presentation given to the European Association for Evolutionary Political Economy, November 1996. Accessed 20 July 2015. http://web.mit.edu/krugman/www/evolute.html.

Kuhn, Thomas. *The Structure of Scientific Revolutions*. Chicago: University of Chicago Press, 1962.

Kurki, Milja, and Colin Wight. "International Relations and Social Science." In *International Relations Theories: Discipline and Diversity*, 2nd ed., edited by Tim Dunne, Milja Kurki, and Steve Smith, 14–35. New York: Oxford University Press, 2011.

Kuznets, Simon. "Economic Growth and Income Inequality." *American Economic Review* 45 (March 1955): 1–28.

LaFerrière, Eric, and Peter J. Stoett. *International Ecopolitical Theory: Critical Approaches*. Vancouver: University of British Columbia Press, 2006.

Lakatos, Imre. *The Methodology of Scientific Research Programmes: Philosophical Papers*. Vol. 1. Cambridge: Cambridge University Press, 1978.

Lake, David A. "Anarchy, Hierarchy and the Variety of International Relations." *International Organization* 50.1 (1996): 1–34.

———. "International Political Economy: A Maturing Interdiscipline." In *The Oxford Handbook of Political Economy*, edited by Barry R. Weingast and Donald Wittman, 757–77. New York: Oxford University Press, 2008.

———. "TRIPs across the Atlantic: Theory and Epistemology in IPE." *Review of International Political Economy* 16.1 (2009): 47–57.

Lake, David. A., and Robert Powell, eds. *Strategic Choice and International Relations*. Princeton: Princeton University Press, 1999.

Langley, Paul. "Power-Knowledge Estranged: From Susan Strange to Poststructuralism in British IPE." In *Routledge Handbook of International Political Economy (IPE): IPE As a Global Conversation*, edited by Mark Blyth, 126–39. London: Routledge, 2009.

Laver, Michael, and Kenneth Shepsle. "Divided Government: America Is Not 'Exceptional.'" *Governance* 4 (1991): 850–69.

Leblang, David. "Domestic Political Institutions and Exchange Rate Commitments in the Developing World." *International Studies Quarterly* 43.4 (1999): 599–620.

Legro, Jeffrey W., and Andrew Moravcsik. "Is Anybody Still a Realist?" *International Security* 24.2 (1999): 5–55.

Lenin, V.I. *Imperialism: The Highest Stage of Capitalism*. 1917. Sydney: Resistance Books, 1999.

Leontief, Wassily. "Theoretical Assumptions and Nonobserved Facts." *American Economic Review* 61.1 (1971): 1–7.

Leysens, Anthony. *The Critical Theory of Robert W. Cox: Fugitive or Guru?* Basingstoke, UK: Palgrave Macmillan, 2008.

Ling, L.H.M. "Global Passions within Global Interests: Race, Gender, and Culture in Our Postcolonial Order." In *Global Political Economy: Contemporary Theories*, edited by Ronen Palan, 253–67. London: Routledge, 2000.

Lipset, Seymour Martin. "Some Social Requisites of Democracy: Economic Development and Political Legitimacy." *American Political Science Review* 53.1 (1959): 69–105.

Lohmann, Susan, and Sharyn O'Halloran. "Divided Government and the U.S. Trade Policy: Theory and Evidence." *International Organization* 48.4 (1994): 595–632.

MacIntyre, Andrew. "Institutions and Investors: The Politics of Economic Crisis in Southeast Asia." *International Organization* 55.1 (2001): 81–122.

Macleod, Alex, and Dan O'Meara. "Qu'est-ce qu'une théorie des relations internationales?" In *Théories des relations internationales: Contestations et résistances*, edited by Alex Macleod and Dan O'Meara, 1–17. Montréal: Athéna éditions, 2007.

Magee, Stephen P. "Three Simple Tests of the Stolper-Samuelson Theorem." In *Issues in International Economics*, edited by P. Oppenheimer, 138–53. Oxford: Oriel Press, 1978.

Maliniak, Daniel, and Michael J. Tierney. "The American School of IPE." *Review of International Political Economy* 16.1 (2009): 6–33.

Maliniak, Daniel, Susan Peterson, and Michael J. Tierney. *TRIP around the World: Teaching, Research, and Policy Views of International Relations Faculty in 20 Countries*. Williamsburg, VA: Teaching, Research, and International Policy (TRIP) Project, 2012.

Maliniak, Daniel, Amy Oakes, Susan Peterson, and Michael J. Tierney. "International Relations in the US Academy." *International Studies Quarterly* 55.2 (2011): 437–64.

Mansfield, Edward D., and Jack Snyder. *Electing to Fight: Why Emerging Democracies Go to War*. Cambridge, MA: MIT Press, 2005.

Mansfield, E., H. Milner, and B.P. Rosendorff. "Why Democracies Cooperate More: Electoral Control and International Trade Agreements." *International Organization* 56.3 (2002): 477–514.

Mansfield, Edward, Helen V. Milner, and Peter Rosendorff. "Free to Trade: Democracies, Autocracies, and International Trade." *American Political Science Review* 94.2 (2000): 305–21.

Martin, Lisa L. *Coercive Cooperation: Explaining Multilateral Economic Sanctions*. Princeton: Princeton University Press, 1992.

———. *Democratic Commitments: Legislatures and International Cooperation*. Princeton: Princeton University Press, 2000.

———. "Interests, Power, and Multilateralism." *International Organization* 46.4 (1992): 765–92.

Martin, Lisa L., and Beth A. Simmons. "Theories and Empirical Studies of International Institutions." *International Organization* 52.4 (1998): 729–57.

Marx, Karl, and Frederik Engels. *Manifesto of the Community Party*. February 1848. *Marxist Internet Archive*. Accessed 27 July 2015. https://www.marxists.org/archive/marx/works/download/pdf/Manifesto.pdf.

Mastanduno, Michael. "Do Relative Gains Matter? America's Response to Japanese Industrial Policy." *International Security* 16.1 (1991): 73–113.

———. *Economic Containment: CoCom and the Politics of East–West Trade*. Ithaca, NY: Cornell University Press, 1992.

———. "Economics and Security in Statecraft and Scholarship." *International Organization* 52.4 (1998): 825–54.

Mattli, Walter. "Private Justice in a Global Economy: From Literature to Arbitration." *International Organization* 55.4 (2001): 919–47.

McDonald, Patrick. "Peace through Trade or Free Trade?" *Journal of Conflict Resolution* 48.4 (2004): 547–72.

McGillivray, Fiona. "The Party Discipline As a Determinant of the Endogenous Formation of Tariffs." *American Journal of Political Science* 41.2 (1997): 584–607.

McNamara, Kathleen, R. "On Intellectual Monocultures and the Study of IPE." *Review of International Political Economy* 16.1 (2009): 72–84.

Mearsheimer, John. "Back to the Future: Instability in Europe after the Cold War." *International Security* 15.1 (1990): 5–56.

———. "The False Promise of International Institution." *International Security* 19.3 (1994–1995): 5–50.

———. *The Tragedy of Great Power Politics*. New York: W.W. Norton & Company, 2001.

Milner, Helen V. *Interests, Institutions and Information: Domestic Politics and International Relations*. Princeton: Princeton University Press, 1997.

———. "Rationalizing Politics: The Emerging Synthesis of International, American and Comparative Politics." *International Organization* 52.4 (1998): 759–86.

———. "Reflections on the Field of International Political Economy." In *Conflict, Security, Foreign Policy, and International Political Economy: Past Path and Future Directions in International Studies*, edited by Michael Brecher and F.P. Harvey, 623–36. Ann Arbor: University of Michigan Press, 2002.

———. *Resisting Protectionism: Global Industries and the Politics of International Trade*. Princeton: Princeton University Press, 1988.

Milner, Helen, and B. Peter Rosendorff. "Democratic Politics and International trade Negotiations: Elections and Divided Government as Constraints on Trade Liberalization." *Journal of Conflict Resolution* 41.1 (1997): 117–47.

———. "Trade Negotiations, Information and Domestic Politics: The Role of Domestic Groups." *Economics and Politics* 8.2 (1996): 145–89.

Mishra, Ramesh. *Globalization and the Welfare State*. Cheltenham: Edward Elgar, 1999.

Mitchell, Ronald, and the IEA Database Project. *International Environmental Agreements (IEA) Database Project (Version 2014.3)*. Accessed 27 August 2015. http://iea.uoregon.edu/page.php?file=home.htm&query=static.

Mitra, Devashish. "Endogenous Lobby Formation and Endogenous Protection: A Long Run Model of Trade Policy Determination." *American Economic Review* 89 (1999): 1116–34.

Mitrany, David. *A Working Peace System: An Argument for the Functional Development of International Organization*. Oxford: Oxford University Press, 1943.

Moravcsik, Andrew. "Liberal International Relations Theory: A Scientific Assessment." In *Progress in International Relations Theory: Appraising the Field*, edited by Colin Elman and Miriam Fendius Elman, 159–204. Cambridge, MA: MIT Press, 2003.

———. "Taking Preferences Seriously: A Liberal Theory of International Politics." *International Organization* 54.1 (1997): 513–53.

Morrow, J.D., R.M. Siverson, and T.E. Tabares. "The Political Determinants of International Trade: The Major Powers, 1907–90." *American Political Science Review* 92 (1998): 649–61.

Mulvale, James P. *Reimagining Social Welfare: Beyond the Keynesian Welfare State*. Aurora, ON: Garamond Press, 2001.

Murphy, Craig N. "Do the Left-Out Matter?" *New Political Economy* 14.3 (2009): 357–65.

Murphy, Craig, and Douglas Nelson. *Global Institutions, Marginalization, and Development*. London: Routledge, 2005.

———. "International Political Economy: A Tale of Two Heterodoxies." *British Journal of Politics and International Relations* 3.3 (2001): 393–412.

Murton, Robert. *Social Theory and Social Structure*. Detroit, MI: Free Press, 1968.

Mutti, John H. *Foreign Direct Investment and Tax Competition*. Washington, DC: Institute for International Economics, 2003.

Myrdal, Gunnar. *Against the Stream: Critical Essays on Economics*. New York: Random House, 1972.

Narang, Vipin, and Rebecca M. Nelson. "Who Are These Belligerent Democratizers? Reassessing the Impact of Democratization on War." *International Organization* 63.2 (2009): 357–79.

Nesvetailova, Anastasia. *Financial Alchemy in Crisis: The Great Liquidity*. London: Pluto Press, 2010.

———. *Fragile Finance: Debt, Speculation and Crisis in the Age of Global Credit*. Basingstoke, UK: Palgrave Macmillan, 2007.

Nye, Joseph S. *Bound to Lead: The Changing Nature of American Power*. New York: Basic Books, 1990.

———. *The Paradox of the American Power: Why the World's Only Superpower Can't Go It Alone*. New York: Oxford University Press, 2002.

Nye, Joseph S., and Robert O. Keohane. "Transnational Relations and World Politics: An Introduction." *International Organization* 25.3 (1971): 329–49.

O'Brien, Robert. *Global Unions? Theory and Strategy of Organized Labour in the Global Political Economy*. London: Routledge, 2002.

———. "Labour and IPE: Rediscovering Human Agency." In *Global Political Economy: Contemporary Theories*, edited by Ronen Palan, 91–102. London: Routledge, 2000.

Ohmae, Kenichi. *The End of the Nation State: The Rise of Regional Economies*. New York: Simon and Schuster, 1995.

Onuf, Nicholas. *World of Our Making: Rules and Rule in Social Theory and International Relations*. Columbia: University of South Carolina Press, 1989.

Oye, Kenneth A. *Cooperation under Anarchy*. Princeton: Princeton University Press, 1986.

Palan, Ronen, ed. *Global Political Economy: Contemporary Theories*. London: Routledge, 2000.

———. "The Proof of the Pudding Is in the Eating: IPE in the Light of the Crisis 2007/8." *New Political Economy* 14.3 (2009): 385–94.

Palan, Ronen, and Barry Gills, eds. *Transcending the State-Global Divide: A Neostructuralist Agenda in International Relations*. Boulder, CO: Lynne Rienner Publishers, 1994.

Palan, Ronen, and Jason Abbott with Phil Deans. *State Strategies in the Global Political Economy*. London: Pinter, 1996.

Palan, Ronen, Richard Murphy, and Christian Chavagneux. *Tax Havens: How Globalization Really Works*. Ithaca, NY: Cornell University Press, 2010.

Paquin, Stéphane. "La mondialisation et les politiques publiques." In *L'analyse des politiques publiques*, edited by Stéphane Paquin, Luc Bernier, and Guy Lachapelle, 357–86. Montréal: Presses de l'Université de Montréal, 2011.

———. "La mondialisation n'est (toujours) pas coupable." In *Social-démocratie 2.0: Le Québec comparé aux pays scandinaves*, edited by Stéphane Paquin and Pier-Luc Lévesque, 51–74. Montréal: Presses de l'Université de Montréal, 2014.

———. *La nouvelle économie politique internationale*. Paris: Armand Colin, 2008.

Paterson, Matthew. *Understanding Global Environmental Politics: Domination, Accumulation, Resistance*. London: Palgrave, 2000.

Paul, Darel E., and Abla Amawi. *The Theoretical Evolution of International Political Economy: A Reader*. 3rd ed. New York: Oxford University Press, 2013.

Pauly Louis, W. "The Political Economy of Global Financial Crisis." In *Global Political Economy*, 2nd ed., edited by John Ravenhill. Oxford: Oxford University Press, 2008.

———. *Who Elected the Bankers? Surveillance and Control in World Economy*. Ithaca, NY: Cornell University Press, 1998.

Peterson, Susan, Michael J. Tierney, and Daniel Maliniak. "Ivory Tower." *Foreign Policy* (Nov.–Dec. 2005): 60–2.

Peterson, V. Spike. "How (the Meaning of) Gender Matters in Political Economy." In *The Theoretical Evolution of International Political Economy: A Reader*, edited by Darel E. Paul and Abla Amawi, 309–23. Oxford: Oxford University Press, 2013.

Peterson, V. Spike, and A.S. Runyan. *Gender Issues in the New Millennium*. 3rd ed. Boulder, CO: Westview Press, 2010.

Phillips, Nicola, ed. *Globalizing International Political Economy*. Basingstoke, UK: Palgrave Macmillan, 2005.

———. "The Slow Death of Pluralism." *Review of International Political Economy* 16.1 (2009): 85–94.

Picciotto, Sol. "Political Economy and International Law." In *Paths to International Political Economy*, edited by Susan Strange, 164–82. London: George Allen & Unwin, 1984.

Pierson, Paul. *Dismantling the Welfare State? Reagan, Thatcher and the Politics of Retrenchment*. Cambridge: Cambridge University Press, 1994.

———. "Irresistible Forces, Immovable Objects: Post-industrial Welfare States Confront Permanent Austerity." *Journal of European Public Policy* 5.4 (1998): 539–60.

Pieterse, Jan Nederveen. "Trends in Development Theory." In *Global Political Economy: Contemporary Theories*, edited by Ronen Palan, 206–23. London: Routledge, 2000.

Piketty, Thomas. *Capital in the Twenty-First Century*. Cambridge, MA: Belknap Press, 2014.

Pinter, R., and A. Hoogvelt. *Globalization and the Postcolonial World*. London: Macmillan, 1997.

Pirages, Dennis. "An Ecological Approach." In *Paths to International Political Economy*, edited by Susan Strange, 53–69. London: George Allen & Unwin, 1984.

Polanyi, Karl. *The Great Transformation: The Political and Economic Origins of Our Time*. New York: Farrar & Rinehart, 1944.

Popper, Karl. *Conjectures and Refutations*. London: Routledge, 1963.

———. *Objective Knowledge: An Evolutionary Approach*. Oxford: Oxford University Press, 1972.

———. "On Clouds and Clocks: An Approach to the Problem of Rationality and the Freedom of Man." In *Objective Knowledge: An Evolutionary Approach* by Karl Popper. Oxford: Clarendon Press, 1972.

Powell, Robert. "Absolute and Relative Gain in International Relations Theory." *American Political Science Review* 85.2 (1991): 1303–20.

———. "Anarchy in International Relation Theory: The Neorealist-Neoliberal Theory." *International Organization* 48.2 (1994): 313–44.

Putnam, Robert. "Diplomacy and Domestic Politics: The Logic of Two-Level Games." *International Organization* 42.3 (1988): 427–60.

Putnam, Robert D., Peter B. Evans, and Harold Jacobson, eds. *Double-Edge Diplomacy: International Bargaining and Domestic Politics*. Berkeley: University of California Press, 1993.

Ravenhill, John. "International Political Economy." In *The Oxford Handbook of International Relations*, edited by Christian Reus-Smit and Duncan Snidal, 539–57. New York: Oxford University Press, 2008.

———. "The Study of Global Political Economy." In *Global Political Economy*, 3rd ed., edited by John Ravenhill, 3–28. New York: Oxford University Press, 2014.

Rawls, John. *A Theory of Justice*. Cambridge, MA: Harvard University Press, 1971.

Rees, William. "Ecological Footprints and Appropriated Carrying Capacity: What Urban Economics Leaves Out." *Environment and Urbanization* 4.2 (1992): 121–30.

Reich, Robert. *The Work of Nations: Preparing Ourselves for the 21st Century Capitalism*. New York: Alfred A. Knopf, 1991.

Reus-Smit, Christian, and Duncan Snidal, eds. *The Oxford Handbook of International Relations*. New York: Oxford University Press, 2008.

Riker, William H. "Editorial Comment." *American Political Science Review* 68.3 (1974): 73–4.

RIPE. "Editorial: Forum for Heterodox International Political Economy." *Review of International Political Economy* 1.1 (1994): 1–12.

Roberts, J. Timmons, and Bradley Parks. *A Climate of Injustice: Global Inequality, North-South Politics, and Climate Policy*. Cambridge, MA: MIT Press, 2006.

Rodrik, Dani. *Has Globalization Gone Too Far?* Washington: Institute for International Economics, 1997.

———. "Les débats sur la mondialisation: Leçons du passé." *Politique étrangère* 63.3 (1998a): 567–85.

———. "Les idées l'emportent sur les intérêts." *Project Syndicate*, 26 April 2012. http://www.project-syndicate.org/commentary/ideas-over-interests/french.

———. "Why Do More Open Economies Have Bigger Governments?" *Journal of Political Economy* 106.5 (1998b): 997–1032.

Rogowski, Ronald. *Commerce and Coalitions: How Trade Affects Domestic Political Alignments*. Princeton: Princeton University Press, 1989.

———. "Institutions as Constraints on Strategic Choice." In *Strategic Choice and International Relations*, edited by David A. Lake and Robert Powell, 112–36. Princeton: Princeton University Press, 1999.

———. "Political Cleavages and Changing Exposure to Trade." *American Political Science Review* 81.4 (1987a): 1121–37.

———. "Trade and the Variety of Democratic Institutions." *International Organization* 41.2 (1987b): 203–23.

———. "Power and International Relations: The Rise of China and Its Effects." *International Studies Perspectives* 7.3 (2006): 31–5.

Rosecrance, Richard. *The Rise of the Virtual State: Wealth and Power in the Coming Century*. New York: Basic Books, 1999.

Rosecrance, Richard, Bertrand Badie, Pierre Hassner, and Pierre De Senarclens. *Débat sur l'État virtuel*. Paris: Presses de Sciences Po, 2002.

Rosenau, James, and Mary Durfee. *Thinking Theory Thoroughly*. 2nd ed. Boulder, CO: Westview Press, 2000.

Rosendorff, Peter B. "Stability and Rigidity: Politics and the Design of the WTO's Dispute Resolution Procedure." *American Political Science Review* 99.3 (2005a): 389–400.

———. "Voluntary Export Restraints, Anti-Dumping Procedure and Domestic Politics." In *The WTO and Anti-Dumping: Critical Perspectives on the Global Trading System and the WTO Series*, edited by Douglas R. Nelson and Hylke Vandenbussche. London: Edward Elgar, 2005b.

Rosendorff, Peter B., and Helen V. Milner. "The Optimal Design of International Trade Institutions: Uncertainty and Escape." In *The Rational Design of International Institutions*, edited by Barbara Koremenos, Charles Lipson and Duncan Snidal, 69–98. Cambridge: Cambridge University Press, 2003.

Rowe, David. "The Tragedy of Liberalism: How Globalization Caused the First World War." *Security Studies* 14.3 (2005): 407–47.

———. "World Economic Expansion and National Security in Pre–World War I Europe." *International Organization* 53.2 (1999): 195–232.

Ruggie, John G. "International Regimes, Transactions, and Change: Embedded Liberalism in the Postwar Economic Order." In *International Regimes*, edited by Stephen D. Krasner, 379–415. Ithaca, NY: Cornell University Press, 1983.

———. "What Makes the World Hang Together? Neo-Utilitarianism and the Social Constructivist Challenge." *International Organization* 52.4 (1998): 855–85.

Rupert, Mark. *Ideologies of Globalization: Contending Visions of a New World Order*. London: Routledge, 2000.

———. *Producing Hegemony: The Politics of Mass Production and American Global Power*. Cambridge: Cambridge University Press, 1995.

Russett, Bruce, and John Oneal. *Triangulating Peace: Democracy, Interdependence, and International Organizations*. New York: W.W. Norton & Company, 2001.

Sabatier, Paul A., and Edella Schlager. "Les approches cognitives des politiques publiques: Perspectives américaines." *Revue française de science politique* 50.2 (2000): 209–34.

Samuelson, Paul A., and William D. Nordhaus. *Economics*. 19th ed. New York: McGraw-Hill, 2010.

———. "Where Ricardo and Mill Rebut and Confirm Arguments of Mainstream Economics Supporting Globalization." *Journal of Economic Perspective* 18.3 (2004): 135–46.

Sapir, André. *An Agenda for a Growing Europe: The Sapir Report*. Oxford: Oxford University Press, 2005.

Scharpf, Fritz. "Negative Integration: States and the Loss of Boundary Control." In *The Welfare State Reader*, edited by Christopher Pierson and Francis G. Castles, 223–6. Cambridge: Polity, 2006.

Schattschneider, Elmer E. *Politics, Pressures and the Tariff*. New York: Prentice-Hall, 1935.

Schechter, Michael G. "Critiques of Coxian Theory: Background to a Conversation." In *The Political Economy of a Plural World: Critical Reflections on Power, Morals and Civilization*, edited by Robert W. Cox and Michael G. Schechter, 1–25. London: Routledge, 2002.

Schelling, Thomas C. *Arms and Influence*. London: Yale University Press, 1966.

———. *The Strategy of Conflict*. Cambridge, MA: Harvard University Press, 1960.

Schelling, Thomas C., and Morton H. Halperin. *Strategy and Arms Control*. New York: The Twentieth Century Fund, 1961.

Schlosberg, David. *Defining Environmental Justice: Theories, Movements, and Nature*. Oxford: Oxford University Press, 2007.

Schumpeter, Joseph. *Capitalism, Socialism and Democracy*. New York: Harper & Row, 1950.

Shaw, Martin. "Historical Sociology and Global Transformation." In *Global Political Economy: Contemporary Theories*, edited by Ronen Palan, 239–52. London: Routledge, 2000.

Shepherd, Laura J., ed. *Gender Matters in Global Politics*. New York: Routledge, 2010.

Sil, Rudra, and Peter J. Katzenstein. *Beyond Paradigms: Analytic Eclecticism in the Study of World Politics*. Basingstoke, UK: Palgrave Macmillan, 2010.

Simmons, Beth A. "Capacity, Commitment, and Compliance: International Institutions and Territorial Disputes." *Journal of Conflict Resolution* 46.6 (2002): 829–95.

———. "Compliance with International Agreements." *Annual Review of Political Science* 1 (1998): 75–93.

———. "The International Politics of Harmonization: The Case of Capital Market Regulation." *International Organization* 55.3 (2001): 589–620.

———. "The Legalization of International Monetary Affairs." *International Organization* 54.3 (2000): 573–602.

Simmons, Beth A., and Lisa L. Martin. "International Organizations and Institutions." In *Handbook of International Relations*, edited by Walter Carlsnaes, Thomas Risse, and Beth A. Simmons, 192–211. London: Sage, 2001.

Sinclair, Timothy J. "Beyond International Relations Theory: Robert Cox and the Approaches to World Order." In *Approaches to World Order*, by Robert W. Cox with Timothy J. Sinclair, 3–19. Cambridge: Cambridge University Press, 1996.

———. *The New Masters of Capital: American Bond Rating Agencies and the Politics of Creditworthiness*. Ithaca, NY: Cornell University Press, 2008.

Sinclair, Timothy J., with Lena Rethel. *The Problem with Banks*. London: Zed Books, 2012.

Singer, David. "The Level-of-Analysis Problem in International Relations." In *The International System: Theoretical Essays*, edited by K. Knorr and Sidney Verba, 77–92. Princeton: Princeton University Press, 1961.

Small, Melvin, and David Singer. *Resort to Arms: International and Civil Wars, 1816–1980*. Beverly Hills, CA: Sage, 1982.

Smith, Steve. "Introduction: Diversity and Disciplinarity in International Relations Theory." In *International Relations Theories: Discipline and Diversity*, 2nd ed., edited by Tim Dunne, Milja Kurki, and Steve Smith, 1–13. New York: Oxford University Press, 2011.

———. "Positivism and Beyond." In *International Theory: Positivism and Beyond*, edited by Steve Smith, Ken Booth, and Marysia Zalewski, 11–43. Cambridge: Cambridge University Press, 2008.

———. "The United States and the Discipline of International Relations: 'Hegemonic Country, Hegemonic Discipline.'" *International Studies Review* 4 (2002): 68–85.

Smith, Steve, and Patricia Owens. "Alternative Approaches to International Theory." In *Introduction to the Globalization of World Politics: An Introduction to International Relations*, edited by John Baylis, Steve Smith, and Patricia Owens, 174–91. New York: Oxford University Press, 2008.

Spar, Debora, and David Yoffie. "Multinational Enterprises and the Prospects for Justice." In *Debates in International Political Economy*, edited by Thomas Oatley, 148–76. New York: Pearson Education, 2010.

Spero, Joan. *The Politics of International Economic Relations*. New York: St Martin's Press, 1977.

Spiro, David. *The Hidden Hand of American Hegemony: Petrodollar Recycling and International Markets*. Ithaca, NY: Cornell University Press, 1999.

———. "The Insignificance of the Liberal Peace." *International Studies Association* 19.2 (1994): 50–86.

Stein, Arthur A. *Why Nations Cooperate: Circumstance and Choice in International Relations*. Ithaca, NY: Cornell University Press, 1990.

Steinmo, Sven. "The Evolution of Policy Ideas: Tax Policy in the 20th Century." *British Journal of Politics and International Relations* 5 (2003): 206–36.

Sterling-Folker, Jennifer. "Neoliberalism." In *International Relations Theories: Discipline and Diversity*, 2nd ed., edited by Tim Dunne, Milja Kurki, and Steve Smith, 116–34. New York: Oxford University Press, 2011.

Stopford, John, and Susan Strange, with John S. Henley. *Rival States, Rival Firms: Competition for World Market Shares*. Cambridge: Cambridge University Press, 1991.

Strange, Susan. *Casino Capitalism*. Oxford: Blackwell, 1986.

———. "*Cave! hic Dragones*: A Critique of Regime Analysis." *International Organization* 36.2 (1982): 479–96.

———. "The Future of the American Empire." *Journal of International Affairs* 42.1 (1988a): 1–17.

———. "ISA As a Microcosm." *International Studies Quarterly* 39.3 (1995): 289–95.

———. "International Economics and International Relations: A Case of Mutual Neglect." *International Affairs* 46.2 (1970): 304–15.

———. *Mad Money: When Markets Outgrow Governments.* Ann Arbor: Michigan University Press, 1998.

———. "The Persistent Myth of Lost Hegemony." *International Organization* 41.4 (1987): 551–74.

———. Preface to *Paths to International Political Economy*, edited by Susan Strange. London: George Allen & Unwin, 1984.

———. *The Retreat of the State: The Diffusion of Power in the World Economy.* Cambridge: Cambridge University Press, 1996.

———. Review of *Production, Power, and World Order: Social Forces in the Making of History* by Robert Cox. *International Affairs* 64.2 (1988b): 269–70.

———. *States and Markets: An Introduction to International Political Economy.* London: Pinter Publishers, 1988c.

———. "Territory, State, Authority and Economy: A New Realist Ontology of Global Political Economy." In *The New Realism: Perspectives on Multilateralism and World Order*, edited by Robert W. Cox, 3–19. Basingstoke, UK: Palgrave Macmillan, 1997.

———. "Wake up, Krasner! The World Has Changed." *Review of International Political Economy* 1.2 (1994): 209–19.

———. "The Westfailure System." *Review of International Studies* 25 (1999): 345–54.

Stubbs, Richard, and Geoffrey R.D. Underhill, eds. *Political Economy and the Changing Global Order.* 2nd ed. New York: Oxford University Press, 2006.

Sutton, Robert I., and Barry M. Staw. "What a Theory Is Not." *Administrative Science Quarterly* 40.3 (1995): 371–84.

Swank, Duane. *Global Capital, Political Institutions and Policy Change in Developed Welfare States.* Cambridge: Cambridge University Press, 2002.

———. "Tax Policy in an Era of Internationalization: Explaining the Spread of Neoliberalism." *International Organization* 60.4 (2006): 847–82.

Tickner, J. Ann. "Ann Tickner on Feminist Philosophy of Science: Engaging the Mainstream and (Still) Remaining Critical in/of IR: Theory Talk #54." *Theory Talks*, 22 April 2013a. http://www.theory-talks.org/2013/04/theory-talk-54.html.

———. "Gender in World Politics." In *The Globalization of World Politics*, 5th ed., edited by John Baylis, Steven Smith, and Patricia Owens, 262–78. Oxford: Oxford University Press, 2011.

———. "On the Fringes of the World Economy: A Feminist Perspective." In *The Theoretical Evolution of International Political Economy: A Reader*, edited by Darel E. Paul and Abla Amawi, 297–308. Oxford: Oxford University Press, 2013b.

———. "You Just Don't Understand: Troubled Engagements between Feminists and IR Theorists." *International Studies Quarterly* 41.4 (1997): 611–32.

Tickner, J. Ann, and Laura Sjoberg. "Feminism." In *International Relations Theories: Discipline and Diversity*, 2nd ed., edited by Tim Dunne, Milja Kurki, and Steve Smith, 206–22. New York: Oxford University Press, 2013.

Tooze, Roger. "Perspectives and Theory: A Consumer's Guide." *Paths to International Political Economy*, edited by Susan Strange. London: Allen & Unwin, 1984.

———. "Susan Strange: Academic International Relations and International Political Economy." *New Political Economy* 5.2 (2000): 280–9.

———. "Susan Strange et l'économie politique international." *L'Économie politique* 10 (2001): 101–12.

Tooze, Roger, and Christopher May. *Authority and Markets: Susan Strange's Writings on International Political Economy.* Basingstoke, UK: Palgrave Macmillan, 2002.

UNCTAD. *World Investment Report.* New York: United Nations, 2012.

Underhill, Geoffrey R.D. "State, Market, and Global Political Economy: Genealogy of and (Inter-?) Discipline." *International Affairs* 76.4 (2000): 805–24.

Van der Pijl, Kees. *Transnational Classes and International Relations.* London: Routledge, 1998.

Vernon, Raymond. *Sovereignty at Bay: The Multinational Spread of U.S. Enterprises.* New York: Basic Books, 1971.

Viner, Jacob. "Power versus Plenty as Objectives of Foreign Policy in the Seventeenth and Eighteenth Century." *World Politics* 1.1 (1948): 1–29.

Wackernagel, Mathis, and William Rees. *Our Ecological Footprint: Reducing Human Impact on the Earth.* Gabriola Island, BC: New Society Publishers, 1998.

Wade, Robert. "Beware What You Wish For: Lessons for International Political Economy from the Transformation of Economics." *Review of International Political Economy* 16.1 (2009): 106–21.

Waever, Ole. "The Rise and Fall of the Inter-Paradigm Debate." In *International Theory: Positivism and Beyond*, edited by Steve Smith, Ken Booth, and Marysia Zalewski, 149–85. Cambridge: Cambridge University Press, 2008.

———. "The Sociology of a Not So International Discipline: American and European Developments in International Relations." *International Organization* 52.3 (1998): 687–727.

Wallerstein, Immanuel. *The Essential Wallerstein.* New York: The New Press, 2000.

———. *The Modern World-System I: Capitalist Agriculture and the Origins of the European World-Economy in the Sixteenth Century.* New York: Academic Press, 1976.

———. *World-Systems Analysis.* Durham, NC: Duke University Press, 2004.

Waltz, Kenneth N. "Globalization and American Power." *The National Interest* 59 (2000): 46–56.

———. *Man, the State and War: A Theoretical Analysis.* New York: Columbia University Press, 1959.

———. "The Myth of National Interdependence." In *The International Corporation*, edited by Charles P. Kindleberger, 205–27. Cambridge, MA: MIT Press, 1970.

———. "A Response to My Critics." In *Neorealism and Its Critics*, edited by Robert O. Keohane, 322–46. New York: Columbia University Press, 1986.

———. *Theory of International Politics.* Boston: Addison-Wesley, 1979.

Walzer, Michael. *Guerres justes et injustes.* Paris: Folio Essai, 2006.

Watson, Matthew. *Foundations of International Political Economy.* Basingstoke, UK: Palgrave Macmillan, 2005.

———. "The Historical Roots of Theoretical Traditions in Global Political Economy." In *Global Political Economy*, 3rd ed., edited by John Ravenhill, 25–46. New York: Oxford University Press, 2014.

Weick, Karl. "What a Theory Is Not, Theorizing Is." *Administrative Science Quarterly* 40.3 (1995): 385–90.

Weiss, Linda. *The Myth of the Powerless State: Governing Global Economy in a Global Era.* New York: Oxford University Press, 1999.

Wendt, Alexander. "Anarchy Is What States Make of It: The Social Construction of Power Politics." *International Organization* 46.2 (1992): 391–425.

———. *Social Theory of International Politics.* Cambridge: Cambridge University Press, 1999.

Wightman, David. "Why Economic History?" In *Paths to International Political Economy*, edited by Susan Strange, 23–32. London: George Allen & Unwin, 1984.

Zacher, Mark, and Richard A. Matthew. "Liberal International Theory: Common Threads, Divergent Stands." In *Controversies in International Relations Theory: Realism and the Neoliberal Challenge*, edited by Charles W. Kegley, 107–50. New York: St Martin's Press, 1995.

Index

Abbott, Jason, 176
"act locally, think globally," 189–90
actors in IPE: and interests, 111–14, 119–20, 127; in liberalism, 79–80, 82; orthodox *vs.* heterodox, 19, 20–2
American school: *vs.* British, 13–14, 31–2, 40, 176–7, 179–80; criticism of, 162–3; description, xi, xii; in theory, 16–17; *see also* orthodox school
anarchy, 52
Axelrod, Robert, 99–100

Barbieri, Katherine, 62–3
behaviourism, 29–30
Boehmer, Charles, 89–90
bounded rationality, 21
bourgeoisie, 136–9
Bretton Woods Agreement, 1–2
British Empire, and power, 170
British school: *vs.* American, 13–14, 31–2, 40, 176–7, 179–80; criticism of orthodox school, 161–5; description, 16, 135; and finance, 176–9; on globalization, 164, 165–8; and markets, 173–6; multidisciplinarity in, 159–60, 161–2, 163–5; and structural power, 168–73; *see also* heterodox school
Brooks, Stephen G., 88–9

Cameron, Angus, 167–8
Cameron, David, 123–4
capital, and structural power, 152–5
capitalism, 125–7, 136–9, 140–1
causal theories, 32–4, 36
civil society, 147–8
Clift, Ben, 31–2
Cohen, Benjamin, 11, 27, 28–9, 33, 205; American *vs.* British schools, 13, 16, 177, 179–80, 201
complex interdependence, 91–3, 97
comprehensive theory, 32, 33
concentrated interests, 112
conflict, and economy, 61–4, 84, 85
constitutive theories, 34
constructivism, 15, 105, 128
cooperation: and environment, 185; in liberal institutionalism, 93–101; prisoner's dilemma, 98–9
cores, semi-peripheries, and peripheries, 140–1

corporations. *see* multinationals
Cox, Robert: influences on, 145–6, 147; as neo-Gramscian, 143–5, 146, 149–51; ontology and heterodox views, 18–19; place and role in IPE, 16, 143, 146, 156–7; and theory, 35–6, 40–1, 42–3
critical green theory, 188, 189–91
critical theory, 35–6, 39, 40–1, 142

democracy, and peace, 85–6, 90
democratic peace theory, 63–4, 85, 175
dependency theory, 138–40
developing countries, and dependency theory, 138–40
diffuse interests, 112
disciplinary neoliberalism, 154
distribution of power, 53, 56, 80
domestic politics perspective: concern of and categories in, 108, 109, 110; and globalization, 110, 121–2; and ideas, 127–30; as paradigm, 14–15, 51; "second image reversed" approach, 108, 121–7; "three-*I*" approach, 110
Doyle, Michael, 85

ecological footprint and shadow, 190
economists, and IPE, 8–12
economy and trade: and capitalism, 125–7; and conflict and wars, 61–4, 84, 85; and domestic policies, 124–5; and environment and pollution, 184, 185, 188–90, 191; and globalization, 61–3, 84, 121–2; integration, 86–7; and interests, 112–14; international negotiations, 120–1; openness to, 123–4; and peace, 61–4, 84, 87–90; and power, 54–5, 64–71; and production, 88–9; and public policy, 117–18; and women, 195; and world-system theory, 140–1; *see also* free trade
Engels, Frederik, 138–9
environment: and economy/trade, 188–90, 191; institutions and agreements, 185–7, 188; tragedy of the commons, 184–5; *see also* green IPE
environmental injustice, 190
environmental regimes, 185–6, 188
epistemic community, 128–9
epistemology: and feminist IPE, 196–7; in IPE, 27–9, 201–2
explanatory theories, 32–4, 36

facts, and theory, x, 43, 177
feminist IPE: epistemology in IPE, 196–7; ontology in IPE, 191–6; orthodox views, 198; overview, 182–3, 191; place in IPE, 191, 198; variants, 196–7
finance: in heterodox school, 176–9; in orthodox school, 201; *see also* economy and trade
financial crisis of 2008, 177, 180, 201
firms, 126–7, 174–5; *see also* multinationals
Fordist model, 155–6
formal modelling, 28
free trade, 68, 70, 89, 112–14
functionalism, 86–7

gains, 53, 71–2
Gartzke, Erik, 89–90
gender. *see* feminist IPE
gender neutrality, 193–4
Germain, Randall, 179
Gill, Stephen, 151–5
Gilpin, Robert: economy and conflict, 63; globalization myth, 56, 58–61; on power, 54, 56, 66–70; theoretical perspectives of IPE, 12–13
globalization: British and heterodox schools, 164, 165–8; domestic politics perspective, 110, 121–2; and economy/trade, 61–3, 84, 121–2; and IPE's rise, 3; and liberalism, 84, 90–3; and neo-Gramscians, 151, 156; and policy, 121–2; of production, 88–9; and realism, 56–61, 73–4; and states, 60–1, 121–2; and transnationalism, 90–3; and welfare state, 121–5
global multinationals, 58–9
global political economy, 7
Goldstein, Judith, 129
government. *see* state
Gramsci, Antonio, 146–9, 156
green IPE: and heterodox theories, 187–91; as orthodox approach, 183–7; overview, 182–3; place in IPE, 183, 197
Grieco, Joseph, 72
Grossman, Gene, 184

Haas, Ernst, 86–7
Haas, Peter, 128–9
Hall, Peter, 126–7
Hall, Peter A., 130
Hamilton, Alexander, 55
Hardin, Garrett, 184–5
hard power, 83
hegemonic power cycles, 67–8
hegemonic stability theory: basic assumptions, 64; economy and power of states, 64–70; and liberal institutionalism, 97;

and liberalism, 82–3; Strange's views, 169–70
hegemony, in neo-Gramscians and Gramsci, 142, 146–50, 153
Helleiner, Eric, 177, 178
heterodox school: criticism of, 202; description, xi–xii, 18–19; on finance, 176; and globalization, 164, 165, 166; and green IPE, 187–91; *vs.* orthodox school, 17–23, 59, 159, 177, 179–80, 200–3; and positivism, 26–9, 31–2, 40, 47; and the state, 18–19; synthesis with orthodox school, 202, 205; theory in, 32, 39–40, 47, 177; *see also* British school
Hirschman, Albert, 9, 70–1
historical materialism, 144–5
historical structure, 145
historicism, 40–1
holism, orthodox *vs.* heterodox, 19–20
hyperliberalism, 150

ideas, and domestic politics perspective, 127–30
IMF (International Monetary Fund), 72
imperialism, 137
information, and liberal institutionalism, 96, 100–1
institutionalism, in liberal perspective, 93–101
institutions: influence, 114–15; policy in open economy politics, 114–21; rational design, 101–3; *see also* international institutions
INTELSAT, 72–3
interests and interest groups, 111–14, 119–20, 127
international agreements, 102–5, 120–1, 186–7, 188
international institutions: and compliance, 103–5; and cooperation, 94–101; in Cox and neo-Gramscians, 150; and environment, 185–6, 188; and liberalism, 101–3; organization of, 102–3; and peace, 86–7; and realism, 53–4, 56; role, 100
international law, 83–4
international negotiations, 119–21
International Organization journal, 3–4, 179
international policy, and domestic structures, 115–17
international political economy (IPE). *see* IPE
International Political Economy Group, 161
international regimes, 55–6
international relations: complex interdependence, 91–2; and constructivism, 128; and IPE, 3–7, 160, 163–4; key perspectives, 14–16; levels of analysis, 109; liberalism in, 78; and positivism, 27, 29–30; and realism, 50, 51–2; theory in, 36, 46

interstate relations and cooperation, 70–3, 93–101
IPE (international political economy): birth and history, 1–5, 11–12, 17, 160; core ideas, 8; definition, 5–8; and economists, 8–12; key perspectives and theories, 12–17; publishing on, 205; role and importance, 200

Jensen, Nathan M., 125

Kant, Immanuel, 85, 90
Katzenstein, Peter, 115, 117–18, 202
Keohane, Robert: on complex interdependence, 91–3, 97; criticism of orthodox school, 201–2; globalization and transnationalism, 91–2; hegemonic stability theory, 82–3; IPE in US, 3–4; liberal institutionalism, 94–5, 96–9; ontology, 20
Kindleberger, Charles, 64–5
Kohr, Leopold, 189
Koremenos, Barbara, 102–3
Krasner, Stephen: on complex interdependence, 93; criticism by Strange, 163, 165–6; economy and power, 65–6; on globalization myth, 57; on IPE, 6; and positivism, 31; and power relations, 54, 56; and theory, 46; weak and strong states, 115–16
Krueger, Alan, 184
Krugman, Paul, 8
Kuznets curve, 184

labour, 126–7, 136–7, 140–1, 193
Lakatos, Imre, 38
Lake, David, 110, 111, 135–6
Law, David, 152
Lenin, Vladimir, 137
Li, Quan, 89–90
liberal feminism, 196
liberal perspective (liberalism): basic assumptions, 78–84; compliance with agreements, 103–5; and economy/trade, 87–90; and feminist IPE, 194–5; on globalization, 84, 90–3; and green IPE, 184–7, 188, 190; and institutionalism, 93–101; and international institutions, 101–3; and international law, 83–4; in IPE, 12–13, 15, 50–1, 77–8; and peace, 84–90; and power, 80–3, 92; and transnationalism, 90–3; variants, 78, 79
Lipson, Charles, 102
List, Friedrich, 55

McDonald, Patrick, 89
marginalization of women, 193–4
market civilization, 155

markets, in heterodox and Strange's views, 173–6
Martin, Lisa, 94, 95, 96, 120–1
Marx and Marxism, 136–9, 196
Marxist perspective, in IPE, 12–13, 15, 134–8, 144–5
mass production, 155–6
Mastanduno, Michael, 116–17
Mattli, Walter, 103
mercantilism, 54–5
methodological individualism, 19–20
methodology, and positivism, 28, 30–1, 200
Milner, Helen, 119–20
Mitrany, David, 86
monetary policies, and peace, 89–90
Moravcsik, Andrew, 79–80
multinationals: delocalization and production, 88–9; and globalization, 61; and markets, 174–5; nationality of, 58–9; power, 67, 82; types and impact, 58–9; see also firms

nation-state. see state
neoclassical economics, 10
neofunctionalism, 86–7
neo-Gramscians: Cox and Gramsci in, 144–51; and globalization, 151, 156; in IPE, 134–5, 141–2, 146–7, 156–7; and mass production, 155–6; power in, 146–7; and structural power of capital, 152–5; theory in, 40–3
neoliberalism and neoliberals, 97, 98, 154–5
neo-Marxism, 138, 140
neorealism, 52, 95–6, 97, 99, 144–5
Nesvetailova, Anastasia, 178
new international political economy, 7
Nixon, Richard, 1–2
normative theory, 34–5
North–South relations, 138–40
Nye, Joseph, 3–4, 82–3, 91–3

Oneal, John, 90
ontology, 17–18; and feminist IPE, 191–6
open economy politics: concern and focus of, 108, 109–10; and institutions, 114–21; and interests, 111–14
orthodox school: criticism of, 161–5, 200–2, 203–4; description, xi, xii, 18; in feminist IPE, 198; on finance, 201; and green IPE, 183–7; vs. heterodox school, 17–23, 59, 159, 177, 179–80, 200–3; and positivism, 26–32, 47; synthesis with heterodox school, 202, 205; theory in, 32, 36–9, 46, 47, 177; see also American school

Palan, Ronen: American vs. British schools, 176–7, 180; on finance, 176, 178; on globalization, 167–8, 176; IPE views, 162

panopticon, 154, 155
paradigms, and policy, 130
parsimonious theory, 37
Pauly, Louis, 178
peace: and democracy, 85–6, 90; and economy/trade, 61–4, 84, 87–90; and international institutions, 86–7; variables of, 90
peripheries, semi-peripheries, and cores, 140–1
Phillips, Nicola, 161–2
Polanyi, Karl, 9
policy: change in, 130; and domestic structures, 115–17; and economy/trade, 117–18; and globalization, 121–2; and ideas, 129–30; and institutions, 114–21; and interests, 111–14; and political regime, 117–18, 120–1
political market failure, 97–8, 100
political regime and systems, and policy, 117–18, 120–1
pollution, 184, 185
Popper, Karl, 37–8
positivism: and feminist IPE, 197–8; and methodology, 28, 30–1, 200; and neo-Gramscians, 41, 42–3; orthodox vs. heterodox schools, 26–32, 40, 47; postulates, 29
postpositivism, 34, 47, 196, 197
power: distribution of, 53, 56, 80; and economy/trade, 54–5, 64–71; and interstate relations, 70–3; in liberalism, 80–3, 92; in neo-Gramscians and Gramsci, 146–50; and neoliberalism, 154–5; and non-trade issues, 72–3; in realism, 53, 56, 81; soft and hard, 83; and state (see state and power); structural power, 152–5, 168–73
prisoner's dilemma, 98–9
problem-solving theory, 35–6, 40–1
production, 144, 155–6
protectionism, 55, 112–14
public policy. see policy
Putnam, Robert, 119

rational choice theory, 20–1, 22, 195
rationalism, 20–2
realism: basic assumptions, 51–6; criticism by British school, 164; economy and war/peace, 61–4; and feminist IPE, 195–6; and globalization, 56–61, 73–4; and green IPE, 184, 187; hegemonic stability theory, 64–70; and institutions, 53–4, 56; and international relations, 50, 51–2; and IPE, 4, 15–16, 50–1, 73–4; main debates, 56; and mercantilism, 54–5; and

positivism, 29–30; and power, 53, 56, 81; and states, 51–3
reflectivism and reflective theories, 20, 42
relational power, 171
relative gains, 71–2
Review of International Political Economy (RIPE), 162, 163–5, 166–7, 205
Rogowski, Ronald, 113, 117–18
Rosamond, Ben, 31–2
Rosecrance, Richard, 87–8
Rowe, David, 61–2
Ruggie, John, 124–5
Rupert, Mark, 155–6
Russett, Bruce, 90

scientific culture, xi
security issues, 6–7, 50, 52–3, 88
semi-peripheries, peripheries, and cores, 140–1
Sil, Rudra, 202
Simon, Herbert, 21
Sinclair, Timothy, 179
Smith, Adam, 54
Smith, Steve, 27, 29, 30–1
Snidal, Duncan, 102
social forces, 150–1
social learning concept, 130
social science, theory in, 45
soft power, 83
Soskice, David, 126–7
Spiro, David, 63
state: and compliance, 103–5; cooperation, 93–101; and globalization, 60–1, 121–2; in Gramsci and neo-Gramscians, 149–50, 151; and IPE, 9; in liberalism, 79–80; and markets, 174–6; orthodox and heterodox views, 18–19; and power (see state and power); in realism, 51–3; and territory, 87–8
state and power: distribution of power, 53, 56; in economy, 54–5, 64–70; interstate relations, 70–3; in liberalism, 81–2, 92; weak and strong states, 115–16
Stolper–Samuelson theorem, 113–14
Strange, Susan: birth of IPE, 3, 4, 7–8, 11, 16, 159, 160–1; criticism of orthodox school, 162–3; criticized in US, 179–80; on decline of US, 169–71; on globalization, 165–6; on markets, 173–5; ontology, 19, 21; and structural power, 168–73; theorizing, 43–6; works on IPE, 3, 6, 7, 161, 162–3, 175
structural power: and capital, 152–5; Strange's views, 168–73; structures of, 172–3
Swank, Duane, 125

territory, 87–8, 169–70
theory: absence of, 43–4; definition, 26–7, 32, 33; and facts, x, 43, 177; goal and role, 44–5; heterodox school, 32, 39–40, 47, 177; and neo-Gramscians, 40–3; objectivity and bias, 42; orthodox school, 32, 36–9, 46, 47, 177; refutability, 36–8; and S. Strange, 43–6; typology in IPE, 12–17, 32–6; *see also* specific theories
"three-*I*" approach, 110
Tickner, J. Ann, 193–6, 197, 198
trade. *see* economy and trade; free trade
tragedy of the commons, 184–5
transnationalism, 90–3
transnational relations, 4
Trilateral Commission, 153–4
TRIP project (Teaching, Research, and International Policy), 14–15, 203

UNCTAD index, 58–9
United States: decline of empire, 2–3, 69–70, 169–71; IPE in universities, 203–5; key perspectives in IPE, 14–15; positivism in, 27–8; public policy, 115–17; structural power, 169–71, 172–3; *see also* American school
universities, and IPE, 203–5
USSR, and power, 170

Wallerstein, Immanuel, 140–1, 165
Waltz, Kenneth, 61–2, 109
war, and economy, 61–4, 84, 85
Watson, Matthew, 13
welfare state, and globalization, 121–5
women. *see* feminist IPE
world politics, 19, 136–7
world-system approach, 140–1